The Paragon

The Paragon

Odyssey of the Nazarene

JOSEPH EMMRICH

© 2017 Joseph Emmrich
All rights reserved.

ISBN: 1545137528
ISBN 13: 9781545137529

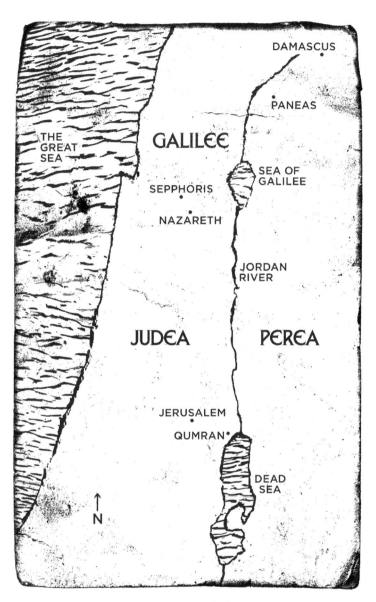

Modern era place name keys at end of text

One

**The Present Time
In the Court of Herod Antipas
In the Early Years of the Reign of the
Emperor Tiberius
Yeshua is Twenty-five Years Old**

It was the age of occupation and corruption. It was the time of a culture in decline. It was a time without redemption, when the leaders of the people whored themselves for personal gain; and the common people, beyond family and village, existed as every man for himself.

The Roman overseers had ultimately confirmed Herod the Great's last will and testament, dividing Judea into four, to end the internecine squabbling of sibling pretenders to his throne. Each of the four was called tetrarch and was king or queen enough in his or her own realm to sit atop the pyramid of wealth and orchestrate the dirty deeds beneath.

From time to time someone would arise who claimed to be the long-promised Messiah to his people, to save them from the morass of Roman rule and corruption in which they wallowed.

Herod Antipas feared these messianics above all others. It was not in any Jew's interest, especially his, to challenge Roman rule.

The Qumran monastic community, near the Dead Sea, was a hornet's nest of sedition as far as he was concerned. His spies had made that clear. The problem was he couldn't send men into Judea, the territory of his brother, Archelaus, to lay waste to the place. If, however, unfortunate things happened to the worst of them, he could have the best of both worlds: keeping the favor of Rome and quelling the urge for popular uprising.

Antipas paced the marble floor of his throne room, the grandest salon in the grandest palace in the eastern part of the Roman Empire. He had inherited his father's penchant for building opulent structures. His guard snapped the butt of his spear to the floor, cracking an echo in the rotunda above them and announcing the approach of his regent.

Sesipedes, the regent, was the king's backbone, in the same way a snake has a backbone. Kill them all. Let them fear you. That was the counsel he often gave and was only too happy to execute, but today his advice was more nuanced.

"Right now, your majesty, there are two monks at Qumran we need to be concerned about. They're Galileans from Nazareth, called Yonnah and Yeshua. We need to find a way to eliminate them. Maybe they could meet with some accident on the road when they're returning to Nazareth or even be killed by 'highwaymen.'

"Perhaps the same thing could happen in Perea," Sesipedes continued, "where this Yonnah preaches. Of course, Perea, across the Jordan, as well as Galilee, are your territories, and your brother would have no concern about what happens there, but these two are clearly who we need to watch. We have time. We can be patient."

"I've been patient, Sesipedes," Antipas said. "Others have warned me about these two, and I'm ready to see it done. Find me two men from the Royal Guard who trust each other and who I can trust, and bring them to me."

"Your Majesty," Sesipedes replied, "I suggest Kefir, second in command of the Guard and his son Ptolemy, the fittest and best fighter. He adores his father and will be completely loyal to him and to your mission. The reason you can be assured of their loyalty is that you'll find them extremely motivated, and you'll see how easily you can manipulate that motivation."

"Of course, Kefir. I know his story well," Antipas said. "In fact, I brought him to the Court before your regency. He'd been loyal and deserved some reward because of his personal tragedy. Bring them here. I want to instruct them myself."

In Nazareth
Ten Years Earlier

Yosef awoke well before first light. He shuffled across the central room of his home, the one where the family gathered for meals and such, and made his way to the hearth to get a flame from last night's embers to light a lamp.

His house was modest but sturdy. He'd built it himself of stone and brick. It was a bit larger than some of his neighbors', large enough to accommodate his parents. It had three rooms in addition to the central one, and an outbuilding behind the main house for the animals.

Yosef and his son, Yeshua, had been home for a few days, waiting for supplies to arrive in Sepphoris, so they could finally finish their work there. If they kept a brisk pace, they could make the walk to Sepphoris in less than two hours. It was too far to do every day, so they often stayed in the dormitories provided by the king, but they were among the lucky ones who could make the trip home whenever they wanted or needed to.

Yeshua awoke at Yosef's second calling. He sat up, rubbed his eyes, and made his way to a bowl of water, where he took a drink and splashed some in his face. With the waking process now begun in earnest, he was able to bring good humor to his first words. "Good morning, Father."

"Good morning, Son. We need to move, so we aren't late for work."

Without a verbal response, Yeshua made his way to the barn to feed and water the animals, while saying his abbreviated morning prayers to himself.

Antipas had conscripted Yosef, and who knew how many others, for his project to build a magnificent capital in Sepphoris. The family owed the king two years of labor, but with father and son working together, they could fulfill the obligation in one year. It wasn't exactly slavery. The king paid them, albeit a pittance, about half of what Yosef could make as a builder working on private jobs, but it was a hardship in an already hard life.

Yosef's wife, Maryam, awoke with them. She served them some bread she'd made the day before, along with a little cheese,

The Paragon

enough to sustain them on their trek. She herself would soon go to work on her parents' small farm. She worked at least as hard as her men.

Whenever her duties in the field or with the animals were finished, Maryam helped whoever needed it whether or not they were family. Yosef loved her for this. She'd always helped whomever she could, even as a child, running errands, doing chores, caring for the sick. She never ran out of energy. It was as if everyone was her family, and she was beloved in Nazareth.

As father and son walked the dusty path to their job, they passed the time in a variety of ways, sometimes bursting into song, sometimes playing games of observation, such as who could be the first to spot ten hawks, or sometimes just conversing father to son. Yosef had been angry about this conscription. Not only did it ruin his business, it interfered with his son's education. Most young people got only a little schooling, and mostly at the local synagogue, but Yeshua seemed to have a gift for learning and speaking, and Yosef would do anything he could to nurture that gift.

"Yeshua, this servitude will only last a while longer," Yosef said. "You're my able helper, but we both know your future is as a rabbi and possibly an influential one. I expect you to remain humble as I say this, but you have an exceptional mind, and you need to have education beyond what you've gotten in Nazareth, and as much as I hate to admit it, from this time you've spent in Sepphoris.

"I know," Yosef continued, "you seem interested in the Essene sect. You're fifteen now. You've shown your mother and me you'll walk your own path. Most parents would consider you incorrigible; but since your rebellious behavior has always been constructive, we've allowed you more freedom than most children. Have you thought about where you want your path to take you when this job is finished? I'd love to keep you in Nazareth with me, but that's a selfish wish I can't justify. You have good to accomplish beyond Nazareth."

As they trudged up a hill, two men on mules passed them, and the four exchanged pleasantries. It was the day after *Shabbat* and people were returning to business. The closer they got to Sepphoris, and the higher the sun rose, the more encounters they could expect.

"I've thought about what you said, and I agree," Yeshua rejoined after the brief interruption. "For my calling, this kind of learning is like driving nails or setting bricks is to your business. So, yes, I've been thinking about joining the Essenes at Qumran. It wouldn't cost you anything other than my absence and loss of my labor. I appreciate the sacrifice it would mean for you to let me do this, but I sense you'd be agreeable and even encourage it. I've talked to some Essenes, and I think the monks could teach me well."

"I agree," Yosef replied. "I think your mother will too. I also hope you can convince your cousin, Yonnah, to go along with you. He's a strange one. He withdraws from people, and seems to have an unholy flirtation with the Zealots."

Yosef was now aware of more and more people on the road. The sun was fully risen, the sky cloudless, all signaling the likelihood of a crowded market in the new city.

"In your cousin's mind the answer to our misery is rebellion," Yosef continued, "and in a young man's idealism, he has sympathy for the radicals, because he agrees with their goals. He may not be ready to adopt their methods, but when they commit some atrocity, he's too willing to blame the victim."

"I think you're right about that," Yeshua said, "and I'll try my best to convince him to join me. Despite his aversion to people, it's not because of shyness. It may be his form of demon, albeit benign. He can speak to people with passion. I don't pretend to understand his behavior, but I think he'll be a great preacher someday. He needs some direction to his voice, as I do myself. We're both young and have a lot to learn."

"A young man who can say that is wise beyond his years," Yosef responded. "I hope you keep that attitude."

As they walked the last rolling hills into Sepphoris, they were in as good a mood as men could be on their way to a job they despised. The day went well. The sun was warm enough to make Yosef sweat. The colors of spring splashed his view from the blossoming trees on the hillsides, all the way down to the tiny blooms in the nooks and crannies of the job site.

They were working on an amphitheater near the market. It was a big day for buying and selling, perhaps because it was the first sunny day in a while. The women of Sepphoris and surrounding villages, packed shoulder to shoulder and elbow to elbow, all seemed to be shopping for something. This was the largest market in the area, rivaled only by Jerusalem, and today was a terrific day for business.

The workers were taking a short break. Yeshua was watching people, imagining where the man in the turban was from, what life was like for the hunchbacked old woman, was this pretty girl married?

Suddenly, his focus shifted to men in hoods. It wasn't a day for hoods. There were four of them. They came from different parts of his field of view, but they seemed to be converging on a single point.

"Father, look . . . those men." They were close enough now to be seen together as one group with a common purpose.

"Yeshua, stay here."

He did as he was told and watched his father run toward the men. He wouldn't be in time. The four of them set upon a woman who looked to be Egyptian, took daggers from under their cloaks, and began to stab her as if they had a personal hatred of her. She was with a young boy, probably her child. Yosef screamed, "Zealots among us!" The crowd parted as the men hacked. Yosef broke through and grabbed the child, whisking him back into the crowd.

As the men finished with the mother, they seemed to realize they'd been denied the life of the child and to understand they were now observed. After a quick glance, they ran and lost themselves in the crowd. Almost immediately soldiers converged on the spot. Yosef was trying to comfort the young boy, who was maybe eleven or twelve years old, when the soldiers grabbed the boy and hustled him away.

Yeshua watched in horror at the murder, in fear for his father's life, and in agonizing sorrow for the boy, who had witnessed his mother slain so brutally. When Yosef returned, he was breathing heavily. He was angry to the point of rage. "May God damn them all to hell!" he exploded. "These are the Zealots who fascinate your cousin. They'd kill an innocent woman and a child, probably because she's married to a Jew. These are the murdering bastards who claim to be men of God and speak for Judaism. If you ever have anything to do with them, I'll denounce you to everyone."

There was no need to worry about that. For although Yeshua always listened to his cousin's opinions with an open mind, including about the Zealots, this settled his own opinion and wrote it in stone. This was evil, pure and simple. There could be no justification for it.

He might want to be rid of the Romans and the corruption they brought, but better to wait. Eventually, he felt, Roman rule would collapse under its own weight. No need to try to hasten the day with murder and making yourself worse than a beast.

At the Same Time as the Murder in Sepphoris
In the Palace of Izates I, King of Adiabene
In Hadyab, in the Northern Tigris River Valley

The slave girl's father slapped her to the ground. She didn't cry. She was used to this kind of treatment. She felt only resentment toward him.

Her mother was worse in her eyes, weak and groveling, concerned more for her own welfare than her daughter's, always willing to kiss King Izates's feet for whatever small favor she could wrest from him.

"Meryam, you little bitch, you've done it now," her father bellowed. "We'll all pay for your stupidity."

"What would you expect me to do, Father? How can I even call you *father*?" She drew out the word in sarcasm. "You care nothing for me."

"You question me?" he thundered. "What don't you understand about our slavery? You were born a slave. Izates owns you. If you want to be fed and housed--in short, if you want to live, and if you want your parents to live--you do his bidding and the bidding of his people."

"You're parents to me in name only." Meryam growled the words. "I despise you as much as I despise Izates. He at least has no reason to love me. When the overseer of the kitchen tried to force himself on me, no, I wouldn't have it. I grabbed the nearest knife and plunged it into his filthy body. Now you blame me. I spit on you."

Her father raised his hand to her again. Her mother stood by expressionless, looking down, staring at her fingernails. Instead of striking her, her father kicked her toward the door. "Get out." He spat out the words. "Go now to Izates, as he commands, and meet your fate. We're through with you. I only hope we're spared for the crime of spawning you. Get out."

Although her defiant attitude was more than a veneer, she was afraid to die and now believed that would surely be her fate. A guard took her arm and led her down a long colonnade to the opposite end of the palace. Each marble pillar she passed seemed like the counting down of moments to the end of her life. She had nothing to sustain her but that well of defiance inside.

Meryam was Jewish by heritage, but that was another part of her life that existed in name only. Her parents had taught her nothing of Judaism's tenets or of its possibility to give a sense of community or hope to her. She'd heard there were many free Jews in Adiabene, but whatever events had brought her parents to slavery had happened before she was born, and they told her nothing of them.

As far as a sense of belonging or feelings of love were concerned, there was nothing in this palace to fulfill those needs. Izates bestowed favors in such a way as to encourage envy and jealousy among the slaves. No one seemed to form any bonds of friendship or love, certainly not with her. She'd seen mothers of the court caring for their babies, acting as a family with their husbands. That was the only way she knew what love might be.

The guard brought her into the throne room. She was unimpressed by the silk draperies and gold appointments, but the faint echo of everything spoken, off the cold marble walls, produced a sonorous tone of authority that compounded her fear. He threw her to the tiles at the feet of Izates. She was almost oblivious to the pain of it.

"Leave us now," Izates instructed. There was no emotion in his command.

Meryam lay at the king's feet saying nothing. All she could see was Izates' sandals and the hem of his royal robe. She could smell the oil in his hair and spiced perfume on his body.

After some moments of silence, designed to intensify her uncertainty and fear, she assumed, and having that effect, Izates spoke without emotion. "This is not a discussion or an opportunity for you to plead your case or beg for mercy. I've decided your fate. The kitchen overseer will live, and for that reason so will you.

He tried to use my property for himself and will receive punishment accordingly."

"You, on the other hand . . ." the king continued. "I'm through with you. You're in your fourteenth year. You've lost your virginity before this, which decreases your value. You're also incorrigible. Before this incident, I know you've set fires, befouled my food, and done everything you could to express defiance and lack of gratitude. I should kill you and do it now, but that would be a waste. Instead I'm going to sell you to a caravaneer I'm acquainted with. I've described you as 'feisty' to him." Izates grunted in contempt of his own understatement.

"I've made a good deal for myself. I'll receive a camel, some silk, and some spices. It's more than you're worth. The guard will take you to the gate to meet your new owner immediately. Don't bother about your parents. As I'm sure you know, they care nothing about you. They'll be glad to be rid of you and will be spared from punishment because of your departure. Now get out.

"Guard!" Izates shouted. "Take her to the gate."

That was it, then. So simple; no preparation or goodbye. Thank God I'm out of this place, she thought. Whatever my new life is, it can't be any worse.

On the Road in Adiabene

Meryam had become the caravaneer's sex slave, pure and simple. Mithros, by name, had made his orders clear and direct. "I hear you're quite willful," he said at the outset. "Well, this is paradise, and you have choices. If you wish to eat and have a modicum of comfort, you will come to my tent every evening after your chores. You will first clean yourself and then give me pleasure. You may leave when I tell you I'm finished. There's no need for you to respond. Just do as you're told."

Meryam held her tongue, came to his tent in the evenings or at his beckoning, and did everything he asked of her. She boiled inside with hatred, however, and knew there'd be a day when she'd get her revenge or die attempting it.

After some weeks of his personal cruelty, he decided it would benefit him to share her, so he rented her to others as a prostitute. She learned how to please men even as she learned to despise them.

At last her opportunity came. One night after all the men were passed out from heavy drinking, Meryam sneaked into his tent as Mithros slept off his drunkenness. She crept close to where he lay. She could smell the wine coming from the depths of his body as he snored like a pig. She saw his knife hanging from a pole and silently removed it from its sheath. She went back and stood over him, clutched the knife tightly in both hands, and plunged it into his black heart.

Mithros was too heavy to move easily, so Meryam slit the back of the tent and got a horse. She returned to the tent and bound his feet. There was so much blood. She rolled the mat he'd slept on around his disgusting carcass and tied a rope around it. Then she dragged the body away as she escaped.

Meryam didn't know if the others would care enough about him to pursue her for her crime, although she knew she'd be of some value to whoever captured her. She thought, however, that if the body was missing, they might spend some time looking for him, time she could use to get far away.

She dragged the body through the night, passing two separate crossroads that would make it more difficult to follow her. Meryam had a horse. She had his coins, which were a considerable sum. She kept going. It helped that dragging the weighted mat behind her seemed to obliterate her trail. Before first light she concealed the body in some higher rocky terrain well off the road.

Looking back in the morning, she could see vultures circling the distant hill where she'd left her tormentor, and she felt pleased with herself. Meryam relished her first taste of freedom. She didn't know exactly what to do or where to go, but she'd heard there were Jewish people to the south in the marshes around Nehardea, who at least would be something like her. They were robbers, true enough, but so was she.

The Present Time At Qumran

Yeshua awoke before the sun. He began his morning routine with the first crowing of the cock. It was a time of silence. He'd been almost ten years with the Essenes, both here at Qumran and in Jerusalem.

Although others were awake, no one spoke until the breaking of bread. He rubbed his eyes and shuffled into a small room near the one where he slept. He took one of the scrolls of the Torah from the jar in which it was stored and read silently. The familiar smell of the kilns, toasting clay vessels, brought him peace, as did the sound of the water from the spring, tumbling from the upper to the lower cistern.

All the words were familiar to him. He'd studied them for years, first as a child in Nazareth at the temple and now for the years at Qumran. When he finished the verses he chose for the day, he returned the scroll to the jar and sat in meditation, allowing the stillness to fill his spirit. He lived the story in his mind, pictured it vividly, and allowed his mind to go to a place where he thought of nothing. It was in that place he knew the underlying truth of the verses would come deeply to him, where it would inform his daily behavior, bring him peace, and leave words inside to explain its truth to others.

When about one hour had passed, he ended his morning session with a prayer to Yahweh. "Make me your instrument," he'd beseech. "Let me bring your people who've lost their way closer to you, so we may all live in the safe harbor of your peace." When he finished, he went to tend the animals, which was his duty.

Yonnah, his cousin, also read, but as he did, his mind raged amid thoughts about the corruption of the Sadducees and of the Roman enslavement and brutal taxation, which institutionalized that local corruption. He prayed in a different way. "Lord," he begged, "give me the strength to inspire your people to cast off their oppressors. May it be your will to restore the dignity of Israel and renew your sacred rule."

Although he was still a young man, he could move people with his fiery rhetoric. Yonnah would occasionally go across the Jordan to Perea, at first just to practice his preaching, but he soon developed a following among the villagers near the river. He'd begun a practice of inviting people to be baptized, and the villagers were beginning to respond. The response came partly out of a sense of novelty and partly because of Yonnah's powers of persuasion. Some even referred to him as 'the Baptist.'

Yeshua would sometimes go with him but didn't preach himself. Not that he was incapable; far from it. Yonnah appreciated this and understood Yeshua refrained out of respect for him, but he realized Yeshua was the gifted one. He believed a time would come when he'd do everything he could to promote Yeshua to the people. In the meantime, he needed to get his cousin to realize his duty to lead.

When the morning chores were done, the men gathered for breakfast: an herbal tea, some goat's cheese, and fresh, hot bread. It was simple and delicious. Yonnah and those with more ascetic sensibilities thought it an indulgence, but by now he accepted the fact that Yeshua loved it.

Some Days Later
In Jerusalem

Yeshua had studied more than the Torah. The monks at Qumran also kept scrolls they'd acquired from caravans coming from the east. Yeshua had read them, and they filled him with new ideas that he wanted to understand better.

He also spent time in Jerusalem and other cities where he had discussions, or even debates, with the Sadducees and Pharisees.

The Paragon

He developed a taste for city life in Jerusalem and a fascination for the stories the arriving caravaneers brought with them.

In Jerusalem, he volunteered his time caring for the sick. There were a few wealthy people who used their money to do good and who'd established homes for those unable to care for themselves and were without family. One of them was a man named Nikodemos. Yeshua and he became friends over the years, and Nikodemos would gladly have taken Yeshua in and let him enjoy his lifestyle, be his patron as it were.

Most other Essenes either stayed in the city or lived permanently at Qumran. Yeshua was an exception. The community held him in high esteem, and no one criticized his coming and going. Lately, when Yeshua was in Jerusalem, he stayed with a group of Essenes. He arose at first light and meditated with the others, then went to work at the *officina medica,* as the Romans called it.

One morning his meditation wandered to a specific question about his future. He'd been thinking about it for some time. When he finished his duties with the sick, he went to see Nikodemos. He needed to talk to someone about his tentative decision.

The house of Nikodemos was in a wealthy part of town. Nikodemos had become well-off as a trader. Although he did not go abroad himself, he often did business with caravaneers who had been to all parts of the Roman and Parthian empires.

"Come in, Yeshua." One of Nikodemos's servants answered Yeshua's knock and invited him in. "Master is on the balcony and will be delighted to see you. I anticipate his request for tea."

Yeshua showed himself to the balcony that looked out on the Jordan Valley and desert beyond. "Yeshua, my friend, please sit," Nikodemos offered. "I never grow tired of this view."

"Thank you. The city and countryside are beautiful. It belies the misery below," Yeshua said, bursting a bubble of complacency.

Nikodemos sighed. "It's my escape. The misery is the fault of many who live in this neighborhood. Most of my neighbors, the tax collectors, landowners, priests, got rich at the expense of the poor. I like to think my own wealth was well earned, and I do what I can to help the less fortunate, but I know I can do more."

"You're a generous man, Nikodemos," Yeshua said. "You've been good to me personally, including your invitation to allow me to live in this beautiful home, but I'm a man of the poor. I'm afraid these trappings of wealth would corrupt me and my message. Although I see myself speaking mostly to the poor when I begin my ministry, I know the wealthy need a spiritual awakening like everyone else, probably more so."

The servant arrived with tea and served it to the men in fine glass cups. They were a deep blue color, matching the pitcher from which the beverage was poured. Glass was becoming more popular and affordable, even to those of more modest means, but these were exquisite, with white ceramic blossoms all around completing the design.

As the men sipped, Yeshua got to the point of his visit. "My friend," he began, "I'm close to a decision I know will change my life."

"Is this about the journey you've mentioned to me?" Nikodemos asked. "It's more than a young man's dream, then?"

"Yes," Yeshua said. "I want to go to the east and meet the thinkers and sages whose ideas I've read at Qumran and discussed with you. I've talked with some of their followers here in Judea and Galilee, but I want to get to the root of these beliefs in a way I can only do by visiting their cradles."

"I'm thrilled for you, Yeshua," his friend said. "I wish I could go with you. The Royal Road of Parthia can take you far, even to the cities of Merv and Maracanda. I urge you to do it."

"Your encouragement gives me confidence. I'll miss you," Yeshua said.

"As I'll miss you, my friend," Nikodemos replied. "Now, don't even think about refusing this offer, but I intend to provide you with financial support to help you do this. That's decided."

"Thank you, Niko, but I'm going to work as I go." Yeshua said.

"It's a good idea to work, if you can find work," Nikodemos agreed, "but I want to be sure you have something in reserve if you need it. Please accept my gift."

"I accept with much gratitude, Niko," Yeshua said, "and I'm eager to begin. I'm convinced this will make me a better minister to my people."

"I agree," Nikodemos replied. "Go safely."

Some Days Later
In Nazareth

"Yeshua," Yonnah railed, "this is a terrible idea. We both need to be here to begin our ministry."

"Cousin, I've decided to do it. I wish you were happy for me."

The cousins sat by a rivulet at the bottom of the hill from the village. Yeshua's wish for his cousin's approval left them in an uncomfortable silence. Yonnah took a deep breath from the breeze that carried the familiar scent of the animals, then exhaled.

"Although I don't like it," Yonnah finally said, "I feel a duty to go with you. For the sake of your parents and your people, you need to return alive. I fear the worst for you, but I'll go if you'll have my company. Have you told your parents?"

"Not yet, Cousin. Come with me to break the news."

Yeshua and Yonnah trudged up the hill to the cluster of buildings at the top, making their way to Yosef and Maryam's home. The day's chores were done. Yosef was perfecting the evening fire with an iron tool. Maryam was shaping the bread whose comforting aroma would soon fill the family dwelling like love itself. Yeshua knew there was no good time to break this news, but he had to do it.

"Mother, Father," he began, "I've thought about this and prayed, and I'm going to leave Galilee and travel to the east. I want to meet the men whose writings I've read and learn from them."

His father was the first to voice concern. "You're of age, Son, so you'll go where you please, but I'm troubled by your decision. If you go beyond the protection of Rome, I fear you won't return."

"Cousin, do not do this thing." Yonnah tried one last time to change Yeshua's mind. "The people need you. You're destined to lead them in casting off this Roman rule that corrupts even our own institutions. The people are suffering, even your own village, even your own parents. It's your duty to unite them under the Law and the Prophets, and no one understands and explains that better than you. You can't leave for these unknown and dangerous places."

"Yonnah, Mother, Father," Yeshua began, "I go to the temple and debate with the Pharisees and the others, and I begin to feel as if I'm no different from them. They say, 'This is so.' I say, 'That is so.' In my heart I believe there's something more than 'this' or 'that.' I need to find out what the 'more' is. If I don't, and I go preaching among the people, telling them only 'this' or 'that,' then what have I accomplished? I'd be a preacher who speaks for his own gratification, so those who hear me can say, 'What a wise and learned man he is.' Rather than turn into such a man, I'd abandon preaching and teaching and pick up the carpenters' tools like my father and go to Sepphoris when Antipas bids me."

Yeshua quickly realized he'd poked an open wound. "Son, you speak with scorn for my profession and my acceptance of Antipas's conscription." Yosef's face was getting red, which was not a good sign.

"No, Father, I intend only respect for what you do," Yeshua replied, "and how it's provided for us, and I know that refusal to go to Sepphoris for a year would have meant death. I'm only saying if I chose the building trade, I'd be the best I could at it, and like you, would have no choice but to do the king's bidding. But I feel there's something more for me to do, and I'm frustrated I don't yet understand what it is."

Everyone went silent. In that instant Yeshua smelled his mother's robe as she passed him; then a bouquet of smells: his father's sweat, the bread, the dung. He heard the birds chirp, the domestic animals rustle and snort, the children playing in the street. He looked at the room around him. Rather than anyone's words, these impressions of familiar things were the most powerful arguments against his plan.

But he would not be deterred. He hadn't come to his parents to be talked out of his decision. For him it was written in stone. He would go. But he'd go with eyes wide open, fully understanding what he was forsaking and risking.

"The things I've learned from reading," Yeshua continued, "aren't all I need to know to serve the people. There are ideas I need to understand and wisdom to gain. The only way I can do that is by meeting the people from these places and enduring the challenges of life without the shield of those who love me here. Only after that kind of experience would I feel competent to take up the mantle I think you expect of me; so I'll leave after next *Shabbat*."

"Yeshua," Yonnah interjected, "It's clear you won't change your mind, and I understand, without you, I'm just a voice from the wilderness. So I'm saying to your parents, as I have to you, that I'll go with you as your family and your friend. I hope my company keeps you mindful of your duty."

"Yonnah, I welcome your company," Yeshua said. "I've learned endurance of hardship from you beyond what we knew growing up together as children, and I know this won't be easy. I know we don't always see the world through the same eyes, but we'll be comfort and support to each other."

The Paragon

"How will you communicate with these people?" his mother asked.

"Since the conquests of Alexander, many people speak Greek, just like here in Galilee, and as I've learned to do," Yeshua responded.

"And how long will you be away from us?" Maryam continued.

"Emmi, I don't know," Yeshua said. "I want to go to the city of Maracanda, which is far from here, farther than Rome is, and spend what time I need there. You and Father are in strong health, and I expect to find you well when I return, but I can't say how long that will take. Be assured, though, I leave my love with you and take yours with me. You've raised me well, and the things you've taught me will serve me well. I promise you'll see me again."

When *Shabbat* had passed and the day for his departure came, Maryam kissed him goodbye like all mothers, saying, "Travel safely, Yeshua. Say your prayers and mind your temper."

"Of course, Mother. I'll carry your reminder as well as your love."

"Mind your temper, Yeshua," Yonnah teased in a singsong voice when they left the house.

"My temper can make me explosive, but it takes long or drastic abuse to engage it," Yeshua mused.

"You are your father's son," Yonnah said. "I remember when word came that Antipas had conscripted him to work at Sepphoris."

"Oh, yes," Yeshua recalled, picturing the scene. "He nearly tore his workshop apart with his bare hands."

"Cursing and throwing things at the walls," Yonnah rejoined. "I'm sure he didn't want us to see that."

"No," Yeshua said. "He was ashamed when he realized we were watching from across the road. He became more conscious of controlling his demon and always counseled me to do the same. I think demons go from parents to children. Mother's correct; I need to be vigilant against it; but Father's temper had its advantages for the family.

"Mother told me about the circumstances of her pregnancy and my birth," Yeshua continued, "so I wouldn't be shocked if I heard talk, but there was little tongue-wagging around the village. For the most part it was out of respect for my mother, but a healthy fear of my father didn't hurt anything. No one wanted a problem with him."

"The townspeople love your mother. There's no end to her giving to others," Yonnah said.

"You're right about that, Cousin. I can only hope I live up to her standard. For now, let's get to Damascus. I'm sure we'll find a fine caravan heading east."

Two

In Damascus

It took Yonnah and Yeshua nearly two weeks to get to Damascus. They traveled by local path to the Sea of Galilee, where they stopped at the village of Magdala to stay with relatives and say goodbye. Then, following the shore of the Sea, they joined the valley road that ascended to the north to Caesarea Paneas. From there they crossed the mountains and made their way across some dry lands to the Barada River, which led them into the city.

They knew Damascus was old, even older than Jerusalem, even before the time of Abraham. Some said Abraham came from this land. They approached it with awe and even reverence for the history it held, but when they entered, they found chaos.

This wasn't Nazareth. This wasn't even Jerusalem. Yeshua got over his initial shock and became mesmerized by the cauldron of commerce, the great mix of faces, strange to him and surely to each other, the crush of beggars tugging at his tunic.

They'd entered the city at a large market. Yeshua learned there was another market on the other side of town where a person might find a caravan heading east. "Isn't this amazing, Yonnah?"

Yonnah was cowering on the perch of his donkey at this vision of hell. "That isn't the word I'd choose, and the sooner we leave here, the better. Give me a quiet place by a river or even an empty desert."

"As we speak, we ride beside the river Barada," Yeshua observed.

"Right," Yonnah groused, "but we ride on streets lined with the shanties of the poor and the desperate, streets fouled with human and animal waste. The stink of rotting garbage fills our nostrils. The dust of the road mixes with all of it, and I do not wish to breathe, even if I could."

"It seems the Romans haven't brought their fabled sanitation to this neighborhood yet," Yeshua said. "I'm sure there are more pleasant parts to this city, but I don't want to linger here in any case."

"How can I thank you, O Wise One?" Yonnah said.

Yeshua laughed for the first time on the journey. His cousin's sarcasm amused him.

"Yonnah," Yeshua said, "when I begin my ministry, it will be people like this I speak to, so I don't shrink from them. It hurts me that there's nothing I can do to alleviate their physical misery. We were comfortable growing up, but even being poor in a small town like Nazareth or in the more remote countryside is nothing like the hopelessness of being poor in the city. We had a well. We had food and fresh air. There weren't ten of us in a single room."

"I'm comforted someone like you will minister to them, but if they want to hear me," Yonnah huffed, "they can find me far from the crowd."

The two made their way across the city and found the bazaar on the other side. There was a much larger camel market there, with caravanserais and inns close by to serve the merchants and travelers who came to do business. It was easy, therefore, to

The Paragon

inquire among the innkeepers where they might find a caravan going east they could join.

Yonnah let Yeshua attend to this chore. He found a quiet spot farther up the road out of town and asked Yeshua to get him when it was time to leave. Then, after only a few inquiries, an inkeeper directed Yeshua to a caravaneer called Hadi Ba'riel. He would be next to leave.

Hadi Ba'riel was a swarthy man who laughed at almost anything with a sound that seemed to resonate from the depths of his rotundity. "Yes, you've come to the right man," he said. "I've led caravans ten times over the length of the Royal Road from here to Maracanda and back, and before that, I assisted or led shorter routes both here and in Parthia."

"I want to go all the way to Maracanda," Yeshua said.

"Ambitious," Hadi observed. "Do you travel for amusement? You don't seem to be a merchant or a man of means."

"I suppose I'm traveling in quest of ideas," Yeshua replied. "And I have my cousin with me as well."

"Oh, 'ideas,' is it?" Hadi mused. "Well, I hope you find ideas that sustain your mind, but my immediate concern is how you'll sustain your body, and more important, mine? In short, how will you pay for this adventure?"

"I have some money friends in Jerusalem gave me," Yeshua answered. "We'd sell our donkeys and buy mules or a camel. I'd ask for work tending the animals. My cousin is an unusual man. He likes to live apart from people. He's an ascetic monk with minimal needs and will beg for alms when we're in a town."

"Very well," Hadi announced. "I like you, and your mission intrigues me. Maybe I could even introduce you to some people you'd find interesting. I think we can do business. I do need to hire someone for the animals. For the most part each man sees to his own beasts, but we take some others for sale or trade under my auspices. It's those you'll be most concerned with.

"This will be a large caravan," he continued. "One hundred twenty beasts to start, some camels, some horses, mules, one hundred . . . and two men, a few with their wives. I'll take my first wife on this trip. The other two remain here in Damascus. They alternate." Hadi Ba'riel laughed that laugh. "You don't bring wives, then?"

"No," Yeshua replied. "My cousin has vowed never to marry and probably wishes I'd do the same. But I'm sure when I return, my parents will have some plan for me, which I hope is to my liking."

"You seem to take everything seriously," Hadi said. "It's good to be sober-headed on the Royal Road because, especially in the cities, there are those who would rob, cheat, or harm you, out of desperation, drunkenness, or a perverse sense of pleasure. But laughter is good for the soul."

"I admit there isn't much humor in Galilee," Yeshua offered, "but it seems I've found an able teacher."

"Maybe we'll teach each other some things," Hadi said. "We leave in two days. The rules are simple. I'm the boss. The law of talion applies once we leave Roman rule, and I see to its administration. We come and go when I say. We don't wait for anyone. Everyone has some contract with me, which incorporates that understanding. Any questions?"

Yeshua noted Hadi's transformation from jokester to businessman. He felt comfortable with him. No questions. "We have a deal," Yeshua agreed.

The Paragon

Talion: "Do unto others as they do unto you." It wasn't very satisfying to Yeshua. But it was better than the law of savagery: "Do unto others *before* they do unto you." The Torah had its roots in talion, but Yeshua looked for a different formulation, one rooted in love. Maybe, do unto others as you want them to do unto you, he'd mused. He'd also found that concept in the Torah, but it seemed the rabbis had lost it in a Babel of legalistics.

In two days Yeshua awoke with the cock's first crowing. The morning air was crisp and the morning star glowed like a bright ball in the eastern sky, as if pointing the way. He went to Hadi Ba'riel and prepared the animals as instructed, giving them food and water, and arranging them in line. The various owners packed the others quickly and efficiently, having done it often, and took their places as they were ready.

At first light Hadi walked down the line, making a visual check to insure everyone was present and each animal was properly loaded. He had twenty rough-looking armed men for protection leading the way. In Roman or Parthian lands, guards weren't widely needed, but they were a necessary precaution for those places where the government had a weak presence.

"Let's go, then," he ordered, and so they were off. They would turn northeast to Palmyra, rather than due east to Ctesiphon. Ctesiphon was the Parthian capital and the first of its great cities on the Royal Road. The most direct route was across the desert, but on this Palmyra route, after a short desert crossing, they'd stay in fertile land. This would be much easier on the animals and the humans as well.

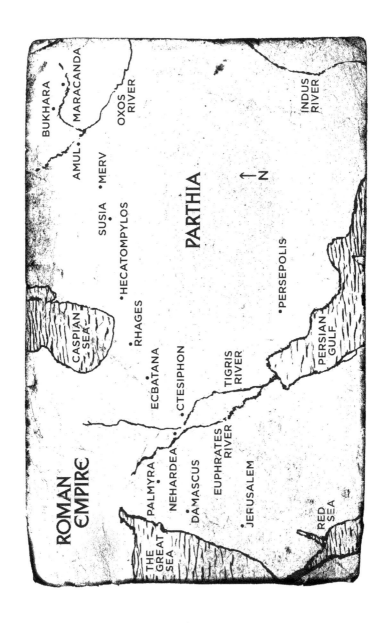

At Palmyra

Like many of the towns they would encounter on the Royal Road, Palmyra was built on and around an oasis. One could say it *was* an oasis. Palmyra was located at a major commercial junction between west, east, and south. It was once a simple Bedouin settlement where the population, if threatened, could collect all their belongings and scamper across the Euphrates River, frustrating their attackers, but now, under the Romans, it was becoming a beautiful and prosperous city.

As they approached Palmyra, through the part of the oasis that was farmed, the caravan stopped for water and rest. After seeing to his duties, Yeshua noticed some local children playing in the stream that fed the fertile land. He approached and watched them laugh and play. They had a ball fashioned out of goatskins. They kicked and tossed it in a game that seemed to have neither an object nor rules, but entertained them nonetheless.

He watched until they stopped. They ran over to him. "Hello, mister. Where you from?" They attempted their meager Greek with him. He sat and talked with them for a while, sharing his bread. One of the boys ran among the palms and returned with dates from his family garden to share with Yeshua and the others.

Yeshua thought about things he'd missed as a child. He remembered laughing and playing when he was young, but as he got a little older, his parents noticed his love of learning and his gifted mind. They made sure he was educated, and he gravitated to the company of older people, more serious than his peers. He wouldn't change the path his life had taken, but sometimes he was wistful about the childhood that had eluded him.

His encounter and his musings were soon interrupted. "Yeshua, come here. I need you." Hadi wanted him for some chore. "I see you get along well with the little ones. You should be more like them: free in spirit, full of laughter. They can teach you more about humor than I can. Come. I need help with one of the animals. As planned, we stay here one night and then on to the Euphrates and down the river to Nehardea and Ctesiphon."

The caravan made its way across another finger of desert and eventually came to the Euphrates River. Across it lay Mesopotamia, the land between the two rivers. The Tigris was the other. It was, along with the Nile Valley, the other great cradle of western civilizations, as well as one of its breadbasket.

Once they forded this river, they would leave Roman jurisdiction. They'd be entering Parthia, nominally an empire, but whose integrity was more subject to the vagaries of local politics than the more cohesive Rome.

That was the advantage of traveling with a man like Hadi Ba'riel, Yeshua realized. He knew the local satraps and had goodwill with them. He knew who to ply with baksheesh, or information, or even to make trouble between rivals if it was to his advantage. Often, the political situation shifted as quickly as the desert sands, and Hadi was nimble if nothing else.

The capital of Parthia was wherever the king chose to live, which wasn't always the same place. There were any number of large cities that mostly sprung from the river of commerce that the Royal Road provided. Any one of them, Ctesiphon, Ecbatana, Hecatompylos, had the infrastructure to accommodate the royal presence. For now, it was Ctesiphon, but before they reached the capital, they would stop at Nehardea.

This Royal Road, and its extension beyond Parthia into Seres and Sinae, the Land of Silk and the Land Below the Yellow River, was rather a web of routes that connected east to west. It facilitated trade in all manner of goods: carpets, spices, seeds, silk, wool and cotton fabric. The caravans carried finished goods as well, not to mention horses, camels, gold, and stones--almost any product you could think of.

Yeshua knew this kind of trade would change the lives of everyone touched by it, but the trade that would change men most was the trade in ideas. Great thoughts of great thinkers made their way across this web, contending and mixing with one another.

The Parthians, who controlled the heart of the route, were practical men, oriented to commerce. The economics of trade trumped any feelings they may have had about ideology or religion. If they made money, everyone who helped them do that was welcome to come and go and, short of sedition, believe and talk as he wished.

In Nehardea

The governor at Nehardea had a problem. He had a substantial population of Jews, including a band of aggressive brigands who dwelt primarily in the marshlands, but these criminals also had a loyal following in the towns and cities of the region. Many of these Jews had a long family history in the area, but some had come recently in response to the opportunity for wealth and mischief.

Hadi had a camel that came up lame. He'd need to try to sell it there, either to someone who believed he could nurse it back to health or for meat. Unless he got lucky and sold it in the caravanserai, there'd be a camel market in a week that would certainly bear fruit.

At dawn on their first morning in Nehardea, Yeshua went to the well near the caravanserai. The well was a three-foot-wide hole with a wooden cover that sat in an open field near a crossroads. There were houses nearby, but the field itself was barren except for small, scattered weeds. The dust made a whirlwind that swirled the hair of a woman who was there to draw water. Her steely eyes flashed frustration as she slammed the bucket to the ground.

"Is there a problem, sister?" Yeshua asked. "Can you not draw water?" His soothing tone mollified her.

"Sir," she answered, "the water is too low, and this rope will no longer reach it."

He surmised by her looks she was Jewish, probably from the local Jewish community. He thought he'd seen her last night and was certain she was a prostitute. "Sister, if you'll be patient, I'll return to the caravan and bring a longer rope."

"Sir," she replied, "my husband will be here soon, so don't trouble yourself on my account." Her tone betrayed suspicion.

"I think you're Jewish like me," Yeshua said. "Where are you from?"

"From the town of Magdala in Galilee," she replied, apparently thinking the place so obscure that she couldn't be doubted. She must have constructed her lie from what she'd learned about Galilee and Judea from her associates.

The Paragon

Yeshua smiled. "Sister, I know the town and people of Magdala well, and I'm certain you aren't from there, and we both know you don't have a husband. Don't be afraid. I mean you no harm. I need water as well. I'll be back in a few minutes."

Yeshua sensed sadness and vulnerability under her frosty exterior. He saw it in her eyes, and it attracted him to her. The anguish in her spirit was palpable to him. He wanted to salve it.

He returned with a longer rope and drew water for both of them. "Thank you, sir. I'd return the favor by preparing a meal for you. You're right. I'm not from Magdala and have no husband, but I provide for myself well enough that I can offer you hospitality. Sorry I lied to you."

"I'd like that very much," he said. "I'll come in the early afternoon, if that's all right. I know you lied out of fear, but there's no need to fear the truth."

"Thank you for putting me at ease," she responded. "I'll make some bread, and see you after midday."

It pleased him to see her smile.

Yeshua found his cousin and told him about the encounter.

Yonnah was furious. "Yeshua, you go to the home of a whore? Will you do this in Galilee and Judea? What are you thinking? Does the road turn you from your God?"

"So many questions from my cousin," Yeshua said. "I'm not in the business of judgment, and I won't teach the people to judge. I forgive as I expect to be forgiven. Who are you to say she's this or she's that, and condemn her? She'll be judged by the whole of her life. It's never too late for anyone to amend."

"You speak of forgiveness," Yonnah said. "For what do you need to be forgiven?"

"If you look inside yourself," Yeshua responded, "you'll understand we all need to forgive each other, because demons lurk in our hearts that cause us to do things we aren't proud of. How we repay and amend is how we'll be judged."

Yonnah took his leave and went out from town to the stream where he stayed while the caravan paused. He sat under a tree and prayed over the words his cousin had spoken, and he understood them, although he did not trust this whore.

Yeshua arrived at Meryam's house. It was a simple building: one room, built of mud bricks with a thatched roof. The floor was strewn with mats, skins, and silk-covered pillows. It was finery, to be sure, beyond what he expected to find in such a modest house, surely the "gifts" of caravaneers with whom she'd socialized in the past.

They drank wine together and talked. Yeshua told her about his life in Galilee. This might have caused her shame over her own story, but with him she felt not shame, but comfort.

"Yeshua, my parents weren't free Jews. A local king, far north of here, owned them. I was born into slavery. My parents had only known slavery themselves, and they'd lost their souls. Every woman slave, including my mother, was a concubine to our lord at his pleasure.

"She wasn't a part of the harem, but whenever he wanted a little something different, she was at his beck and call. The rest of the time she spent doing assigned duties like everyone else, the mundane chores of a household: cook, clean, come, go, fetch me this or that. She had no interest in me, nor any time to be what a mother's supposed to be.

"My father." Her face tightened in a sneer of contempt. "If there was ever a time in his life when he had any spirit or any spine, I never knew it. He didn't give a rat's tail if I lived or died. There was never a moment of affection between us, not that I remember, and, I assume, not before I have memory."

She told Yeshua the whole story of how she was sold into sexual slavery and of her murderous escape.

Yeshua swallowed hard. Her story horrified him while it made him cry inside for her. "Your life has been more difficult than many could bear. Don't let your heart be hard and blind to the goodness in the world."

"Yes, that's the challenge of my life," she replied, "and I see that goodness in you. I know you want nothing from me, but you've touched me in a way that I'd give you anything you asked."

After their repast and a little more wine, Yeshua returned to the caravanserai. No immediate sale of the camel meant the caravan would remain in Nehardea, but there was talk of rebellion in the city. Two Jewish brothers, Analai and Asinai, were the supposed ringleaders. Hadi tried to be in the good graces of both sides. He'd bribed the locals to spare the caravan from pillaging, and even though Hadi had done this before, he was never sure how much goodwill he exactly bought.

During that time, Yeshua grew closer to Meryam. He spent every morning in prayer and meditation and, during the day, earned money by tending the animals and helping the innkeeper and his neighbors. Usually, that meant carpentry work, and although he hadn't honed his skills as his father had, he knew enough to be useful. He'd usually visit Meryam in the late afternoon.

Yonnah, as was his custom, stayed outside the town, slept under trees, ate insects, and when necessary, begged for alms after morning prayers. He sometimes came to visit the caravanserai to talk to Yeshua after begging. Yeshua sensed Yonnah's annoyance over his growing friendship with Meryam. Yeshua even brought his cousin to her home one day, hoping to enkindle some warmth between them.

"Yonnah, this is my friend, Meryam. Meryam, my cousin, Yonnah." Yeshua's introductions began an hour of sitting on the floor with bread, and wine, and silence that seemed like half a day to him and probably to his companions.

"Would you pass the bread, please?" was Yonnah's contribution to the conversation.

"Yes, I hope you enjoy it," Meryam responded with equal enthusiasm.

Yeshua was at a loss as to how to encourage conversation. He realized the two had nothing in common. What kind of insects did you have for breakfast? he imagined her asking. How much money did you make last night sleeping with other sinners? Yonnah might inquire. Although he was annoyed with the two of them, his internal sarcasm took the edge off his pique and allowed him to hope the passage of time might occasion some opportunity for connection.

The Paragon

"Thank you for your hospitality," was Yonnah's emotionless farewell. Yeshua knew it was forced politeness spoken for his sake. When they left, Yeshua didn't criticize his cousin. There was nothing further for him to say just now.

The next morning, as the two cousins stood outside the caravanserai, Yeshua decided it was time to be direct. "Yonnah, I sense a wall of jealousy between you and Meryam, and I cannot have it."

"Jealousy? I hope I don't need to be jealous of a whore," Yonnah shot back. "Oh, I beg your forgiveness, of a poor misguided woman who needs only some understanding. I'm sorry. I've prayed over this since you admonished me not to judge, but I have a bad feeling about this woman.

"Do you think you can change her ways?" he went on. "Not even you, with all your gifts and charisma, can bring her to God, and besides, what does it matter? We leave here in a few days."

"Yonnah," Yeshua said, "I think I'll ask her to come with us."

Yonnah was stunned into silence. At last, he spoke. "Have you lost your reason? Have you lost your focus?" Yonnah threw up his hands. "Well, at least she can support herself."

"Enough of that, Yonnah!" Yeshua stormed. "I won't hear such talk again, or I'll go on without you."

Yonnah gave no quarter in the argument. "So there, now you flash your father's temper. Hear this, Yeshua: I will go where I please. If I need to follow you to spare you from your own soft-headedness, I'll do it. I promised your parents."

"I need no keeper, Yonnah," Yeshua barked, "especially an antisocial ascetic. Individuals are important, more important than 'saving a nation.'"

Without warning, a cascade of water came pouring out of an open widow above them, followed quickly by the bucket that once contained it. "People are still sleeping, damn you. Take your argument someplace else." Yeshua didn't recognize the voice, and although he was mortified, did not disengage.

Yonnah didn't move either but shifted his volume to a hard whisper. "You'd better not turn your back on that nation. You know how the people are suffering, and you can't turn your back on your duty just to save a . . . This journey of yours is indulgence enough."

"It's your asceticism that's itself an indulgence," Yeshua responded at the same volume. "You lust for self-deprivation. You can't get enough of it. But I've heard more than enough."

Yeshua went into the caravanserai, slamming the door behind him. When he got inside, he closed his eyes and exhaled. He calmed himself and went back outside to find Yonnah. He was standing where Yeshua had left him.

"I know your thunder passes quickly," Yonnah said calmly. "I'm sorry I provoked you."

"And I'm sorry I allowed you to, and for what I said about your life choice." Both men grunted a laugh, and though Yeshua had expressed regret to his cousin, in his heart he believed there was an element of truth to what he'd said about his asceticism.

"Yonnah, I'm not even sure that Meryam will want to come with us, but I ask you to give her a chance," Yeshua pleaded. "If she jeopardizes our journey, I'll leave her in a safe place. She'll come as my friend, and I hope soon enough, our friend. She'll understand what I mean to do and accompany us only with that understanding."

The Paragon

The next day during Yeshua's visit, he walked with Meryam to draw water from the well.

"Why did you come to Nehardea?" he asked her.

"Because they'd have me," she said. "I had nowhere else, so I fell in with these robbers. They're my people. Soon, my friends, Analai and Asinai, will lead a revolution, and we'll rule this place as our own land.

"My parents were weak," she continued. "They did the bidding of our owner. My looks and my attitude have made me wonder if I'm indeed my father's daughter, but whatever I am, I have no interest in returning to those who abused and abandoned me, my parents or the bastard who owned us. I would die before I'd sacrifice my self-respect." It seemed she couldn't conceive of any other options.

"But what respect do you get from others or yourself as a prostitute?" His tone was kind and inquisitive, not accusatory.

"I drink with the men. I have whored. I have robbed. I have done every bad thing you can or cannot imagine. I've done these things to survive. I heard of this place and knew it would be a refuge for me. I've been welcomed here by these 'criminals.' I've had to fight, especially at first, and there are some men who are no longer with us by my hand, but now I have respect from these people, and having earned that, I can respect myself. What would you have me do, return to Magdala, the home of my invention?"

"There are worse choices," Yeshua responded. "It's a town of honest, hard-working people with good hearts. Sister, I feel the anger and pain in your heart. I've nothing but admiration for you and the way you survived alone, but haven't things changed?

You've proved to yourself you're a survivor, but I feel you've let your heart grow cold.

"Yet I think your hardness is only a veneer," he continued, "a façade you project because you think it keeps you safe. I've felt another side of you. I sense that underneath is a person who wants to give love and be loved. At some point, I think that's all every person wants, but some never admit it."

She shook her head as a half-smile stretched her lips. "You seem to know everything about everyone, don't you? But you don't know what I want. What do you think I want? Tell me."

"Now you tease," he said. "You tell me."

"Yeshua, more than anything I want to be a mother." There were a few seconds of silence. "Does that surprise you?"

"Not that you want love in your life," he replied, "but the form you'd have it take. Although after a second's thought, no, it doesn't surprise me; but how can you have that here?"

"Well, the physician says I won't have it anywhere," she said. "It's impossible for me have children."

"But even to have some normal life full of love?" Yeshua questioned. "The men here live hard lives and think only of themselves. Even those with a family prey on others for their livelihoods."

"What else can I do?" she asked with a tone of resignation.

"Come with Yonnah and me," Yeshua said. "We're going east where I mean to learn the ideas of other traditions. We, I mean, I'd like your company, and you can see what else the world has to offer."

"Yeshua," she responded, "I'm afraid I won't be a welcome companion to your cousin. Will he continue with you?"

"Yes, he'll continue, but I've discussed this with him, and he'll accept it." Yeshua intentionally omitted the word *possibly* or *probably* from his assertion. "It's my mission," he continued, "to ensure the two of you will not be jealous of each other. Trust me. This situation won't be uncomfortable, if you both show goodwill."

She considered his assurances, not denying her own jealousy, and said, "Your proposal interests me. Let me think on it.

"Tomorrow," she continued, "Analai and Asinai are hosting a feast in the tavern on the road to the marsh villages. I'd like you to come for a while and meet them."

"Perhaps another time," Yeshua answered. "I've been neglecting duties, and I'd rather visit you during the day. Will I see you tomorrow in the afternoon?" He had a bad feeling about what would probably become a debauch in the marshes.

"Yes, of course," she agreed.

The next day Yeshua went to Meryam's house. Meryam prepared a meal, and after they ate, he asked her again to come to Maracanda.

"I'm still thinking on it, but I tell you this in secret. The revolution will begin in three days with an attack on the governor's garrison. There'll be blood in the streets, and loyalists will be slaughtered, so I advise you and your group to get your business done and leave as soon as you can. It won't be safe here.

"I tell you I'm torn," she continued. "These are my people now, and they want and need me to fight, but I'm drawn to you as well. Tonight, I'm going to the celebration. I'm sure there'll be more talk of revolution, and I'll know my own mind better once I hear what the people are thinking."

Yeshua began to speak. "Stop," she said. "More talk isn't useful. I'll decide. If I don't go with you, you'll understand why, but go now and be safe." She kissed him on the cheek. "Go."

Yeshua left with his mind spinning. He'd surprised himself by how strongly he wanted her to come with him, but he needed to act quickly. If civil order broke down, no one would be safe here. Ba'riel was nowhere to be found, but there should be enough time to act, if he told him first thing in the morning.

He wouldn't have to wait. He wasn't sure what time it was. Since it was still dark, he guessed about the beginning of fourth watch. His door crashed open and Hadi had an urgent tone in his voice. "Wake now, Yeshua. Prepare the animals as quickly as you can. We're leaving."

"What's the matter?" Yeshua asked.

"The governor has attacked the celebration of Analai and Asinai, and the fight is on." Hadi said.

"I heard there wouldn't be a rebellion for three more days," Yeshua said.

"I heard the same, but no one thought the governor would surprise attack. We need to go," Hadi responded.

"Sir, there's someone I'm concerned about," Yeshua said.

"The whore? I make it my business to know the business of my people," Ba'riel said, responding to Yeshua's look of surprise.

Yeshua resented the description as much from Hadi as from his cousin but held his tongue. "Meryam, yes, she was with the brothers tonight."

The Paragon

"Yeshua," Hadi said, "I fear the worst for her. You cannot go to that place. You'd be killed. You need to forget her and do your job and prepare to leave, so that the greater number is saved."

Yeshua had grown to care deeply for Meryam as a friend and would have gone to try to find her, but Hadi was right. That would be suicidal. His heart was heavy with sadness and guilt as he prepared the animals. Maybe she would escape the attack. Maybe she hadn't gone to the celebration. She'd know the caravan would be leaving. Maybe she'd come. Yes, she would come.

Yeshua wasn't too concerned about Yonnah. He was outside town near the road in the direction of travel. He sent one of the boys who traveled with the caravan to roust him.

Everyone moved with quiet, deliberate speed. No one panicked. This apparently wasn't the first time these veterans of the Royal Road had to make a quick getaway from some nasty situation. At last they were assembled on the edge of town. Yonnah arrived, and Yeshua explained more fully what was happening.

"Let's move then," the master bellowed.

"No, sir," Yeshua pleaded, "I pray you, not yet."

"Why not yet?" Hadi asked.

"I still have hope," Yeshua said.

"Save your hope," Hadi countered, "and besides, she wouldn't be good for the caravan."

"Sir," Yeshua argued, "if she comes, I know she'll be a benefit. She won't come as a whore, but as my friend, whom I'd keep safe."

"There's no waiting, Yeshua," Hadi said. "The soft glow in the east is first light, and the glow in the city behind us is fire. We're going." And the caravan began to move.

Yeshua's heart sank. Yonnah exhaled in apparent relief. They and the great entourage marched out of the city bound for the capital, Ctesiphon.

In the Court of Antipas
A Month Prior

"I've summoned Kefir and Ptolemy, Your Majesty," Sesipedes, the regent, spoke. "With your indulgence, I respectfully ask why you have so much concern for these would-be messiahs rather than the Zealots, who wreak more havoc?"

"Sesipedes, the Zealots are brutes. I don't ignore the Zealots, but they're my second problem. The people don't support them because they act contrary to the Torah, but most of the people believe a messiah will come to liberate them from their 'oppressors,' which besides Rome, include you and me.

"Whenever someone claims the title 'Messiah,'" Antipas said, "he draws a following among the people, and that's what's dangerous. I don't know which of these two, Yeshua or Yonnah, will become the most popular, but we need to erase both of them; and as far as Kefir and Ptolemy are concerned, we speak only of Zealots."

Sesipedes saw the two men approaching and announced them formally: "Kefir and Ptolemy are here to report to Your Majesty."

"Come forward, sirs," the king invited, "and you may remain standing. Kefir, you've served me well for many years, and I expect someday you'll become First Commander of the Royal Guard.

For now, I have a special mission for you. I expect it will coincide with your own interests.

"I know, of course, what happened to your wife," Antipas continued. "The Zealots murdered her in the streets merely because she was a pagan, Egyptian if I recall, and because she was married to you, a Jew."

Kefir didn't need to be reminded. Even though ten years had passed, the wounds to his spirit had never been salved. He harbored a fierce hatred of the Zealots and an unquenched desire to take revenge against them.

Ptolemy was a man now, and with this reminder, his expression grew dark. The murder had never seemed to eat at him daily as it did Kefir. Putting it in the back of his mind, he thought, was a child's, at least his son's, way of dealing with the horror. Kefir never brought it up. He didn't want Ptolemy to grow up wallowing in hatred. It was enough that one of them did.

"I thought you might be interested to know that we've arrested a leader of the Zealots," the king continued, "and under . . . extreme persuasion . . . he was kind enough to confess his knowledge of the murder of your wife and the burning of your farm."

"Was he the one?" Ptolemy's expression perked up beyond what it already was due to being in the royal presence.

"Oh, no, he wasn't the murderer," Antipas answered, "but he told us who two of them were. We know they're now with the Essenes. They were young Zealots at the time, and were two of the four who carried out the attack. As king, I have an interest in removing these two annoyances, without public trial, and I thought you might be interested in the opportunity to exact revenge."

"Your Majesty," Kefir responded, "I've always been grateful for the way you treated me after the attack. As commander of the Sepphoris garrison, I had a good job. I had some acreage as a reward for past service and a fine son who stands with me now. The Zealots also burned my land and house and left me with nothing, only my son who was rescued by my soldiers. My son lives, but not because of any mercy on the Zealots' part.

"After my tragedy," Kefir continued, "you kindly promoted me to your Royal Guard, and gave me new land. I'll be forever grateful for that, so I'd do as you ask only for the asking; but now you tell me I have a chance for revenge as well. When can we begin?"

Ptolemy spoke, although the king hadn't directly spoken to him. His eyes wandered at first, perhaps flashing back to that day at the market. "I never saw the faces behind the hoods that day, Your Majesty," Ptolemy's voice was halting at first, but grew more confident as he continued. "I can only say that the assailants were boys themselves, not much older than I was. I could never imagine why they'd kill my mother. It was an evil thing to do. I'd be happy to join my father in taking revenge now that it seems possible."

The king explained how he wanted the mission to be carried out. "I want you to take care of this in disguise," he said. "I don't want it traceable back to the royal court. Sesipides will brief you about their movements. Their names are Yeshua and Yonnah. They're Nazarenes and cousins. Go now and rid me of them."

The Paragon

The two men set off to find the Nazarenes. They adopted the tattered clothing of common laborers and began to scour the countryside at the cousins' known locations. They claimed to have heard of Yonnah's preaching and told those they asked they wanted to meet and follow him. They knew if they found Yonnah, they'd find Yeshua as well.

Although they'd often talked father to son, as they trod the road from Sepphoris to Nazareth, they spoke to each other about the one subject they'd avoided for many years. "Son," Kefir began, "I know you've never expressed the bitterness that I have over your mother's murder."

"I know," Ptolemy responded. "After it happened, I was sullen for months, but with Aunt Euginia's counsel, I finally decided mother wouldn't want me to live an unhappy life."

"Perhaps I'd have done better to follow your lead," the father mused, "but I couldn't get past it. Every month some Zealot atrocity reinforced my attitude. Those crimes were news I'd never let you hear until you were old enough to train as a soldier."

"My memories of mother sustained me in those years," Ptolemy recalled. "She always made me laugh and fired my imagination with her stories of the places she'd been, Egypt, Rome, Greece. Along with wanting to be a soldier like you, I wanted to see the world like her."

"Hopefully, you won't have to do both those things at the same time. A soldier's life in a foreign campaign is not at all glamorous," Kefir offered. He was tough and loyal but now content to be part of the Royal Guard.

Joseph Emmrich

When they got to Nazareth, they found Yosef. Since ten years had passed, Ptolemy and Yosef didn't recognize each other. "We've heard about your nephew and son's preaching," Kefir said, "and we'd like to follow them. All we know is they're from Nazareth. Are they here?"

Yosef had a bad feeling about the men. He couldn't put his finger on it, but he felt lying to them was the right thing to do. "No, they're not here," he said, "You could probably find them by the Jordan in Perea or in Qumran, but I can't rule out them being in Jerusalem." As far as he knew, some people by the river listened to Yonnah, but neither of them had any far-reaching reputation. He wondered how these two had heard of their preaching. No need for them to know about his son's journey.

Kefir and Ptolemy went to Perea first, to inquire in the towns along the east bank of the Jordan. They came to a village nestled along the riverbank near some shoals, where the water spilled from a deeper pool until it rejoined the channel some yards below. Fertile farms surrounded the cluster of homes, shaded by palms and willows. Cows waded in the shallow waters. Children ran and jumped in from a high bank. The people seemed to move more slowly here, belying how hard they worked.

"There's something pure about farming," Kefir said in a near whisper. "This is the peaceful life I want for myself at the end of my career, but for now we have a job to do."

The Paragon

"Yes, I know who you're talking about," more than one villager told them. Inevitably, these inquiries pointed them in the direction of Qumran.

Qumran was back across the river in Judea, the territory of Archelaus, their king's brother. Their inquiries at Qumran bore some fruit. "Yes, they left here several weeks ago, headed for a visit home to Nazareth," a monk told them. "Yeshua had spoken of taking some kind of journey to the east. He would be searching for ideas. No," he further responded, "I'm not certain what he meant by that."

"We must have just missed them at Nazareth. What bad luck," Ptolemy said when they left.

"Or treachery; let's get back to Nazareth quickly to see what else we can find out," Kefir urged.

When they returned to Nazareth, they spoke again to Yeshua's father. Yosef was now even more suspicious of the men, but he was sure they would neither follow nor find his son. Nonetheless, he told them nothing. "Maybe Jerusalem," was his disinterested response.

The assassins didn't trust Yosef either. Kefir was certain he'd lied to them before, so they asked others after they left his house. More than one villager told them they thought he was bound for Damascus, and from there they weren't sure, maybe Parthia.

When they returned to Antipas, they spoke first to Sesipedes, whose expression made it seem the king would not receive their information with a smile. He told Antipas they were present and ready to report.

"Yes, yes," Antipas said, "I'm anxious to hear from them. Send them in."

"Your Majesty," Kefir began, "we've done as ordered. We've gone, clothed as ordinary villagers to Perea. We've gone to Qumran. We've even gone to Nazareth twice and learned the two you ordered us to kill have left Judea and Galilee, bound for Damascus. Since they've left, does this end our mission?"

The king didn't know what the Nazarenes were up to. Did they somehow know of his intention to have them killed? Were they going into hiding? Were they plotting with expatriated Jews in nearby areas to overthrow him? He'd heard some of them, like the two brothers in Nehardea, even commanded men under arms.

"This is how you obey my orders?" Antipas thundered. "I commanded you to kill them. Leave me, and go do what you were told in the first place. Follow them--to Damascus or the ends of the earth if you must. Bring me their heads or I'll have yours in their place."

"Your majesty, you misunderstand. My fire for revenge still burns," Kefir pleaded. "I only feared it wouldn't be in your interest for us to operate so far outside your jurisdiction or that you might have greater need for us here in Galilee."

"No, Kefir," Antipas retorted, "and in the future, you'd do well to carry out my orders rather than guess my will. Go now, and do as I've told you."

So, Kefir and Ptolemy left the king. "Damn!" shouted a crestfallen and angry Kefir. "I can't believe he questioned our loyalty. I've never given him any reason to doubt me. Let's find these bastards quickly and finish them off."

Ptolemy was outwardly mirroring his father's attitude. But beyond revenge, he was inwardly excited about where this quest might take him and secretly hoped it might last a while.

For now, it was off to Damascus to track down the Zealots. Ptolemy realized the king had changed them from soldiers to spies, even in their own lands; so, they said goodbye to their comrades and loved ones, such as were left to them, and prepared for a journey they weren't free to discuss.

The next day they left for Damascus. It seemed Damascus might not be their ultimate destination, but it would be their starting point. Kefir had little hope of finding Yeshua and Yonnah there, but he'd been to Damascus once before and believed if he inquired at all the inns and caravanserais in the city, they could follow the men's route and catch them at some point. There was, however, no time to waste.

It took Kefir and Ptolemy only about five days to reach the ancient capital, frequently changing horses along the route. When they arrived, they spent a night drinking, whoring, and inquiring.

Kefir got the information he needed from a tavern keeper. "The men you're looking for went with a caravan, led by a man named Hadi Ba'riel," he related. "His caravan is bound ultimately for Maracanda, which is across and beyond the Parthian empire at the mountain gateway to Seres, the Land of Silk. One of the men you're looking for seemed to be interested in making the entire journey."

"Did they go directly to Ctesiphon?" Kefir asked him.

"No," the man replied. "They headed to Palmyra and down the river valley by way of Nehardea to Ctesiphon, but you'd best be careful if you go that way. There's been a revolution in Nehardea."

Kefir believed they could get to Palmyra on their own, but after that they'd need to attach themselves to caravans and leap ahead whenever the opportunity presented itself. This revolution would make their mission more dangerous. Although they could avoid Nehardea and go directly to Ctesiphon, he reasoned, they needed to follow the route of the caravan.

Three

With the Caravan toward the Zagros Mountains

The caravan had lost time in Nehardea. For a journey of such great length, a day here or a day there didn't seem to matter much, but Hadi had a rough schedule, at least early on. He wanted to limit the unexpected delays as much as possible. It was important to cross the Zagros before winter set in, but once that was done, time would no longer be a concern. Trading opportunities would determine their pace, along with any unforeseen annoyances or disasters that might befall them. The road would work its will.

Hadi, therefore, decided to stay in Ctesiphon for only one night. The lame camel had gotten better over the days in Nehardea, but Hadi still thought it better to sell it. Since there was more commercial activity in the capital, that proved an easy task, so they pressed on.

The caravan with all its animals lumbered out of the Valley of the Two Rivers. Verdant Mesopotamia morphed into a harsher land. Although they were following a river into the mountains, its twists and turns afforded fewer and fewer meadows for cultivation the closer it came to its rise into the highlands.

The mountain ranges were arranged in rows running northwest to southeast, like perfect waves on the sea. The road went between the waves, traversing a plain that spared them from having to cross at a high elevation. If all went well, they could be in Ecbatana in three to four weeks.

Yeshua was profoundly unhappy over the events at Nehardea. He'd been sure that Meryam would come with him and was devastated by her rejection. A woman of the street, he thought. How could I be so stupid? This gift of empathy I believed I had has completely failed me. I was wrong about her. She loved her life of whoring and mayhem more than she wanted to amend. He continued this torrent of thought which was more self-berating than directed at her.

Yonnah was only too happy to reinforce it. He hoped nothing like Nehardea ever happened again.

As the first day ended, the mountains were still so distant they were but a jagged edge to the horizon. They camped at an oasis and marveled at the sliver of a moon, with a bright star near one of its horns, chasing down the sunken sun; but in that darkening western expanse a solitary figure on horseback approached.

Hadi saw it first. He was none too happy about it.

Yonnah saw it second, and his expression darkened even as his face turned white. He grudgingly called attention to the thing he knew would animate his cousin. "Yeshua, look yonder."

He knew, as they all did, that it was she.

As she came closer, Yeshua's unbridled joy received a jolt of horror. She was covered in dried blood, both from wounds of her own and from the damage she'd inflicted on the governor's guard. She had a blank gaze as she dismounted. Yeshua ran to her and embraced her.

In Nehardea
Some Days Earlier

It was a raucous feast. The tables were filled with roasted goats and pigs, succulent fruits, a cornucopia of vegetables, and fresh aromatic breads that the women had spent the day creating. Wine flowed from a limitless store of jars, and the hundreds of revelers were in a celebratory mood over what they all believed would happen in a few days.

"Meryam, please come with us," Analai beckoned. "We want to discuss our plans, and we need any information you've come by in the course of 'business.'" He, along with his brother and a small trusted cadre, made up the war council. There would be more time to celebrate after they finalized a course of action.

The group settled around a sturdy wooden table in a small back room of the tavern. Asinai began to address the group. "Friends, we're proposing to begin the revolution in two days.

At the same time we attack the garrison, we'll send an emissary to the king to assure him that he'll get his due, if he leaves us to otherwise govern ourselves. We think because of our strength and the terrain in the marshes, he'll agree. It would be too costly to try to put us down."

Analai rose to begin outlining the battle plan when the group heard a commotion in the tavern. The singing and laughter turned into screams. "We need to get out!" Analai shouted. One by one the plotters clambered out a back window. It was clear they were under attack.

Most of them carried small arms but ran to a shed behind the tavern where other weapons had been stored. They found comrades already distributing swords and spears to many others who had rallied there. Those inside had barred the front door of the tavern and soldiers of the governor were trying to break through.

Analai grabbed a young man by the shirt. "Son, run to the marsh and rally the people. We need men and weapons. Don't waste any time."

"Father," the young man argued, "give me a weapon. You need me to stay and fight."

"I need no such thing," Analai shouted. "This is no time to argue. Run. Grab a horse if you can do it without being seen. We need help or we'll all die. Go now."

Analai's son ran into the darkness while the rest joined the fight. They raced to the front door and attacked the flank of the invading force, driving them back from the tavern. Those inside opened the door and poured out to help their leaders.

The Paragon

They only had enough time to arm themselves and get organized when the governor's troops counterattacked. This second wave brought greater numbers, more than the rebel forces. The battle was joined in earnest. It wasn't a battle of lines of soldiers. It was chaos. The clang of swords, the groans of mortally wounded bodies, the cursing, the flying and splashing of blood gave no hint of who was winning or losing.

Eventually, the governor's forces began to push the rebels back toward the tavern. Meryam was in the thick of the melee. She was skilled with a sword and wreaked death on her enemies. She relished the fight and the bloodshed but was becoming exhausted by the length of the battle.

"Analai," she screamed, "I don't know how much longer we can endure."

"Fight, sister," he screamed back. "If we don't prevail, we all die. We cannot surrender, and they wouldn't accept it."

As their situation grew more desperate, Analai was astonished to see his son beside him wielding a sword. "Father, I ran ahead. Help is coming."

No sooner had he spoken, when he saw torches moving swiftly up the road toward the tavern. Fully a thousand men, fresh and well-armed, stormed the rear of the attackers. The tide of battle had turned for good.

Once those who had besieged the tavern were either killed or on the run, Asinai shouted the order: "On to the garrison, men!"

The rebels overtook the governor's retreating troops and slaughtered them all, hacking them without mercy. They surrounded the garrison and burned it to the ground. After another fierce fight, they won the ultimate prize, the head of the governor.

It was over. The groaning was now muffled. The odor of smoldering fire and spilled blood filled the air, and first light gave a glimpse of devastation and carnage beyond Meryam's imagination. Beyond physical exhaustion, Meryam was stripped of any ability to have an emotional response. She surveyed the scene around her, dropped her sword, and began walking away, without intention or direction, from this macabre vision of victory.

With the Caravan

"I had to help Analai and Asinai," Meryam explained, to herself as well as Yeshua. "It was my duty. The battle lasted for hours, and we killed every last one of them, even those who would surrender. The matter was going badly for us when a thousand men came from the marshes and turned the tide in our favor. Once we routed the attackers, we followed them to the garrison and finished the job. Nehardea is ours now . . . theirs.

"Even though I've shed blood in my life, the horror of this battle was more than I could bear. It will haunt my dreams. I took this horse and left my friends to their spoils. I think there's no forgiveness for what I've done."

The Paragon

"There can always be forgiveness," Yeshua whispered, "but forgiveness is for tomorrow. For tonight come by the stream, and I'll clean you up. I'll find you fresh clothes, and you can sleep away your exhaustion. When you're rested, you can begin your life anew. Come with me."

Yeshua slept by her side that night. Twice, she awoke suddenly, screaming, once in rage, once in horror. Yeshua held her. "Be still, Meryam. Everything will be all right." It didn't seem like enough, but it was all he knew to say.

When morning came, she sat on the ground where she'd slept. She looked out over the desert with the same blank stare she'd arrived with and began to cry. She looked at Yeshua. "This bloodshed wasn't justified. How can I be forgiven?"

He knew she had true remorse for what she'd done. Since she'd arrived, she'd spoken only of forgiveness. It was as if her mind had become blocked by her sin, and she couldn't go forward without someone bringing her peace.

"If you wrong a person," Yeshua consoled, "and if you can ask and receive forgiveness from him, that's best; but that isn't possible here. The men most wronged are dead, and you can't go back and seek out their families to ask them. They would kill you; but you can pray to God and ask his forgiveness. To receive that forgiveness, however, you need the purpose to amend your life, and show it by giving love and doing good works. You'll best understand your own sincerity and know in time if you're forgiven, but be confident that God will let it be so."

"I swear to you I'll amend," she vowed. "I've descended as far as I can bear."

Meryam went apart from the caravan and in her heart renounced her sins: her whoring, her murder, her robbery. She confronted herself, denying or excusing nothing. She pledged to God to live a life of helping others. She prayed the demons inside her that made her do these things would be banished forever; and as the days passed, joy returned to her heart with a peace she'd never known. Then she prayed it would last.

After some days, the caravan emerged from the mountains on the path that opened onto the Nisaean Plain. The route would be flat all the way to Ecbatana. The traverse of the Zagros had been cold, but not unbearably so, and as expected, any snows remained in the higher elevations.

By the time they neared Ecbatana, the moon was a crescent again, but now in the morning sky. They were about two days away and stopped at an oasis for the evening. There was another caravan already encamped, headed in the opposite direction. The two traveling parties mingled, exchanged stories, and shared some of the local palm wine.

The atmosphere was convivial, but it troubled Hadi to learn there was sickness in Ecbatana. It began, the other master told him, with people having fever and vomiting, but now the situation was getting worse, and people were beginning to die in great numbers. The caravan's need for supplies meant there was no way to avoid Ecbatana, but Hadi told everyone the stay would be much shorter than planned. They'd need two nights, but that would be all.

At Ecbatana

As they approached the outskirts of Ecbatana, Yeshua saw perhaps a hundred men gathering brush some ways from the road. More wood was being brought on carts. When they drew closer, he could see there were piles of bodies behind the men. They were preparing a pyre to dispose of the victims of this plague that had engulfed the town. This was unusual because Zoroastrianism, the principal religious tradition of the empire, forbade the cremation of dead bodies.

Yeshua had heard some in the caravan were beginning to feel ill, and he feared the worst. He moved to catch up to Hadi and noticed him slouched in his saddle, swaying, as if not in control of his body. "Hadi!" Yeshua shouted.

The master of the caravan snapped to life. "I'm fine."

"No one said you weren't," Yeshua snapped back at him, "but now I'm afraid you're not."

"Yeshua, I do feel ill. There's a caravanserai I know a short distance ahead. It's before we reach the city, and I think that if we stop there, we won't be exposed to the masses of the sick. There are some among us, however, myself included, who aren't so well right now. I think the disease has come to us from the caravan at the oasis. This may be a difficult time."

The caravanserais of the Royal Road were renowned throughout the world. Most were comfortable, but some, like this one near Ecbatana, were lavish. The owners operated under a royal charter in concurrence with the local governor. Sometimes the government even contributed to the enhancement of the facilities to encourage travel and commerce. Of course, this practice brought business to their jurisdiction. More commerce, more tax money; that was the Parthian model.

As they approached, Yeshua could see this one was massive. It had stone towers about forty feet tall on the four corners of its square perimeter, resembling an imperial fortress.

The rest of the wall was brick, covered in white stucco and decorated with monumental images of beasts, real and imaginary. A pair of Zoroastrian angels oversaw the portal. Each looked like a stylized eagle with a human head and spread wings, sporting three rows of interlaced loops, obviously feathers.

The gate was a massive double door, hewn from sturdy, thick wood brought in from the north of the empire. Each half was crossed with iron strips and attached with imposing iron hinges. The gate was open, but somehow, that wasn't saying, "Welcome."

All caravanserais generally followed a similar layout, and this one was no exception, save it was more elaborate than most. First, Yeshua noticed the courtyard could easily host a market equal to any in a large city. One by one he led the animals across the stone pavement and into the stalls that bordered the front half of the courtyard. Even with the size of their entourage, they filled only half of them.

After he finished putting up the animals, Yeshua walked to the back half of the courtyard. It was elevated three steps from the front part and floored with a combination of polished stones and decorative tile. Its principal design, in the color of the blue of the evening sky before it goes fully black, was a large circle with directional points radiating from its center.

The Paragon

Yeshua was chilled by an eerie sense of inactivity as he noticed the sleeping chambers lining the perimeter. Their doors, many ajar, were recessed under a colonnade formed with intricately carved wooden posts and arches. He could see mounds of disheveled bed coverings and personal items like combs, clothing, and shoes, bespeaking abandonment and a hasty evacuation.

He continued walking to the rear of the caravanserai from the sundial in the center of the design and peered into a grand bathing pool, now empty.

The pool sat between two mirror-image terraced gardens. In the warm months, these gardens surely bloomed with all the colors of the rainbow and flowed with fountains and cascades that must have brought serenity to those who took time to linger among their displays. Yeshua could envision this place when the gardens were at their most spectacular, and when it offered the hospitality of a caring owner, but for now, amazement at the structure would have to do.

Along the rear wall, in addition to the chambers, was a large room with a great stone hearth where the gathering, eating, and drinking took place. Yeshua stuck his head into the room. It was as empty as the rest of the caravanserai, save for the trash and dishes that remained on the long wooden tables.

Hadi called out, "Hallo, Hallo, Dariush; Hadi is here!" But there was no answer except the sound of his own voice echoing off the walls. The proprietor, a friend of Hadi's, was nowhere to be found. His wife and children weren't there either. No one was. This was bad news, although the place would be shelter for them when they needed it most.

As they prepared to take over the building, a lone horseman with his face covered approached the caravanserai from the direction of the city. The horseman trotted through the gate toward Yeshua and Hadi, keeping his distance from the caravaneers. "Who occupies this caravanserai?" he demanded.

"Hadi Ba'riel of Damascus, a friend of Dariush, whom I know to be the owner."

"I am Tartinius, representative of the king's governor. Our city is beset by a plague, as you've seen. We order you to remain here and not enter the city. Your friend and his family all died and are being burned with the others. You have water here and some grain. We're sending men to the east and west to prevent others from coming until this has passed, and since you have sick among you, we order you to remain here until all of you are healed . . . or dead."

"Very well," Hadi agreed. "However, I ask your permission to send one person from my caravan into the city to fetch my friend, Varaza. He's a physician and traditional healer. I'd like to bring him here, if he's alive and willing, to try to restore my health and the health of the others of my caravan."

Yeshua volunteered. "I'm among those who aren't sick. Perhaps God or fortune favors some of us, and one of the well should go. I'll do it."

Tartinius granted permission, and Yeshua followed the instructions Hadi had given him to Varaza's house. The neighborhood where he lived seemed almost normal. The houses were finer and more substantial than in the larger part of the city. The brickwork was precise and much of it brightly painted, as were the doors and window shutters. He noticed the streets were clean, devoid of trash and body waste.

The neighborhood occupied a small hill across a stream, which gave it some degree of isolation from the rest of the city. Two bridges provided access, although now the water was low and easily forded. There wasn't as much activity as he might have expected in ordinary times, but Yeshua saw neither anxiety nor desperation on the faces of those he encountered.

He found Varaza's house and introduced himself, explaining why he'd come. "Hadi Ba'riel, yes, my old friend," Varaza said, his face lighting up. "Of course I'll come."

"Why is there no panic in your neighborhood, and no sign of mass death?" Yeshua wondered aloud.

"The sad truth," Varaza explained, "is that there are few physicians in this town, and I don't have the wherewithal to serve beyond my own neighborhood. We're far from the main streets, and the people have put up signs that say 'Zone of Death' to keep others out. I've gone neighbor to neighbor and recruited help to tell the rest the best practices to treat the sick and to protect their own health.

"The most difficult thing," Varaza continued, "is to deal with the people's superstition and convince them there are things they can do to save themselves. The Greek physicians trained me, but many believe I'm the superstitious one, although our relative success is changing some attitudes. So, for my friend, I'll go with you. I take it he comes with a caravan."

"Yes, we're at the caravanserai on the west edge of town," Yeshua responded. "The plague took the owner and his family. Now we occupy it."

"Maybe we have a chance to save your lives," Varaza said. "Let us hope so. Let's go."

Varaza was a spry man for his age. Although there was a slight hunch to his posture, his step was brisk and certain. When the two men returned to the caravanserai, Varaza examined his friend and then the others. "Ba'riel," he said in a staccato rhythm as certain as his step, "here's what you must do. Separate the sick from the well. Choose one person to care for the sick. Make sure that the sick get plenty of water and rest. Cool their heads if they have fever. Make sure the one who treats them covers his face and has as little contact as possible with the infected. Cover their faces as well.

"The others must not wander around town," he continued, "but stay at the caravanserai. Clean this place and yourselves using soap, and bury the filth far from the building. I'll leave some herbs with you to help the sick feel better and to fight the disease. Let everyone know this is a medical problem, not a curse. No, I'll do that myself, before I go."

Yeshua spoke. "Let me be the one to care for the sick."

"Yes." Hadi agreed and made the order. "Give me a private moment with my friend."

Yeshua left the room, and when the two men finished talking, Varaza came to Yeshua. "Take some time to organize the sick into a few rooms. See to their needs as I've instructed you. Then return to my house the way you came before. I need to talk to you.

"You need to understand," he counseled, "all the sick will get worse. It's only the second or third day. Then, some will get better,

The Paragon

and some will die. When someone has been well for two full days, he may leave his room, but give him fresh clothes and burn the old. Good luck."

After getting the sick into rooms and making them comfortable, Yeshua found Yonnah and Meryam. Yonnah spoke up. "I want to help with the sick."

"It's better if there's only one at risk," Yeshua responded.

"No, you'd exhaust yourself in a few days. It could take a month or more for this to run its course," Yonnah countered.

"And three are better still," Meryam volunteered. "One can take the morning, one the afternoon, one the night."

"That settles it, then. We'll fight this thing, and with God's help, we'll win." Yonnah spoke without any reticence. Despite Yonnah's aversion to people, Yeshua knew he'd step forward when the need arose.

Yeshua went back to the physician's home. "Come in and sit," Varaza began. "I want to talk to you about something. I've been studying the healing arts for many years. I've learned about herbs and how they can help heal the body or the mind, and this took many years to learn. In fact, I'm still learning. Then I studied the treatments and techniques of the Greeks, everything from treating a plague to setting a fractured bone, and that took many years to learn. Still I learn. As far as these are concerned, I can only show you some basic aid."

"I've learned some things caring for the sick in Jerusalem," Yeshua said.

"Very good," Varaza responded, "but there are some other arts I have learned. No, not black arts, but techniques of the mind:

mind helping mend the body. I understand you're empathic--that you sometimes feel what another feels inside, body and mind it would seem. I know, as well, you're experienced with meditation. It's also important to me that you're a good person.

"So I'm offering to teach you these techniques," Varaza continued. "They don't take long to learn. You only need to practice once you've learned them. I'm doing this as a favor to my friend, who recommends you, and who probably could use someone with these abilities for the rest of his journey. I'm also doing it because I like you. There's the offer. Do you accept?"

"Of course I do," Yeshua said. "Thank you for the opportunity."

"Good," the physician replied. "We'll begin tomorrow. I treat people in the morning. Arrange your duties at the caravanserai to coincide with mine; then come in the afternoon."

Yeshua went back to tell Meryam and Yonnah what was happening. He arranged to have the morning duty. When he took over from Meryam, she told him that almost everyone was worse off, especially Hadi, and that there were two new cases.

Yeshua went to the well that was housed under a gazebo where the levels of the courtyard split. He drew fresh, cool water and tried to ease the fever of those who suffered. He made them drink as much as they could keep down. He had them urinate and make their body waste in some large clay bowls he'd found. He emptied them beyond even the outbuilding, where they were burying the other filth and trash.

He spent time with Hadi, with whom he was developing a friendship, thanking him for sending him to Varaza as a student.

The Paragon

He tried to conceal his concern for the man and keep his spirits up, but Hadi was suffering and was afraid he was going to die.

How would he comfort him, Yeshua puzzled: with the words of Zoroaster, which he didn't know, or of the prophets? What did Hadi know of the prophets? What about the Pharisees and their resurrection of the dead? Should he talk to him of an afterlife? If so, he'd better tell him to ask for forgiveness of his sins.

Hadi interrupted this rambling paralysis of internal indecision with verbal rambling of his own. "If I die, please take care of my wife. See that she gets home or wherever she wants to go. Everyone knows the order of succession if the leader dies. It goes in order of experience and is written in the contracts; but if . . ."

"Stop it. Enough. You're not going to die. You talk from delirium. Stop feeling sorry for yourself. Rest now and fight this. Do as Varaza tells you and get well. No more talk of matters of death." He had taken a page from Yonnah. It seemed they both needed to hear it.

The route to Varaza's neighborhood was a trail of misery, seeming even worse than his prior visits. Yeshua moved swiftly among the pathetically sick, who were retching in the streets and moaning in their hovels, avoiding the filth and squalor piling up in the byways of the poorer neighborhood. It seemed a vision of the end of days.

There was an unbearable foul odor about the place; a combination of human and animal waste, putrefying trash, and some rotting corpses that for whatever reason had gone unattended. Those few who were walking, pallid, unsteady, shuffled a few steps before supporting themselves on the nearest wall. Some others, though outdoors, were leaning against the front of their houses, heads tilted back, eyes closed, open-mouthed in the hope that the air would give them a breath because they were too weak to take one.

Some people's heads had slumped forward, their neck muscles no longer able to support the weight of their skulls. There seemed no possibility they could breathe in this position. In fact, many of them were dead.

All these signs screamed, do not stop! But Yeshua noticed a child, a girl maybe ten years old, standing, but with her torso draped over a hitching post. He went to her and, although it was dangerous, put his arm around her and said, "My child, are you all right?"

"Yes, sir," she answered. "I've been sick, but I'm feeling better. I was returning home from my uncle's house with some bread for my father and brother. My mother has died. I'm still weak and needed to rest."

"Is it far?" he asked. "Can you make it?"

"Yes, it's just a little way," she said. "If I rest a minute more, I'm sure I can make it."

Yeshua walked the last few yards to her home with her. Her father and brother were sleeping, but they looked better than those he'd seen in the street. "Do you have clean water?" he asked.

"Yes," the little girl said.

He was satisfied their chances to survive were good, despite their surroundings, or so he hoped. "I'll leave you, then," he said. "Be brave and take good care of your father and brother."

The Paragon

"Goodbye, sir," she replied, "and thank you."

He had a duty to the others not to bring back additional infection to the caravanserai, but his heart sank with powerlessness that he couldn't do more here.

When he crossed the bridge and negotiated the barricade that now blocked the entrance to Varaza's street, he had to explain who he was and the nature of his business to some self-appointed guards. Apparently, Varaza had informed them of his visit, because they allowed him to pass.

He entered Varaza's house, and the physician invited him to sit. "Let's not waste any time," he said. "I want to begin teaching you what I can right away. I know you meditate. Your first lesson is what I call 'directed meditation.' Here's how it works: when you take yourself to the meditative state, rather than thinking of nothing or of a mantra, or whatever your method is, make pictures in your mind instead, or even think of verbal suggestions.

"As a simple example," the physician continued, "a person can view pictures in his mind of his favorite idyllic place and suggest to himself that he can feel what it's like to be there: relaxed, mentally sharp, full of energy. He can then keep the feeling but change the picture to circumstances not so idyllic, like a sick-room. When he awakens from the meditative state, he'll find that he can be in the sick-room and keep his spirits high."

Yeshua understood. "When I meditate, I sometimes contemplate the stories of the Torah and picture them in my mind."

"Excellent," Varaza said. "You're probably good at making these mental pictures. Most people don't exercise their imaginations enough to be skilled at visualizing. You have a head start in learning this.

"Now, I've also found," Varaza continued, "you can use this technique to suggest that you, or yes, even another, will experience no pain or diminishing pain." Varaza's claim had Yeshua's complete attention.

"Not only that," he went on. "You can use this technique to make images of a healed body, a healthy body. You can make pictures of the result: seeing the body running, jumping, feeling good. You can also make pictures of the process of the body healing itself from the inside: bones mending, infections receding, healing blood being absorbed by the tissues. And by merely making these pictures, you can accelerate the healing and recovery processes."

"Ah, of course, I understand," Yeshua acknowledged. "But can I alone do this, or can I teach another?"

"It's best . . ."

"Physician, physician. We need you." A neighbor outside the door interrupted Varaza with a tone of urgency.

"What do you need, friend? Has someone taken a turn for the worse?" Varaza inquired. He'd already stood up and reached for his bag of medicines and devices.

"Not exactly, sir," the man said, "but my brother, who's been sick, stood to walk and fell down the stairs. I think he broke his leg."

"I'm coming," Varaza responded. "Show me the way. Yeshua, come along. What I may have to do could be useful to you sometime, and I might need your help. Have you ever seen a bone set?"

The Paragon

"Yes," Yeshua answered, "in Jerusalem. It seemed a painful process, but all I did was watch."

"Let's go," Varaza urged, and the three made their way to a house a few blocks away. When they entered, they saw several people, their faces drawn tight with concern, surrounding a man writhing in pain on the floor. Varaza went straight to him.

The physician lost no time in assessing the injury. He brought some herbs out of his bag and had the man chew and swallow them and drink water. "These herbs will take away some of the pain," Varaza explained to the injured man and all in the room. "They'll also help you relax, so your muscles don't fight me while I put the bone back in place. Try to relax. We need to wait just a few minutes."

When Varaza observed the herbs taking effect, he softened his tone even more. "Yeshua, come here and help me."

He told the man's wife to put his head in her lap and stroke it gently. She did as Varaza instructed and caressed her husband's cheeks while she softly sang to him. Yeshua didn't understand the words of the local language, but it seemed to him a lullaby.

"Yeshua," Varaza ordered, "grasp his leg above the calf. Yes, below the knee. The fracture, as you see, is in the lower leg. You must hold it firmly below the next higher joint or we'll stretch everything and not move the bone. Friends, I need one of you on each side to hold him still. Hold tightly, Yeshua. I'm going to pull hard and suddenly. Don't let me move you."

Varaza grasped the leg below the fracture and yanked with great force. The man screamed in pain. "That's it," Varaza said.

"You're going to be fine now." Varaza took two pieces of wood and secured them tightly on either side of the leg.

"You can't walk on it for several weeks," he explained. "I'll check on you from time to time. In the meantime, take some of this twice a day," he said, handing the man's wife some other herbs, this time in a powdered form.

When they left, Yeshua's heart was racing.

"That one was easy." His mentor sighed. "No open wound; simple fracture; he should be fine. Hopefully you'll never have to do that, but now you know what it takes.

"I know you have to get back to the caravanserai," Varaza continued, picking up the lesson without missing a word, "but as I'd started to tell you, you *can* teach a person to do directed meditation for himself. It might be most effective if you're doing it with him, but you won't be there all the time. There are rules for making suggestions and rules to keep this practice safe. You must always follow the rules, and never teach anyone who won't follow the rules."

The two men continued walking with Varaza setting a brisk pace, although he had no pressing duty to attend to. They paused at his door. "What's the danger?" Yeshua asked.

"Someone could accidentally misinterpret a suggestion," Varaza explained. "In fact, in this relaxed state, the mind takes any suggestion made to it literally. For example, you might suggest to a person he'd be able to take ten steps tomorrow. Now he might have the physical ability to take twenty or more steps, but in the meditative state he accepts your suggestion of ten literally. That becomes all he's able to do. You'd have carelessly limited him. I'll teach you how to phrase suggestions to avoid that.

"I'll bring some people to my house tomorrow," he concluded, "to observe you practice on them. Meanwhile, continue to do as I've instructed with the sick of your caravan. How's everyone doing?"

"Our friend was talking as if he believed death was imminent," Yeshua said, referring, of course, to Hadi. "I didn't know exactly how to comfort him, so I barked at him to stop feeling sorry for himself. Now I fear I was wrong not to show more compassion."

"No, no, that was perfect, for both of you." Varaza reassured him. "Your empathy told you your sympathy would be counterproductive. That was exactly what you needed to tell that old bastard. Keep everyone thinking positive. That won't be easy because, as I told you, some will die, probably the weaker among you, but the rest have a good chance to live, if they believe they will. Give them belief. That's one way what I'm teaching you will help them."

Yeshua and his two companions continued to minister to the sick at the caravanserai. Each day new cases arose. Two people died. Some got worse. Some stabilized. Hadi remained at a low point, but he was not dead yet.

When Yonnah came to take over, he said, "I understand what you're doing with Varaza. Take all the time you need. I'll make sure your watch is covered."

Yeshua continued his lessons and practice and brought his technique to the caravan. He was able to bring a more positive attitude and renewed energy to most of those he worked with.

Some were not amenable, and more died, five in all; but eventually the rest, including Hadi, began to do better.

As the sickness ran its course, Yeshua continued to go daily to learn from Varaza. Occasionally, Varaza would say, "I know we have only a short time together, but if you exhaust yourself, I believe you'll succumb to this disease. Take a day or two off to digest what you've learned and to rest. Don't try to be the hero. Rest, or you'll be no help to anyone."

The day that Yeshua returned, Varaza said, "You're doing well with directed meditation. You can assume a soothing voice that relaxes people and renders them susceptible to suggestion. I think it's time to go a step further. I intend to teach you what I've learned from a man from Seres, although every culture has some version of it. I'll give it to you, and then you practice."

"Don't tease me anymore," Yeshua said. "What are you talking about?"

"Healing by the laying on of hands," Varaza replied.

"I have heard of this and hoped I'd encounter a practitioner on my journey." Yeshua was excited by this prospect. "There was no one in Judea or Galilee, other than pretenders."

"There's no pretense about this," Varaza said. "Your meditation practice, your desire to learn, and your empathy are predictors that you'll be adept at the technique. You must understand two things to begin: one, you'll be a conduit between the one to be healed and the power of the Divine Force, whatever you call it; and two, the power will heal as it will.

The Paragon

"What I mean," he continued, "is that the chief complaint of the person you work with may not be what the universe chooses to heal. It may be some other thing, body or spirit, this power will address. It's not for you to say or request. You're only an intermediary of the power."

Yeshua understood these concepts, although they were beyond his tradition. God worked miracles, he believed, sometimes through the aegis of chosen ones, but this was different, and he was eager to learn about it.

The education took several days. Varaza explained the process, the rules, and the manual techniques. These involved placing the hands in various places on the body in sequence, from head to toe, front and back. To impart the conductive ability to Yeshua, Varaza went into a meditative state and had Yeshua do the same. With both men having the intention, Varaza to impart, Yeshua to receive, Varaza laid hands on Yeshua in the sequence he'd described.

Yeshua's body grew warm wherever Varaza placed his hands. Sometimes he felt a tingling. When Varaza finished, Yeshua returned to normal consciousness. He felt renewed and full of energy. He couldn't wait to practice.

"Remember," Varaza admonished him, "there are levels to this technique. I've taught you the first level. Practice it, and perhaps, as you continue, you can find someone, maybe in Merv or Maracanda, who can show you the next level. Someday, if you return this way, I hope I'll be around to guide you further. Eventually, you'll be able to give this technique to others and use it remotely. For now, you can't do that.

"Remember, also, you're merely a conduit," he continued. "Do this with an attitude of humility and gratitude. You've been given a gift."

"By the way," Varaza added with a gleam in his eye, "there's a place in Maracanda called the Paragon. It would be useful for you to call on the residents there."

"This is the first I've heard of it," Yeshua said. "I'm intrigued. I'll follow your recommendation."

"And Yeshua," Varaza spoke these parting words, "there's one more thing to remember as you travel, the most important of all. It's this: the impossible is possible through imagination."

Yeshua practiced the lessons at the caravanserai. Of course, he couldn't say exactly who was helped or in what way, but as time passed, the number of new cases diminished to zero, people stopped dying, and people got well, including the now cantankerous Hadi, whose last two days in isolation were an aggravation to everyone.

The moon was again in the west in the evening sky. The nights were crisp. The Hunter was ascendant in the celestial sphere. The stars were so bright and numerous they looked like a fog. It was time to move on. The governor had given permission. Ecbatana itself was slowly casting off the curse of the plague. At first light, they'd leave for Rhages, the next city on the Royal Road to the east.

Four

Rhages

The approach to Rhages was spectacular. The city appeared in the distance framed by the crease in two foothills. Behind it, the Elbruz Mountains, rugged, massive, and white, hung like a Persian tapestry. The snow-line was low this time of year and draped the mountains almost to the city itself. Snows were infrequent at this level, but they did occur. The caravaneers were well bundled up against the wind and cold as they shivered their way toward their goal, but now the view before them stirred their spirits and warmed their bodies.

As the beasts trudged along in file and the riders swayed in the rhythm they induced, Yeshua rode in silence, and closing his eyes, heard the music of the Royal Road in his head. It was Persian in its roots, with harps and flutes making the melody, while the drums echoed the camels' walk. He was lost in the composition of his imagination until the caravan stopped.

It was really nothing. The lead camel needed an adjustment in its load, and it couldn't wait until Rhages. It only took a few minutes to correct, but as Yeshua looked around, a man-made structure in the otherwise empty landscape caught his attention.

It was a tall, cylindrical tower set atop an isolated hillock. The tower was about sixty feet tall, made of stone, probably forty feet in diameter. Nothing about this was remarkable in itself, but there was a rim around the top of it, and perched around its circumference were vultures and other birds of prey. Some had full mouths, but occasionally one or two would leave the comfort of the perch to rip some dinner from the contents of the unseen platform that topped the cylinder.

This was a *dakhma,* the place where Zoroastrians disposed of the corpses of the dead. Hadi Ba'riel filled in the missing information. "Zoroastrians believe dead bodies are unclean and burial would pollute the earth. They arrange the bodies on top in concentric circles for men, women, and children. There's a hole in the center where the bones go. It has filters of coal that protect the earth. The process doesn't take very long. The birds work quickly."

"I've heard about Zoroastrianism from travelers," Yeshua replied. "I've never found anything written about it, although I think it's the world's most practiced religion, and its home is Judaism's nearest neighbor. It has a reputation of being based in magic."

"You're correct, except for the magic part," Hadi said. "There's a sect of it that guards an occult tradition, but the mainstream is really quite, if I may say, normal. It has adherents from Egypt and the western reaches of the Roman Empire all the way to the Hindu lands beyond the river Indus. Although it's ancient, nothing is written. All its sacred texts are passed on by word of mouth.

The Paragon

The Gathas are the core of these texts and were composed by the great prophet Zoroaster himself."

"Do the Gathas tell a person how to behave?" Yeshua asked.

"Not the Gathas themselves," Hadi said. "They're more like the Psalms of your tradition, hymns of praise that reveal the nature of the Divine Spirit and man's relationship to it, but I'm the wrong person to ask. I've told you all I know. When we get to Rhages, I know a priest you can talk to. He's a holy man and a scholar. Take a gift of wood for the fire and he'll be happy to talk to you."

The group reached their goal soon enough, a caravanserai near the gate of the walled city. When all were settled in, Yeshua went into town to find the fire temple Hadi had directed him to. Winter had quieted what would normally be a bustling commercial center, but even in the cold, life went on. Yeshua walked through the markets, as he liked to do, greeting merchants and patrons and engaging in pleasant conversation. It was a way for him to spread goodwill and see what he could learn about their way of life.

"Good day, sir," Yeshua said to the rug merchant. He had a street display in front of his shop.

"Hello, my friend," the merchant said. "Come, come. See some of my beautiful rugs from all over the world. No need to buy. Just come in and look. Get warm inside."

Yeshua knew, of course, that this was a salesman's prattle, but he was curious about the man and his wares and could use a warm-up, so he accepted the invitation.

"Friend, I'm not going to buy today," Yeshua said, wanting to be honest, although he realized all merchants took this as a maybe.

"Sit, please," the merchant invited. "My name is Orban."

"I'm Yeshua, and pleased to meet you."

"As am I," replied Orban, who then turned his attention to three little boys who were running around the shop like a pack of wild puppies.

"Pratti, get us some tea," he said to one of them, who instantly interrupted his play to do his assigned chore.

Yeshua sat on a comfortable pillow near a glowing hearth. Orban threw a log onto the fire as Pratti returned with water to prepare his brew.

Orban began the show, spreading one carpet after another on the floor in front of Yeshua, regaling him with stories of their origin. "And this one is my most beautiful. It is made in Maracanda of the finest Seresian silk."

It was truly beautiful, but while Yeshua wasn't sure exactly what the fabric was, he knew enough to know it wasn't silk. Nonetheless he said nothing to change the convivial mood of the encounter.

While he was still looking, one of the other boys ran up to him with a gorgeous ceramic bowl. It had a polished white glaze with a multicolored geometric flower in the center, surrounded by concentric bands of alternating colors, red, blue, and green, each with its distinctive pattern. Yeshua became transfixed, staring into the design that seemed like the deep well of creation itself.

"You like?" Orban said, half statement, half question. "For you, very cheap."

Yeshua laughed. "Orban, I can't buy today." What began as an expression of finality, however, much to Yeshua's surprise, ended in a purchase.

"Orban," Yeshua finally said, trying to extricate himself from the web of hospitality. "I need to go. I'm on my way to the fire temple. Thanks for the warmth and refreshment."

"Yes," the merchant replied, "I noticed your bundle of wood. Just keep going the same way, and please send your friends."

The bundle of wood he carried let everyone assume he was going to the nearby fire temple, and all were happy to direct him there. It was a simple stone tower, square-shaped and tall, with an interior of carpeted floors and hanging lamps that surrounded a large fire urn in the center. Fire symbolized light and the process of creation among other things, and one of the priestly duties was to see that the fire never went out.

"Thank you for the gift," the priest said, bowing slightly at the waist. "As you can see, I have plenty of wood on hand, but I deeply appreciate the symbolism of your gift." Yeshua had brought it, not to endorse any beliefs, but to show respect and goodwill.

The priest's name was Manthran Jahan. Yeshua told him what he knew of Zoroastrianism, little as it was, and that provided a basis for conversation. "So you have one god called Ahura Mazda?"

"Yes, we do," the priest replied. "In the time of Zoroaster, seven hundred years ago, there were many gods. Religion and the priests had become corrupt, in effect competing in the sale of divine influence, and Zoroaster stepped up to change all that." As he spoke, an acolyte shuffled between the larger wood pile, stacking a few logs adjacent to Yeshua's pile near the central fire.

"Was he a monk or a priest?" Yeshua asked.

"Certainly not a monk," Manthran Jahan said. "He had a wife, probably only one, and children. We in Rhages claim him as our son, although others want to dispute that. He probably was a priest, but whatever his occupation, he was a scholar and a poet, and he himself authored the Ghatas."

"We also have one God we call Yahweh, although we normally don't speak his name," Yeshua explained.

"Yes, but our one God is a little different from yours. Ours is within creation, whereas yours is outside of it. Yours is a man, and a vengeful one at that, but ours has a male and female aspect. Our God, Ahura Mazda, has the attributes of *Ahura*, which means being, and *Mazda*, which means mind. Being is physical reality, and mind is consciousness or spirit. Being is the masculine principle. Mind is the feminine. How can you have creation without both?" the priest challenged.

As he finished his thought, Mathran Jahan stood up and took one of the pieces of wood Yeshua had brought and tossed it into the urn. The flame flared up, and sparks rode a swirl of smoke toward an opening in the roof. The sight entranced both men for a second.

The fire had a sweet odor. Cedar, Yeshua thought, as he inhaled a little more deeply. "I've been troubled by the vengefulness of my God," he answered Jahan. "I pray to understand it. If you lived in my culture, you'd understand why God must be a man."

The Paragon

"Well, women aren't much more highly regarded here among the common people," Jahan explained, "but to the true followers, it makes a difference. A woman can be a priest here.

"We believe Ahura Mazda is the source of both the good and the evil principle," Jahan continued, "although the good is stronger. We emphasize people need to do good works to keep evil at bay and that finally a savior will come who'll raise the dead and bring perfection to the world. Do you have such a concept in Judaism?"

"Some of us believe that," Yeshua answered.

"I don't know about yours," the priest said, "but we believe a *Saoshyant* will be born of a virgin, and that as the agent of Ahura Mazda, he'll resurrect the dead. When that happens, our physical bodies will be restored, our spirits will be cleansed, and we'll be reunited with Ahura Mazda. This event will mark the end of time, and the righteous will experience everlasting life."

"Interesting," Yeshua mused. "A thought seven hundred years old. Truth be told, my cousin thinks I'll be a savior and lead the people to political freedom."

The priest shook his head. "Be careful, young man. Political saviors get murdered."

They talked at length for some days, and Yeshua listened carefully. He was more interested in hearing new ideas than proselytizing his own. When it was time to go, Yeshua thanked Manthran Jahan. "You've been kind and hospitable, and your ideas are intriguing."

"One last thing, Yeshua," the priest said. "Since you go to Maracanda, do you know of the Paragon?"

"Yes, brother, I've heard of it."

"It's a special place," Manthran Jahan explained, "where sages from many lands who travel the Great Road gather to exchange ideas. I believe it's a place that would satisfy your quest. You should go there, but remember always, as Zoroaster himself said, 'One need not scale the heights of the heavens nor travel along the highways of the world to find Ahura Mazda. With purity of mind and holiness of heart one can find Him in one's own heart.'"

In Nehardea
At the Same Time

Nehardea was outwardly calm. The king hadn't moved to reassert his power after the revolution, and there was hope, even expectation, among the people that he was too weak to do so. Although there was some civil authority here, it was, after all, a gang of robbers, and the two of them, Kefir and his son, were ostensibly merchants. They needed to be vigilant.

Kefir wasn't happy when he found out there'd be an extended delay here, but the political situation was bound to give rise to the unexpected. He and Ptolemy went to one of the local inns looking for a good time, and they fell in with a group of men casting lots. All were drinking, of course, and the women of the night were draping themselves around those men who appeared interested, whispering words of lust in their ears.

Ptolemy was doing well, winning in the game and attracting the interest of the most beautiful of the women. In fact, it seemed everyone was having a grand time, when, without warning, one of the local men smashed a wine jar on the table, bringing a cold silence to the room. He glared at Ptolemy. "The stranger does well. Perhaps you don't understand we don't cheat in this town."

Ptolemy looked up without changing his expression or elevating his tone. "In my town a drunken son of a whore would hold his tongue unless he could back up that accusation." The accuser, a large brute of a man, lunged across the table, and Ptolemy smashed his own wine jar against the side of the man's head. The fight was on.

Kefir would rather this hadn't happened, but once it had begun, he threw himself into the fray like a good soldier. Bodies and earthenware flew around the room. Tables and chairs crashed with the bodies. The women screamed, adding a layer of hysteria to the melee. Father and son each went for one of the stronger-looking of the enemy and used whatever they could grab as a weapon. An iron fire tool proved handy to Kefir. Ptolemy grabbed a part of a sturdy branch destined for the fire.

The two of them soon rendered the more formidable of their adversaries unconscious, or possibly dead, and the weaker ran away like the whores. When calm returned, they gave some extra money to the innkeeper to cover a share of the damages. Ptolemy surveyed the devastation, looking pleased with himself, but no one any longer thought they were merchants.

"My friends," the innkeeper said, "I'm sure you won't be safe returning to the caravan in the dark, especially with men of ill will lurking in the shadows. I have a room. You can stay until morning. Please accept my hospitality." They were drunk, and Kefir knew the man was right about the danger they'd be in, so he accepted the offer, and father and son went off to bed laughing over their victory.

At some unknown hour, however, the door crashed open, and a gang of men charged in. The soldiers had only a second, no time to even muster a full waking state. They struggled with all the strength they could leverage from on their backs, but there were too many attackers.

"You bastard," Ptolemy bellowed at the innkeeper, who may or may not have heard him. "You set us up! Father!" he screamed.

The men bound their hands and put sacks over their heads. Their struggling was now in vain. The men dragged them down the stairs and out the door.

"Just kill the old one," one of the invaders shouted.

"No! Father!" Ptolemy yelled in vain.

Ptolemy heard his father utter a chilling sound, part scream and part groan. Then there was silence. All that remained was the sound of his own cursing. He believed that he, too, would get a sword through the heart any second, but instead, he felt himself thrown onto a platform. It was a cart, because it began to move. He heard a gate, he believed, shut behind him. The confinement and uncertainty were frightening in a way that physical battle was not, and Ptolemy churned the death of his father over and over in his mind until the monotony of the cart's rolling wheels sent him back into drunken unconsciousness.

To Hecatompylos With the Caravan

The caravan now seemed less like transportation and more like a small town unto itself that crawled slowly eastward across the landscape, locating itself where it would, trading with whoever wanted to make good business. If Yeshua had merely wanted to visit Maracanda, he could have gotten there more quickly, traveling by himself or with one other, trading horse for horse along the way, but he liked the caravan. To him, the experience of the journey was more important than the destination, although his encounters along the way had left him tantalized by what he might find in Maracanda.

They left Rhages bound for Hecatompylos. To their north, the Elbruz Mountains rose in a great arc, separating the caravan from the more northerly routes along the Caspian Sea. To the south, the vast Parthian high desert, barren and inhospitable, spread to cover most of the empire's territory. The road straddled the foothills, winding its way around and between them. This time of year the caravan depended on what it carried to feed the animals and what was available at the caravanserais along the way. Come spring, there'd be plenty of grass for grazing, but in the middle of winter this was a difficult part of the journey.

They were one day out of Rhages when the skies darkened and the snow began. This part of the route climbed to a higher elevation. Hadi was afraid of what was to come but pressed on in the hope they could avoid the worst of the storm. There was a caravanserai he thought they could reach, giving them shelter until the road became more hospitable.

The snow swirled, pulsating in vortices, and began to accumulate under foot. Soon, visibility became a problem, with the wind driving the storm right into their faces. Hadi now realized the elevation would increase ahead, and the road would likely become impassable. The grumbling among the caravaneers had turned to screaming for him to turn back.

Yeshua was unfazed by the storm and the cold. He used the technique that Varaza taught him to project warmth from the center of his body to his extremities. He rode through the blizzard in a meditative state, internally calm. He was concerned about Meryam, but he'd taught her how to direct this warming energy as well. She was not as skilled as Yeshua, who had a lifetime of meditation on which to base his practice, but she could do it well enough to spare herself the pain of freezing feet and hands.

Yonnah was livid. He hadn't been interested in learning how to project internal warmth. He didn't think it a black art. He couldn't conceive of his cousin practicing what would be akin to summoning demons, but nonetheless he mistrusted it and thought it an illusion, a trick of the mind. However, he had nothing to take the place of it, and he was suffering. He rode up to Yeshua and screamed at him. "What's the matter with you? Don't you feel the pain of this icy tempest?"

The wind blew with such ferocity that Yeshua could hardly hear Yonnah, although he was right beside him. He didn't answer, but Yonnah didn't wait for a reply. "Isn't this a sign to end this infernal journey before we all die? Why do you continue to follow that madman, Hadi? He's in this for the money. He doesn't care a wit about the lot of us. Listen to the screams of agony."

When he got no answer, Yonnah fell back in line and continued to pray for deliverance. Those who weren't cursing Hadi were doing the same.

For his part, Hadi finally realized he'd made a serious mistake. There was no way to make it to the next caravanserai, and if he didn't act, there was every chance they'd all perish, so reluctantly, he gave the order to turn around. As they descended and retraced their steps back to the west, the weather abated. The edge of the storm came suddenly after about ten miles. They'd been in the blizzard almost four hours. The earth, quite abruptly, became visible again, and the snow turned to insignificant flurries.

This had been a costly foray. Two men, members of the guard, had feet that were swollen and toes blackened. They all knew what this meant, and they went to a physician who knew what to do. Amputation was a painful process, a last resort, but loss of a toe or two was better than the life-ending infection that would be the alternative.

While the men were being treated, Hadi barged into the physician's house. He fell to his knees and begged the men's forgiveness. They'd known him for many years from many caravans. They knew the risks and didn't hold Hadi responsible. They told him so, and both accepted his apology. They even told him an apology wasn't necessary, but Hadi wasn't satisfied. "Physician, I apply the law of talion to my caravan, and I must abide by it myself. I am responsible for the loss these men have suffered. Therefore, I'd have you take two of *my* toes."

He put his foot onto the table in front of the physician.

"No, Master, no. Do not do this. It isn't necessary. We don't seek retribution," the men pleaded in unison.

The physician spoke up. "Sir, I cannot do this. Because you have no medical need, my oath forbids it."

Hadi grabbed the blade the physician had used on the two amputees. "If you don't do it, I'll do it myself. Does your oath permit that? Do it, I say, so I don't make a mess of it."

The physician relented and prepared to do as Hadi asked. His tone was curt, as if expressing annoyance, as he told Hadi what to do. Snatching the knife from his Hadi's hand, he pointed. "Here," he said. "Lie down on this table."

Hadi did as he was told. Although he was resigned to what was coming, his chest heaved with the labored breathing of a man trying to control himself.

"You two," the physician said, glancing at the guards. "Come here and help me secure him." The two burly men approached like frightened children and wrapped ropes around the master and the table rendering him immobile.

This wasn't Varaza, Hadi thought, but at least he's washing the knife. There was no warm language from the physician to comfort his spirit. His body, however, could feel the heat from the fire where the cauterizing iron was being readied.

The Paragon

When he returned to the table, the physician cinched Hadi's leg tightly above the ankle. "Bite on this," he ordered, shoving a stick into Hadi's mouth.

Hadi bit down hard. Sweat poured down his face. Every facial muscle screwed up tightly despite his self-talk to relax. He couldn't see what the physician was about to do at the foot of the table, and it came without warning.

The master screamed at the cutting and screamed as the white hot cauterizing iron sealed the wound. The smell of his own burning flesh filled his nostrils, but he would now be able to forgive himself. That thought, as well as the end of the procedure, let his breathing begin to soften.

The physician threw his knife and the iron into a tub near the hearth. The water in the tub sizzled and a cloud of steam billowed through the room. "I hope your satisfied," he said in disgust over what he had done.

But indeed, the master was.

They remained in Rhages for almost two weeks while the men healed and until a caravan coming from the east let them know the road was cleared. Then it was on to Hecatompylos. The weather was seasonably cool by then, but Hadi hoped the back of winter was broken.

Hecatompylos was another royal capital and another city made more spectacular by the Elbruz Mountains that rose behind it. They had left King Artabus III behind in Ctesiphon, but there was opulence enough here to sustain his needs if ever he chose to bless the city with his royal highness.

It was known as the city of a hundred gates, and truly, roads came here from all directions like spokes to the center of a wheel. Important ones, besides the Royal Road from the east and west, came over the mountains from the Caspian Sea to the north and another all the way from Persepolis to the south. In addition, lesser roads came in from satellite market towns and oases that ringed the metropolis.

The caravan would be here for a few days because the next city of any size would be Susia, at least three weeks distant. Yeshua asked Hadi if he felt there'd be anything of interest for him in the city.

"Yes, I do think so," Hadi said. "I think this is a good place for you to meet the Hindus. What do you know about them?"

"I know they have a trinitarian god, at least most of them," Yeshua said. "I'm told some believe in many gods, one god, no god. I don't understand how this can be so. It seems like a chaos of beliefs. It makes me curious about what binds them together in a single way of thought."

"Perhaps you'll need to cross the Indus," Hadi offered, "to understand how those people think, but there's a temple here in Hecatompylos with a guru who might help you. Save your breath with the priest. He's only after your money, and he's not what you'd think of as a spiritual man, but seek out Kamini. He's more the kind of person you seem interested in talking to."

"There are priests in Galilee and Judea who are the same," recalled Yeshua with disdain.

Hecatompylos was a grand city full of temples of all religions. Yeshua walked through the main gate that opened to a wide road that was more like a plaza. He had to look up to appreciate the enormity of the place.

On his right a massive wide staircase, which made the people at the top look the size of insects, delivered a supplicant or government official to the king's palace. A tall colonnade fronted the entrance, and two mythical beasts, bull-bodied, human-headed, and eagle-winged, stood guard at the sides. The palace rose behind, formed from great stones from the mountains and decorated with images of the monarch and scenes of his benevolence and the bounty of his reign.

When he looked on the other side of the plaza, Yeshua saw a fire temple, cube-shaped, simple in itself, but sitting atop an ascension of gardened terraces awaiting spring to complete the coloring of their decoration. As he walked on, he saw temples of other religions and lesser palaces of the merely wealthy that astonished him by their number and magnificence. As he gazed forward to the end of the main road, he could see it terminate at the foot of a citadel, small by the standards of many of the cities he'd already visited, but formidably fortressed at its apex.

This city epitomized the brewing pot of commerce and ideas he had expected the Royal Road would offer. It was even better in that respect than he'd ever hoped for and convinced him he'd made a wise decision to undertake this journey.

He'd imposed on Yonnah to accompany him, thinking it might make some positive impression, and Yonnah reluctantly agreed. To Yonnah's eyes, this place was worse than the Babylon of the old texts, a whore in itself, a monument to wanton paganism.

It made him uncomfortable and testy. The sooner he left, the better.

Yeshua found the Hindu temple located in a prosperous neighborhood of tradesmen and professional people. It was modest on the outside, fashioned of brick, glazed the color of cream, and rising in a pointed tower in the center, but the inside was encrusted with gold enough for a king's palace. It was full of bold colors and icons of strange deities, some dancing, some with many arms, some in the image of an elephant. There were statues of female gods as well with naked breasts and adorned with jewels.

Yeshua was spellbound with the visual stimulation, and he became lost in the appreciation of it all. The aroma of burning incense filled his nostrils. That at least was something he was familiar with in Jewish temples. No, this was not the way he would promote a religion, but it was truly stunning.

A priest came out to meet him. He showed him around, explained some of the statues and artwork, and made it clear he'd appreciate a donation. Yeshua had no wish to be cynical, but he was fairly sure the man lived well. While they toured the temple, Yeshua noticed a small man sitting cross-legged in front of one of the statues, wearing only a loincloth girded tightly. Except for his scraggly hair and weathered face, he looked like a bearded baby.

"That's Jitendra. He's a yogi recently arrived from Hindu lands," the priest said. The man opened his eyes and giggled, revealing the absence of a tooth or two, nodded his head from side to side, and then resumed his meditation. "Jitendra will stay with us for some days." The priest seemed annoyed.

The Paragon

Jitendra opened his eyes again and spoke. "Find Kamini. He's in the next building." He giggled again. Yonnah found him to be a strange fellow, but Yeshua thanked him and told the priest he would indeed like to meet Kamini.

"Very well, then," the priest said, turning suddenly cool to the two visitors. "You can find him by going out that door and knocking at the door across the yard."

Yeshua thanked the priest, who went quickly to other business. He and Yonnah followed their instructions and made their way to the house in the rear where Guru Kamini lived. His house was much simpler than the temple, although not austere. The door opened to a hearth room with table and chairs where they sat and talked.

There was also a bedroom, simply appointed, sporting fresh white linens. Another small room, opposite the bed chamber, served as a chapel, with floor pillows covered in silk, arranged in front of a multi-armed, dancing, bronze Shiva. This wasn't the time of year for flowers, but reeds and bowls of burning incense completed the shrine.

Yeshua and Kamini exchanged pleasant conversation, enough to let them know one another. Yonnah was *casually* interested in hearing about the Hindus. He'd heard of them and understood them to be a disorganized lot, accepting all sorts of beliefs about God and dogma. He didn't take them seriously.

Yeshua wondered, in a religion that included people who had such diverse understandings of God, what this teacher believed. "Do you believe Brahman is the One True God?"

"Oh no, Brahman is not god. Brahman existed before all gods," Kamini explained. "I'd say Brahman is like the soul of the universe. Everything springs from Brahman, first of all the gods. I believe there's one god with three aspects: Brahma, Vishnu, Shiva--Creator, Preserver, Destroyer. Then all of creation springs from the gods. So in Hindu we have plenty of gods, hundreds, thousands, and all of us worship those we choose, and some choose none."

"You call that a religion?" Yonnah grumbled.

"Please excuse my cousin. He can be contentious sometimes." Yeshua shot a glance of annoyance in Yonnah's direction.

Kamini stood up, shuffled to the shrine, and took a scoop of incense from a small jewel encrusted jar, refreshing what had almost completely burned. "I hope you like the scent," he said "It's called sandalwood."

"I've become acquainted with it on the journey," Yeshua responded. "Yes, I do like it."

Yonnah rolled his eyes.

"Now that you mention this about Brahman," Yeshua said, picking up Kamini's last idea, "I'm familiar with a strain of Jewish thought that's relatively new to us, not much more than a hundred years old. I've read it in a text called Sefer Yetzirah."

Yeshua rocked back slightly in his chair, rubbing his chin, taking a moment to organize his developing ideas. "Sefer Yetzirah speaks of God in two ways. It says there is 'God in Essence,' called Ayn-Sof, which is unknowable, existing before anything, an utterly simple underpinning for the unity of everything.

"But there's also 'God in Manifestation,'" Yeshua continued. "This is the revealed personification of God through which he relates to humankind. This God takes on all the aspects of divine activity, such as creating, sustaining, and destroying.

"As I recall, there are ten aspects to Ayn-Sof, although they arise from three principles, and as I think about it, Ayn-Sof is not unlike Brahman or even Ahura Mazda."

"Ah, so. That's new to me, that you have this idea in your tradition," said Kamini, beaming. He stirred the embers in the incense bowl to renew the process of purification that the incense represented, as well as drinking in the pleasure of the scent. He returned to his chair and sat.

"It's new to me as well," Yonnah said, furrowing his brow as he looked with puzzlement at his cousin.

"But in our Hindu tradition," Kamini responded, "the idea is thousands of years old."

"Now that I have a better grasp of your ideas," Yeshua continued, "it causes me to revisit the concept of Ayn-Sof. I'd been somewhat dismissive of the idea until recently, but seeing the same idea in completely different traditions makes me more interested in it."

"Good, good; and by the way, I take no offense at your comment, Yonnah," the guru said. "We're more a way of life or a way of looking at things than a religion, but I'd say we're a religion in the sense that our daily ceremonies and our ideas about ethics are generally the same. In fact, we call our religion Sanatana Dharma. Do you know the meaning of it? *Hinduism* only means that it's from the land beyond the Indus River, Hindu lands."

"Isn't *dharma* a path of ethical behavior?" Yeshua answered with a question.

Before Kamini could reply, a noise, not unlike the wailing of a wounded animal, interrupted them. It was Jitendra chanting in the courtyard. Yeshua and Kamini chuckled, while Yonnah scowled.

"Simply put, yes," Kamini continued, getting back to the topic at hand. "Our religion has its roots in the Rig Veda, a text many thousands of years old. Later, maybe seven hundred years ago, holy men authored other scriptures called the Upanishads. In a word, they tell us Brahman pervades everything in the universe, and we are one with it. Sanatana Dharma is our daily quest to keep mindful of the reality of Brahman in everything and every person we interact with. It requires we act ethically in everything we do."

Yeshua took this in and said nothing. This concept of the Divine Spirit all-pervasive within the universe rather than a being outside it was like the Zoroastrians' beliefs and was still new to him. He could understand it intellectually and found it appealing, but for now it was just another idea, although one that was growing on him.

Yeshua always knew when he'd been fed enough ideas, requiring digestion rather than further feeding, so he thanked the guru and left the temple. On the way out, he saw the yogi in the yard. He'd stopped chanting and was assuming strange, contorted positions and poses. He stopped his exercises to acknowledge Yeshua.

Jitendra prefaced his address with his customary giggle. "Yeshua, I hope you found what you were looking for, although I believe some time must pass before you find what you're *really* looking for. What I'm doing is called yoga, and it's but one path of Sanatana Dharma. Practices like this, done with spiritual intent, can lead to a liberating understanding. We call that *moksha*. It frees us from rebirth."

"So you believe in rebirth after death?" Yeshua questioned.

"Oh, yes," the yogi said. "It's a continuing cycle for the soul until one achieves *moksha*. Once we get it right, *poof!* Eternal bliss. The problem is we come to love individual existence in the physical plane so much that we crave to return to it." He finished with a hearty laugh this time. "It's my pleasure to meet you," Jitendra concluded. "I hope we meet again sometime, in this life or in the eternal bliss."

"Thank you, Jitendra," Yeshua said. "I suspect we will." Yeshua had no idea why he suspected that, other than a feeling.

"Yeshua," Jitendra added with a sly look, "the Paragon."

Yeshua merely shook his head and smiled. This constant prodding of his curiosity by mention of the Paragon was having an effect. He knew he had to find it.

Five

The caravan left Hecatompylos at first light. The road to Susia continued along the great curve defined by the base of the Elbruz Mountains on their north side. The vast expanse of the high desert still lay to the south, and the foothills that marked the caravan's path were ready to burst into early spring. This meant plenty of water and grazing for the animals, as well as sustenance and visual comfort for the caravaneers.

It was an unusually warm day. As the sun passed the meridian and began its decline, Yeshua noticed a spot off the road that would afford him a panorama of the great desert's southward expanse. "Yonnah, Meryam, I'd like to stay here for a while to pray and think about what the Hindus said to me. I like the solitude and view. I'll catch up later."

"I don't like the idea one bit," Yonnah argued. "I don't think it's wise for you to be alone here. If some problem arises, there won't be anyone to help you. Please don't do this."

"He's right. Stay with us and just go away from camp tonight if all you want is to be alone," Meryam added.

Yeshua laughed. "See, my decision has already had a benefit. Both of you have agreed to something. I assure you I'll be fine. I appreciate your concern, but I won't be long. I'll catch up to you before dark."

Hadi didn't like the idea either, but he trusted Yeshua and wanted no argument with him. "I can't leave you with a camel. I'll leave one of the horses, but don't linger. I won't allow anyone to return with an animal to find you if you don't show up." He knew by now Yeshua would do what he would do, and he probably wouldn't have any problem, but it was with some reluctance that he left him behind.

When the caravan had disappeared, Yeshua tied up his horse and climbed a little to a spot where he could be comfortable and look out over the vast emptiness. He felt the warm, clean breeze caress his face like his mother's hands. He thought of her and of his father and prayed for them as he did every day. Then he filled his eyes with the expanse of starkly beautiful nothingness, and taking it inside himself, closed his eyes, breathed deeply, and sank into a profound state of meditation.

He'd been there about two hours when the wind began to pick up. The clouds that had been a puffy mix of white and gray, evoking the shapes of mythical birds, suddenly became thicker. Yeshua knew a storm was likely and leaving was out of the question. As he heard the faint rumble of thunder, his horse became agitated. He knew he had to find shelter quickly. He climbed higher, hoping that by moving closer to the mountains, he might find some cave or overhang growing out of a more precipitous part of the upslope.

Overhang it was, and a good one at that, almost worthy of being called a cave. The rain began as he spotted the refuge. The thunder grew louder. He made it to shelter just before the heavens burst open. The horse remained excited but appeared to be as happy as Yeshua about their luck.

He could see lightning now. The more it flashed, the less time there was between flash and thunder until they were almost simultaneous. The thunder no longer rolled. It snapped like God's whip. It was unrelenting. Then, not twenty yards in front of him, lightning split a tree, sending nearly half of it to the ground in a smoldering heap. Yeshua would have held his ears because by now the noise was almost painful, but he needed both hands to restrain the horse and attempt to calm it.

This crashing sustained itself far longer than anything in his experience. It was an extraordinary storm that seemed to stop in place once it had rolled off the mountain peaks. Eventually, the intervals between the thunderclaps increased, but the rain didn't abate, and even as the thunder finally stopped, the rain continued through the night. When it finished, the breeze faded into stillness. The stars eventually appeared, but the night was moonless. He dared not try to navigate the tortuous path that wound through this part of the foothills. Besides, it would be dawn soon enough.

With first light, he knew he had to move quickly to try to catch the caravan. At least drinking water wouldn't be a problem. The streams were swollen from the deluge. There was no waterline above the torrents to indicate a high-water mark. He hoped he wouldn't find himself trapped by a river he couldn't ford.

As he passed the first bend in the road, he stopped abruptly, startled by the sight in front of him. It was another horse standing in the road, saddled, laden with gear, but riderless. All he could think was Yonnah or even Meryam had come to look for him, but what had become of him or her? "Yonnah?" he shouted. "Meryam?"

He dismounted and approached the animal. It was skittish but allowed Yeshua to grab the reins and calm it. Again, he called out the names of his companions. It wasn't lost on him that the road was narrow at this point, and one side dropped off into a steep ravine. Fearing the worst, he looked over the edge. His heart sank as he saw a crumpled body below.

"Yonnah!" he screamed, but as he got no answer and looked more closely, he was sure it wasn't Yonnah.

He got a rope from the gear on the other horse, tied it off on a rock, and began to make his way below. The first few feet were sheer, but then the cliff morphed into a steep slope of gravel and sand. It was a difficult descent, even with the rope, but it helped him move more quickly, and he could see time was of the essence. The man was obviously unconscious and lying face down at the edge of the rising stream. If the water didn't bring him to, it would kill him.

He reached the sand-covered body, rolled the man over onto his back, and dragged him from the water's edge. Yes, he was breathing, but he was seriously injured. It wouldn't be easy to ascertain how badly, unless and until he regained consciousness. Yeshua took part of his own shirt, wiped off the man's face and lips, and gave him water. "Help me," came the forced whisper out of his mouth.

"Try to relax. Yes, I'm here to help you. Where do you have pain?"

"My head, my leg."

Yeshua used all the lessons that Varaza, the healer, had taught him. He first determined the man's neck or back wasn't broken. He felt a large bump on his head, which Yeshua knew was better than a depression. He thought his leg might be broken, and it appeared he needed to set it.

Yeshua was at a loss over how to set a bone by himself. He'd never seen that done and wasn't sure it was possible. He thought about the problem and devised a plan. He found a sturdy forked branch in which he could wedge the man's leg below his calf and above his fracture. He stuck it firmly in the ground and built a pile of dirt and sand to support the lower leg that extended beyond the branch. He found two large rocks and dragged and rolled them so they snuggly blocked the fork from moving forward when he pulled.

As the man seemed to realize what he was doing and why, he spoke again. "Let me sit up. I can help you." The man groaned as he raised himself. He grasped his own leg below his knee. His grip appeared strong, especially considering his condition. "On the count of three," the man said, "we both pull."

Yeshua thought that would work, and the men executed the plan, which included a scream at the moment of truth. The man flopped back to the prone position with his hands on his forehead, passed out again. The procedure seemed to have been successful, and Yeshua fashioned a splint with sticks he scavenged from among the driftwood then tied it off with other pieces of his shirt.

The man was Yeshua's age, maybe a little younger, and fit, other than his present condition. The man's physical and mental

The Paragon

toughness during the bone-setting had impressed him. What he was doing out here alone was a question there would be time enough to answer. For now, the question was how to get them both out of their predicament.

Yeshua assured the man he wasn't going to leave him and began to look around for another route. He soon realized if they followed the stream, it eventually came closer to the level of the road, where it might be easier to climb out.

Yeshua could see a waterline on the rocks now. This meant the level of the stream was falling. It had fallen only a few inches, but the drop would probably accelerate. If the man could muster just a little more strength, they might have a chance.

"My friend," the man finally spoke, "words can't express my gratitude for what you've done to help me, but I know you can't get me out of here, so I urge you to leave me and save yourself."

"You're lucid again," Yeshua replied. "That's a start. You're young and strong, and I think there's a way out for us. No one's going to die today. Relax awhile more, and we can make a try. It won't be easy, but I think we can do it."

Yeshua calmed the man and got him to relax. "I'm going to use a healing technique by putting my hands on you," Yeshua explained, "if that's all right with you."

"Why not?" the injured man responded. "You've already helped me with your hands."

"Well, this is a little different." Yeshua began to explain.

"Do what you will," the man agreed. "I trust you. I have to."

Yeshua did as Varaza taught him, and he also made sure to elevate the man's leg. When he finished, he realized he had to let some time pass for the man to feel well enough to move, but knew if that time extended much beyond midday, they were in trouble. He didn't want to be stuck in the ravine overnight or to lose more time in pursuing the caravan. "Who are you? What's your name?" Yeshua asked him.

"I'm Ptolemy. My father and I are merchants. We were traveling east to trade for silk and spices, but robbers killed him, so now I'm headed to Maracanda. I want to build a stake, enough to restart my business. I was trying to catch up to the caravan that left Hecatompylos yesterday."

"Fortunately, we haven't encountered any robbers," Yeshua said. "I'm traveling with my cousin and my friend. We're also going to Maracanda. I stopped to meditate and got caught in the thunderstorm. I hope we can rejoin my caravan. I'm sure it's the one you're chasing. My name's Yeshua."

In Nehardea
Some Weeks Prior

When Ptolemy came to, he was still reeling, torn inside between grief over his father's murder and the impossibility of his own situation. He had no control over anything. He remained hooded and bound, rolling around the floor of whatever conveyance he was in, not knowing where he was going, nor who was taking him there. He kicked and flailed in anger and frustration.

Eventually, he understood the futility of lashing out and began to engage his brain. It felt cool, and he couldn't sense any light through the sack that covered his head. He had a powerful thirst.

The Paragon

He assumed it was still night. He lay on his side in silence until he heard men talking. They spoke slowly, like men who had just awakened. The movement resumed.

The sense of motion, the sound of rhythmic clomping, and an occasional whinny told him he was in a horse-drawn cart. Although it was open to the air, he could feel he was surrounded by wooden bars. As it grew warmer, he could feel the sun on his left side with his head in the direction of travel. This meant they were headed south or southeast. He heard other clomping and conversation that led him to surmise there were three other men on horseback besides the driver of the cart. There was probably a camel in their entourage as well: a small caravan.

"We probably need to give him food and water," he eventually heard one of the men say.

"Yeah, he won't be worth spit if we bring him in dead," another replied, one with a deeper voice, who seemed to be in charge.

The cart came to a halt, and the banging of wood seemed to mean the back gate was opening. Two men grabbed him and yanked him out of the cart and onto the ground. One of them removed the hood.

"He's young and feisty. He'll fetch a good price." It was the one in charge speaking. He was a large man, bigger than Ptolemy, bearded and dirty, with fierce eyes. Ptolemy could smell him. He reeked of last night's alcohol and body odor. They all did to some degree, but this one outdid the rest, and Ptolemy recognized him. It was the man who'd started the fight in the tavern.

"You," the man grunted to one of the others, not even calling him by name. "Give him some water and a piece of bread. Feed him yourself. I don't want him untied."

The underling did as he was told, shooting an unnoticed glance of disdain at the man who gave the orders, but Ptolemy noticed. After he ate and drank, and they were about to put him back in the cart, Ptolemy spoke. "Will you leave the hood off? It wouldn't be a threat to you."

"As long as he's tied up and locked in his cage, yeah, why not?" the boss allowed.

The entourage moved on. Ptolemy could now see the Zagros Mountains to his left. They were on a road paralleling the edge of the range. They must be past Ctesiphon. Perhaps more time had passed than he initially thought. He could only guess for now where they were headed. As far as he knew, the next major city would be Persepolis.

"Pick up the pace, you lazy bastards," the boss ordered. Do this. Do that. Orders flew from his mouth apparently just for the sake of giving them, always delivered with a tone of superiority.

Ptolemy sensed an opportunity. He initiated conversation. "Where are we going? What will become of me?"

"To the slave market in Persepolis," one of the underlings started to answer.

"Shut up, you," the boss said to the man who'd answered. "It's none of your damn business," he barked to Ptolemy. "Be thankful you're still alive."

This confirmed exactly what Ptolemy had suspected, and he knew he had to act soon. He wasn't sure how far Persepolis was, but he knew the sooner he tried to escape, the better.

The Paragon

"You have a sharp tongue when your prisoner's caged," Ptolemy opened his gambit.

"Damn right, what's your phrase, 'son of a whore?'" he shot back, laughing at Ptolemy.

Ptolemy knew the worst that could happen was that the man would take him out of the cart and beat him senseless while he was still tied up, which might be fatal, although there was one other thing that might be worse. He had to keep trying to goad him into a fight.

"Well, I don't know whose son you are," he said, "but I do know you fight like a whore." Ptolemy noticed this elicited a muffled giggle from two of the others. He was counting on that. The man in charge noticed it, too, and he flashed a glance of irritation in their direction.

Ptolemy then became relentless. "You're bigger than me. Afraid to fight?"

When Ptolemy got no response, he pressed harder. "Did you dip that beard in a shithole?"

The others laughed out loud. Insulting a man's beard was a serious matter in these parts.

"Does it scratch your mother's thighs when you go down on her, you cowardly bastard?" Ptolemy thought that might do it. He was betting on the man's wanting revenge for Ptolemy's smashing a jar on his head. He thought the man was sure he could destroy Ptolemy in a fight, and Ptolemy knew, because of his size, that might be true; but this last insult pushed him over the edge.

"Stop the cart now!" he screamed. "Open the gate. Cut the ropes. How do you want to do this, maggot?"

"I have no weapon," Ptolemy said. "Bare hands seems fair. Your size should make it easy for you, or do you need a weapon to my bare hands?"

The man threw down his sword and the fight began. The others stood by. Ptolemy sensed they were neutral parties now. He noticed two of them making a wager. The combatants circled each other warily until the larger man charged. Ptolemy went low and punched him in the gut. The brute was unfazed.

The man grabbed Ptolemy by the hair and began to pummel him. Ptolemy was no small man himself, but his opponent seemed a giant. Ptolemy kneed him violently in the genitals and doubled him over, then kneed him in the face.

Both men were bloodied and continued trading blows. Ptolemy's advantages were his training and his conditioning. He knew he had to keep the fight going and endure as long as possible. Part of this strategy meant accepting pain.

As the two exhausted themselves punching, pounding, and kicking, Ptolemy saw an opening to move in close. He placed his knee behind his antagonist and threw him to the ground. He kicked him in the head and jumped on his chest. Then he went to the ground with him and worked his way behind him. As he'd been trained, he maneuvered his arm under the giant's neck, made a lever with the other arm, and began to squeeze. He held on for his life as the man flailed and rolled. Ptolemy would not, dared not, let go.

After what seemed like minutes but was probably seconds, the man began to gurgle. The blood from the blows to his face contributed to his asphyxia. Slowly, but surely, Ptolemy choked the life out of him. Soon enough, it was finished.

The Paragon

Ptolemy was spent and badly hurt, but he knew there was more to do. As the others looked on in disbelief, except for the one who won the wager, he staggered to where the man had left his sword. He picked it up and menaced the others. "Run or be killed, you slimy shits." They ran just as they had at the inn.

He pulled himself up onto one of the horses and held on as best he could. With the camel and other horses in tow, he continued toward Persepolis. He soon saw a small town in the distance and hoped he could hang on until he reached it. After what seemed an interminable time, he rode into the village and dismounted, collapsing in a heap. He looked up at the curious people gathered around him and exhaled the word "robbers."

The townspeople nodded understanding and didn't seem to care why, if he was robbed, he still had his animals. Maybe it was because he gave one to the family that housed him. They took him in and nursed him back to health. They seemed to like him and treated him with great hospitality, including one or two of the young women.

He lingered perhaps longer than he needed to and left when he began to feel an undercurrent of resentment from some of the younger men. Apparently, some of the fathers thought he might make a good son-in-law.

When he got to Persepolis, Ptolemy continued to recover and gathered information to help him decide on his best course of action. He was learning enough of the local language to get by if no one spoke Greek. He sold everything he still had except one of the horses and determined to make his way north to Hecatompylos.

Ptolemy planned to reconnect with the Royal Road and try to find the caravan of Hadi Ba'riel. Since he was by himself, he decided it was better to go with a caravan. This meant he'd move more slowly, but it was much safer. He found one leaving in three weeks.

The trip to Hecatompylos was uneventful. When he arrived, he spent a couple of days resting before he began to inquire at the caravanserais about who had come and gone. He was alone now, his cockiness slightly tamed, but his experiences had given him confidence that he could think for himself and survive as a stranger in strange land. He'd lost time and assumed Ba'riel's caravan had probably already passed through.

On his second day of going to the local caravanserais to get information, Ptolemy got a surprise. "Yeah, Ba'riel's caravan left yesterday," the proprietor said. "Fine fellow, Ba'riel. He's on his way to Susia. You can probably catch him, but it's risky going alone, robbers and the like, you know, and a few long stretches without caravanserais."

"I understand," Ptolemy replied, "but I have to catch up. I have news for him from Damascus." He bought supplies and set off, now believing his objective was within his grasp. He'd complete his mission and return to Galilee, a hero to his king.

He soon found the chief problem of going alone would be loneliness. From his start early in the morning until late in the afternoon there was nothing, no one. He amused himself singing the bawdy songs of the garrison, reminding himself of drinking with his comrades, whom he missed.

Ptolemy kept the best pace he thought his horse could endure and noticed that the trail had been recently trodden by a large group of animals. He was confident he could catch the caravan if not this day, then surely the next. That is, until the storm blew up.

In the Ravine

Ptolemy was alert enough to know who Yeshua was, the man who killed his mother, the man he would kill, but he made no sign of it. "Yes, the storm. That was my problem too. It came on suddenly and spooked my horse. He threw me, and I got up from the ground disoriented. I made one false step."

"Before we leave, there's one more thing we need to do. I want you to relax completely and breathe slowly, deeply, and rhythmically." Yeshua began to talk the man into the meditative state and then directed his meditation with images of healing and strength. When he finished, Ptolemy was amazed. "I feel better than I should. I believe we'll make it."

When Yeshua finally suggested they make a go of it, Ptolemy agreed. Yeshua found a sturdy branch, appropriately shaped, and wrapped the rest of his shirt around one end of it to make a crutch. With Ptolemy's other arm around his shoulder, they slowly made their way along the stream and back toward the road.

As they neared the point where the streambed came closest to the road, Yeshua began to puzzle about how they'd negotiate the last few difficult feet. But as he looked up he saw, on the highway above him, a man on horseback.

"Cousin, you look out of your element on that horse. A donkey is more your speed," Yeshua said with a great sense of relief.

"A man can learn, and I didn't know you knew how to climb like a goat, and maybe you don't," Yonnah responded.

"I learned at Qumran, like you," Yeshua joked back, recalling the rugged desert scarp behind the monastery.

"I see you continue to make friends everywhere you go," observed his cousin dryly.

If it was unusual to see Yonnah riding a horse, it was more unusual to hear him making jokes that were actually funny, but while it seemed funny to Yeshua, Yonnah had disapproval in his heart. Between the two of them, they extracted Ptolemy, retrieved the horses, and began to make their way back to the caravan.

When they could see the caravan in the distance, Yeshua was curious. "Why have they waited for us? Hadi said he wouldn't wait or send anyone back with an animal."

"I left without asking permission, and Meryam said I should trust she could make the caravan wait. I asked no questions because I had no choice. Now we see them, so whatever she did was effective."

"I pray it was harmless." Yeshua chuckled.

Yeshua greeted Meryam with an embrace as a husband would when reunited with his wife. This was not lost on Yonnah. Yeshua introduced Ptolemy to her, and they settled around a fire for the evening.

"How did you make them wait for us?" Yeshua asked.

Meryam grinned broadly. "When Yonnah left, and before first light, I untied a camel and walked him away from the camp.

I raised his tail, then took a stick and did what I had to do. He made a horrible noise, took off into the hills, and was soon out of sight.

"I sneaked back to the camp," she continued. "The noise raised a terrible commotion. People were running around trying to figure out what happened. When they realized a camel was gone, they had a general idea of what direction he went, and after some argument, they sent several men out to find him. They returned with him in mid-afternoon, too late to get back on the road today."

Even Yonnah joined the group at the campfire. He felt useful and social, having effected Yeshua's rescue. His disapproval of Yeshua's chosen companions was suppressed that evening in favor of what passed as sociability for him. But a whore? he huffed to himself, and an impetuous young man, frivolous, careless, who probably never had a thought or sensation above the navel in all the years of his life? For Yeshua's sake, he'd try his best to accept them.

Ptolemy, for his part, had resolved not to take his revenge until he was well enough to make good an escape.

Some Days Later

Yeshua liked to talk to Ptolemy. He was a man who enjoyed laughing, and Yeshua, as Hadi had admonished him, needed that in his life.

For his part, Ptolemy churned inside. The man who killed his mother, the man he was ordered to kill, had saved his life and treated him as a friend. He vowed not to betray his inner conflict in face, voice, or attitude. For now, in his crippled state, he could turn his back on this dilemma. He'd lock that conflict in a box and live as if it didn't exist, as if he wasn't under any orders. Later, he'd know what to do.

As the days went on, the two often found opportunities to sit and talk. They talked as friends, and Yeshua found it easy to confide in Ptolemy in a way he couldn't even confide in Yonnah. Yonnah knew nothing of women, and now Yeshua had a woman in his life who was becoming more than an acquaintance or a friend.

"So I see your fondness for Meryam. Have you laid with her?" Ptolemy laughed heartily. The very question made Yeshua squirm, and he could see how that amused Ptolemy.

Ptolemy pressed the teasing. "What? You can't tell me it's a question of her virtue. Isn't she a woman of the street? I think a woman like that would welcome your affection."

Yeshua took no offense, although he could have. He realized Ptolemy was observant about women but had made a mistake about how Yeshua felt about her and about her deepest heart. "As I was raised, marriage must come before the pleasure," Yeshua said.

"Oh, you have a conscience in these matters, but aren't you far from Nazareth?" Ptolemy countered. "This isn't adultery. Neither of you is married."

"My friend the tempter," Yeshua replied. "Ptolemy, I come from a place where it's unseemly for a man to be promiscuous, let alone a woman, and apart from there I've been an abstinent monk. I want to live by the values I was taught, but as you say, out here, the stricter law of that culture can't apply.

"I believe," Yeshua continued, "if we're pledged in a lasting bond we swear to one another and to God, we may lie together as man and wife. So I'm going to ask to betroth her if she'll have me."

"You'd do that? What's wrong with you?" Ptolemy responded, laughing in shock and amusement. "I can't believe a young man's response, so far from home, would be so ethical."

"You tease me, my friend," Yeshua said, "but she's my true love."

A Few Days Later

As the sun went down in the west, the full moon rose opposite to it. First, the eastern sky took on a glow like dawn, and then a white sliver punctured the horizon and began to expand into a breathtaking globe grander than any memory or fantasy. It was as if day had followed day.

"Meryam, please come walk with me," Yeshua asked.

Yeshua was nervous. He'd thought about this for weeks. He thought about what Ptolemy had said and what Yonnah would think. He thought about what his parents would think if he returned home betrothed without family involvement or a contract. He thought about how renouncing celibacy would affect his ministry. He thought about this and that until he decided he was finished with thinking and the time for courage was at hand.

"Meryam, we've known each other for some months and have shared some tough times. I've seen you amend your life, grow in love and turn to a life of service to others. As I've watched this, my love for you has grown."

Meryam wasn't sure what would come out of his mouth next, but his words had captured her attention. She stopped and turned toward him and looked him right in the eye.

"Uh, I . . . I mean . . ." Yeshua stammered.

"The preacher is at a loss for words?" she asked in amusement.

"Yes; I mean, no." He took a deep breath and then blurted a torrent of words. "Meryam, I'd betroth you if you'll have me. We could make our own contract and promise each other to abide by it."

Her eyes sparkled with reflected moonlight. She hugged him tightly. She was thrilled by the proposal. She'd thought marriage would never be possible for someone like her. Yeshua had saved her, and she loved him for it. She composed herself on the inside enough to tease him for his clumsiness. "Let me think, then. What would this contract say? There are no goats nor any other property to exchange. What would we promise to each other?"

"I'd promise to love and honor you for all my days, no matter what difficulties we encountered," Yeshua said.

"Would you feel free to take another wife?" she asked.

"It's permitted," he responded, "but I think one's enough for me. I'd promise not to do it if it pleases you."

"It would please me," she said.

"Then I promise," Yeshua said. "And you know someday when we return to Galilee, I'll have a ministry, and probably go village to village preaching and teaching. Will you support this way of life and, if necessary, maintain a household while I travel around the countryside?"

Meryam grew serious. "I'll support you, but I won't promise blind obedience. I understand the custom that the man is ruler of the household, but I've have had enough of slavery. I see these married women shuffling about, kowtowing to their husbands, more a slave than I ever was. I will not promise this."

Yeshua knew he had to soften her heart. "But if what I ask of you would be a benefit to our family, wouldn't it be your pleasure to do it?"

"Yes, it would be my pleasure," she admitted.

"Do you promise it would be your pleasure?" he asked with a smile.

She rolled her eyes, realizing the man of words had trapped her. "I promise it would be my pleasure."

"I accept your promises," Yeshua vowed. "If you accept mine, we have a contract and are betrothed."

"I do accept yours," she agreed. "I am betrothed to you."

Yeshua exhaled completely. "Maybe when we return to Galilee," he mused, "we could make our home in Magdala. It's a beautiful area by a great sea. As I told you, I have friends and family there. Some are farmers. Many are fishermen. You'd be my dear Magdalena after all."

"As long as you were with me, I'd love that," she cooed.

"So, by custom I'd drink with your father," pronounced Yeshua, returning to the present, "and time would pass between the fulfillment of the financial conditions and the consummation. Then there'd be a celebration. Sometimes, the period of fulfillment lasts months or years."

"None of that applies here," Meryam countered. "We shouldn't spoil this moment by being legalistic."

"What are you suggesting, then?" he asked.

"I'm suggesting you come to my tent tonight. I'm the only unmarried woman in the caravan. We have it to ourselves."

"I need to keep our betrothal secret until I can break the news to my cousin. He won't be pleased, but he'll accept it in the end."

"Fine." She seemed slightly annoyed by this request but not deterred. She added coyly, "I can keep a secret. I'll see you in my tent when the moon is straight up."

They walked back to the camp. Most everyone was asleep by now. Meryam kissed Yeshua. She walked to her tent, and he to his. He thought to take a nap, but he was excited and a little apprehensive. He went to the river and bathed. Yeshua was a lean man of average height who had more the musculature of a man of the building trades than the gaunt look of his cousin.

He stood in the moonlight. His body tingled. He had a new awareness of it. He immersed himself in the river and then slowly rubbed off the dirt of the road, feeling every inch of his skin. As he emerged from the stream, his loins stirred with anticipation. He returned to his tent and donned a clean tunic. Everyone in camp was asleep by now. It would be midnight soon enough.

He waited nervously; then he could wait no more. It was before the appointed hour, but he walked quickly to Meryam's tent. "I'm sorry I've come early. I . . ."

The Paragon

"I'm pleased you've come early," she said, like a woman of experience. "Please lie down while I bring you some tea."

"Tea is good," Yeshua said, "but do you have any wine?"

"Of course." She smiled, repressing a chuckle.

Once he lay down, he looked around and saw her tent was adorned with mats, skins, and silk-covered pillows, like her home in Nehardea. He watched her pouring the wine. She, too, had cleansed the dirt of the road from her body. She'd pulled back and oiled her long black hair and had wrapped herself in a dress of almost sheer yellow silk that made her dark eyes seem like a vortex pulling him in.

She brought the wine and lay next to him. Then she leaned over and softly kissed his lips.

"Meryam . . ." he began to speak.

She put her arms around him and kissed him hard. He opened his eyes wide but soon enough closed them, embraced her fully, and kissed her back. He wasn't sure he'd know how to please her, but she knew exactly what to do.

"Relax," she said. She slowly massaged his temples as he sank deeply into one of the silk pillows. "Here, let me take your tunic." She pulled it off deftly, not disturbing the mood. Then she began to rub his body and touch him in places and ways that he'd never allowed himself to imagine.

The very smell of her, beyond the scented oils she'd applied, excited him in a primal way, and dissolved his passivity. He rolled on top of her, aggressor now, giving in to his new feelings.

"Slower, slower," she said in a hard whisper.

He complied, not in response to the words, but to the tone and cadence of her voice. She told Yeshua what would please her and what to do. He followed her guide, clumsily at first, but when she sighed then moaned with pleasure, they fell into the rhythm of love, until they both shuddered in ecstasy.

Yeshua had never imagined such pleasure of the body. At the same time, his heart swelled like the sea in spring tide with love for his wife in a way he couldn't describe with words. As he lay there, breathing slowly and deeply, his body at once weightless yet unable to move a muscle, he thanked God for the gift He'd given him.

For her part, Meryam, heart still pounding, drifted into a state of unimaginable bliss. For all the sex she'd had in her life, she had never made love. Never. Her world was different now, she thought. This was her salvation.

They separated before first light came and before the others began to stir, in time to hide any sign of their rendezvous. They were exhausted, and this wouldn't be an easy day. They'd agreed to stay separated so as not to arouse suspicion. This was a good plan except for the observant faculties of one.

"Yeshua, you look more than tired," Ptolemy said. "It's as if you haven't slept."

"I tossed and turned all night, Ptolemy," Yeshua replied. "I think it was the full moon." Not exactly a lie.

The Paragon

"Oh, I think it may be for some other reason. I notice someone else who looks tired. Perhaps the moon kept her awake too." Ptolemy just laughed at him.

"My friend," said Yeshua, "if you breathe a word of this before I do, I'll take you back to the ravine where I found you and leave you to the vultures." They both laughed.

Six

Susia

Susia was nestled between two mountain ranges. The lower one, to the east, was the last of the mountains before the desert crossing to the river Oxos and the final slow rise to Bukhara and Maracanda. The caravan would spend a few days here to resupply, to trade, and to rest.

Yeshua and Meryam, on Yeshua's initiative, observed the traditional Jewish holidays. There were a few other Jews in the caravan who would join them. As the days passed, especially when they were away from cities, it was easy to lose track of what day it was. Sometimes that became more a guess than a calculation. They decided, therefore, to celebrate the Feast of Unleavened Bread when they got to Susia.

Furthermore, the exact date of *this* feast depended on when the barley was ready for harvest, and who knew when that would be? Much of the celebration had to do with requirements and customs in a home, which they didn't exactly have. Yeshua and his friends, however, agreed that a seder meal of unleavened bread and a young lamb, together with a remembrance of the flight of

The Paragon

the Jews from Egypt, would provide an occasion for religious fellowship, fulfillment of duty, and fun.

They arrived at a caravanserai southeast of the walled city, close enough to walk to the nearest market. Traders came from that market and others to the caravan. The first day they were there, Yeshua noticed a Seresman among some of the camels that he'd led to a nearby stream. He was elderly but spry and his eyes darted from side to side as he walked. "Good day, sir," Yeshua greeted. "It appears you're either lost or looking for something."

"Someone, I'd say," the man said. "Is there one called Yeshua among you?"

"He's among you as you speak," Yeshua answered. "What business do you have with him?"

"I have a task for someone going to Maracanda, and the master of the caravan tells me you'd be suited for it. My name is Ling Zhi. I need to speak to you to be sure you're the best one for the job. Is it true you have an interest in the spiritual ideas of other cultures?"

"Yes," Yeshua said, "and I intend to go to the Paragon when I get to Maracanda where, I'm told, I can meet great thinkers from traditions other than my own. Based on my experiences so far, I'm sure you know of the Paragon." Yeshua was amused by now at who knew of the place and how he seemed to meet them. He stopped and set down his burden: a shovel draped like a yolk across his shoulders, suspending a bucket on either end, water and a brush in one, dung in the other.

"Yes, certainly," the Seresman responded. "In fact, the task I have for you is to make a delivery there."

"And what would it be?" Yeshua asked. "A camel full of supplies?"

"No, not at all," Ling Zhi replied. "Something more mundane and quite a bit smaller; a codex, to be exact. I've made Susia my home for some time. I've spent several years translating the Tao Te Ching into Greek and have crafted four copies, one to remain here in the library, one to go to the library in Alexandria in Egypt, one for me, and one for the Paragon. Are you familiar with the writing? Go ahead. Finish your duties while we talk."

"I've heard of it," Yeshua said, picking up the water bucket, "but I haven't read it. Can you tell me about it?"

"Of course," Ling Zhi responded. "The Taoist way of looking at things is elegant and simple. The Tao is the Oneness that exists forever. It operates through the interaction of two opposing aspects called yin and yang, representing positive and negative, male and female, good and evil, and so forth.

Yeshua continued working as the men talked. The camel he approached knelt at water's edge in anticipation of its bath. Yeshua took the brush, scrubbing the beast with a circular motion.

"Everything that exists," Ling continued, "arises from the interaction of yin and yang. Everything you know and everything you don't know, from the operation of the cosmos to human behavior, can be understood in this way. A spiritual person should love the Tao and live according to its operation."

"That's it?" a surprised Yeshua asked.

"Yes, that's all there is to it," Ling replied.

"Are good and evil then equal?" Yeshua quizzed.

"Two sides of the same coin," the old man explained. "They're relative conceptions that arise from human observation. How can something be said to be evil without good to compare it to or good without evil to contrast it with?

"Of course, the people need guidance to help them understand how to behave," he continued. "The Tao Te Ching, written by our great prophet Lao Tzu, is the poetic expression of this fundamental truth and offers guidance in acting in accordance with the Tao. It uses paradox to illuminate this understanding."

He walked with Yeshua to the next camel. Before the bath, Yeshua shoveled the camel's dung into the bucket. When dried, it would be used to fuel cooking fires. None of this distracted Yeshua from his intense interest in what the old man had to say.

"We also have a text called I Ching," Ling explained further, "or Book of Changes, which a person may consult like an oracle when his life comes to a crossroads."

"I love the simplicity and clarity of your thinking," Yeshua responded. "If I transport this codex, may I read it?"

"Of course," Ling said. "Come to my house in the city tomorrow morning, and I'll have it ready for you."

"But I'm curious," Yeshua said. "The Tao--is it the same as Brahman?"

"Oh, the Hindu people," Ling answered. "Their beliefs seem complex to me: all those gods, but yes, I suppose there's great similarity between their Brahman and the Tao."

With Ayn-Sof as well, Yeshua thought, and Ahura Mazda.

Yeshua rose early for prayer and meditation. Lately, those practices had begun to meld into one. He asked the Divine Spirit for safe travels for him and his companions but also visualized it. He asked for strength to conquer his demons and the same for his loved ones and visualized their lives in harmony. He believed God never promised to protect the body, but there was always redemption and healing for a soul when someone truly desired it and when she could find a way.

Today he would go into the city to get the codex from Ling Zhi and bring back a year-old lamb for their feast. But something felt strange this morning. He didn't hear any birds, even the cocks. Animals that should have been parading out to pasture were huddled together, making agitated sounds. He felt these things portended something, something bad perhaps. He didn't know what that might be, but as he made his way through the city gate, he learned.

Yeshua fell to the ground as the earth began to shake like the end of days. A shiver gripped his spine as he envisioned the thunderous collapse of Jericho. The dust momentarily blinded him, but what he could hear was disturbing enough: the crumbling of brick, the screaming of women and groaning of men, the sound of the earth cracking, right in front of him as far as he could tell. Without being able to see, he dared not move.

The lintel of the gate crashed but didn't fall onto him. The screaming and wailing redoubled. The shaking intensified. It seemed it would never end.

He was finally able to wipe the dirt from his eyes. The rumbling abated, but he was still trembling on the inside. Through the clouds of smoke and dust, all he could see was rubble. There was a tear in the earth about three feet wide, only steps in front of him. The city gate was collapsed behind him.

Yeshua's heart was racing. His breathing was shallow and rapid. All he could think to do was to find Ling Zhi. The mission he'd been given was still important in his mind, but he also feared for his safety, even his life. He leapt the chasm and proceeded the best way he could figure to Ling Zhi's house. There were mounds of death and misery all around him, dead and dying crushed by the collapse of their own homes. Piles of rubble blocked his path and disoriented him.

It was a windless day, and the smoke from a thousand fires sank into the streets, mixing with the dust into a stifling, unbreathable soup that displaced the air. He pulled the front of his shirt up over his nose. He came to a crossroads and was unsure how to proceed.

The house on the corner where he paused had been reduced to a pile of clay, but amid the chaos he heard a muffled groaning. At first he was unsure of the source but soon realized it was coming from under the rubble. Without hesitation, he began to tear through the pile, casting aside the debris, trying to reach the voice he'd heard.

He couldn't tell if it was a man, woman, or child, or even if there was more than one person trapped. He called out to whoever was buried, "I hear you. I'm coming to help."

His mind was racing with thoughts of Ling Zhi and of his own mission. He thought about his friends back at the caravanserai, wondering if they were safe and certain they would worry about him. Mostly, however, he thought about saving the life whose voice was growing fainter.

He shouted to passers-by for help. Most were dazed. Some were running. Everyone ignored his plea until one man stopped and joined him tearing into the pile. Soon a woman, wiping tears from her dirty face, her bloody leg barely allowing her to walk, was helping them too. They ripped, pulled, and cast aside one brick after another, choking as they gasped for breath to fuel their efforts.

Eventually, they could see a body. It was a man clutching an infant. They were wedged under a table that had two legs collapsed. The rescuers dragged the two out. The baby appeared not to be breathing. Meanwhile, the man kept whispering, "My wife, my wife."

Yeshua took the baby and, remembering what he'd learned from Varaza, laid his hands on her and then lightly pressed her chest above her heart with his fingers, again and again. He put his lips over the child's and lightly gave her breath.

Varaza had told him of this technique. "Another physician," he had said, "told me he'd once seen it used to revive an apparently dead woman. Those who had watched called it miraculous." Varaza himself didn't know if it would work, but it did. The child gasped and began to cry. The astonished crowd that had gathered by now began shouting praise and crying tears of joy.

Meanwhile, the others had uncovered the man's wife. They dragged her out as well, and she was not breathing either, but a bloody gash in her skull had sealed her fate.

Yeshua had done all he could. He knew he had to complete his task and return to the caravanserai as soon as possible. "Does anyone know the way to Ling Zhi's house?" he asked, beginning to calm himself.

The first man who helped spoke up. "This is my neighborhood, and I think I know who you're looking for: a Seresman. Go two more streets down and to the left."

"Thank you, and thank all of you who helped," Yeshua said to the crowd. "Will one of you be able to stay with the man and his child for a while?"

"I can do it." The first woman who'd stopped spoke up.

"Good," Yeshua said. "God will surely bless all of you. You've put aside your own concerns to help strangers."

"You've amazed us. Who are you?" the first man who helped asked.

"I'm Yeshua of Nazareth," he said, "from a land to the west called Galilee. It's you who've amazed me. I have to go now."

He tried to follow the man's directions but had to guess at what was a street. Eventually, he came to the place where he believed Ling Zhi lived. When he didn't see him, he had second thoughts about choosing to go there.

He became more concerned about his companions at the caravanserai. He had to get back. As well as being worried about the others, he knew they'd be worried about him, and he hoped no one would come to look for him.

Just as he made the decision to return, he saw the old man sitting on a collapsed mound of brick that was once a house. He was slumped forward with his face in his hands.

"Ling Zhi!"

"Yeshua, come here." The old man appeared shaken as he slowly raised his head. "I'm all right, and my wife is alive and well. She's gone to her sister's, and I'll join her shortly. I believed you'd come, and I've waited here. This is all I've saved from my belongings. In truth, I didn't have many belongings, but here's the codex."

Ling Zhi unwrapped a goatskin to reveal a bundle wrapped further in a fine red silk that featured two exquisite gold dragons in a twisted embrace. "Please treat it reverently," he beseeched. "Have a look at it, Yeshua."

"What's this material it's written on?" Yeshua asked, marveling at the object even amid the disaster. "So smooth; so thin."

"They call it *paper* here," said Ling, "a corruption of the word *papyrus*. It's a leap into the future over the old material, although we've had it in Seres for some time."

"Where does it come from?" Yeshua continued to fondle it. He'd never seen anything like it.

"We make it in Seres in a secret process using mulberry bark," Ling explained. "I brought a large quantity with me when I came from my homeland. When I left, I thought I'd sell or trade it, but I soon realized creating these codices was my true calling."

"How can I take this if it's the only one you have?" Yeshua asked.

"It isn't the only one," Ling said. "The two in the library, one meant to remain here and one for Alexandria, I believe have been destroyed, but my own copy is in a safe place. Who knows, I may take my copy to Alexandria personally. There's nothing for us here anymore."

The Paragon

Yeshua was skeptical of the old man's ability to make such a journey, even though he appeared to have great vitality, at least before he saw him in this pitiable condition.

"I should stay here and help you and any others I could," Yeshua offered.

"No," Ling said, "you must go. You have a responsibility to your companions, and I'm sure their uncertainty over your fate is torture to them. The caravan will need to leave immediately. What could you do here except help to bury the dead? My family and I will survive. Go to your friends. It's they who need you most."

It broke Yeshua's heart to see so many in need and realize he couldn't help, and that he had a greater responsibility, like Ecbatana revisited. He left Ling Zhi, found his way out of the city by a western gate, and quickly moved to return to the caravanserai. As he approached it, he saw one wall partially collapsed, but the rest of the structure appeared to be intact. The people and animals were gathered outside the walls, and they cheered when they saw him.

He told them what he'd seen, and they told him how they'd felt the shaking but had escaped without injury. The damage he viewed here was nothing like he'd experienced within the city walls. The caravanserai could be rebuilt, but for now, they had no choice but to be grateful they were all alive and to leave as quickly as possible. As soon as people got over their shock and appreciated their deprivation, they'd begin to look on the caravan with desperate eyes.

Of course, Yeshua had not brought back a lamb for their feast, so Meryam passed around the bread she'd made, which they stood and ate while they prepared to leave.

This next part of the trek would be difficult. The weather was turning hot. When they left the mountains after Susia, they would be in the desert all the way to the Oxos except for the great oasis city of Merv. It would take the caravan about ten days to make that first leg of the journey.

The mountain range to the east of the city diminished as the ridge ran southeastward. They chose the flatter route around the mountains rather than cutting across the rugged peaks. Even though that made the distance traveled somewhat longer, it was a far easier route.

They had just begun to move from the caravanserai when the earth began to shake again. Some tried to calm the animals, some wailed, and some sank to their knees to beg whatever god they prayed to, to make it stop and forgive their transgressions.

"Yeshua, do you think God is punishing us?" Ptolemy asked with apprehension in his voice.

Yeshua himself was uncertain of their fate but felt he had a duty to project calm. "Can we say everyone in our caravan is equally deserving of punishment?" he responded. "Yet this disaster affects us all. Can we say the whole city of Susia is more wicked than all of us? They're wasted to rubble, and there are good people among them.

"I think God allows horrors like this randomly," Yeshua continued, "but if someone wants to use this event to be reminded of his own mortality and judgment to come, that's fine. If it causes him to repent from personal wickedness and amend his life, I wouldn't discourage it. A man never knows when his possessions or his life will be taken from him."

As the periodic shaking diminished and finally stopped, they moved onto the desert plain. Leaving the green banks of the foothills was like sailing out of sight of land into the vast emptiness of the ocean. Only an occasional tuft of scrub gave any hint life was even possible here. It was flat, hot, and devoid of any odor except their own. They covered up against the sun and dust and sank into the rhythm of the movement of their beasts.

There were oases at regular intervals and a larger one about three days out of Merv. They stopped there for water and to set up camp for the night.

Yeshua had been out in the desert talking to Yonnah and was returning to his tent. It was mostly dark by now. The serenity of night had fallen over the camp. The animals acknowledged him with friendly sounds as he passed them. Then he heard a woman scream and then again.

It was Meryam, and the sounds were coming from her tent. He ran to it, pulled open the flap, and heard a man's voice. "Come on, now. Spread your legs for Darab." It was one of the guards, and he was on top of her.

"What's the matter? You don't want it now?" He was obviously drunk, and Yeshua set upon him in a rage. He ran at Darab and knocked him off her. Then he grabbed his staff and began to beat Darab's head.

By then others had heard the commotion and ran for the tent. Hadi was first to enter, brandishing a sword. "Desist, Yeshua. I'm the law here."

Ptolemy, who entered next, guessed the situation and allowed Yeshua one more blow before hobbling over and restraining him. In truth, Yeshua let himself be restrained.

"What's happened here?" Hadi demanded.

"I found him on top of her," Yeshua fumed. "You pig; we cared for you when you were sick and near death. This is how you repay us?"

Darab cowered in the corner. His size didn't spare him from the intimidation of those arrayed against him. He turned to Meryam. "You wanted it before."

"I screamed for you to stop."

"When you heard someone coming."

"Liar."

"Bitch."

"Stop it, all of you," Ba'riel commanded. "Meryam, I know you're a woman who's lived a life without virtue, and you're not married or betrothed."

"Not so, sir." She contradicted the master.

"Yeshua, although you tend animals for me," Hadi said, referencing the code of talion in his mind, "I regard you as being of the priestly class. Nonetheless, you have no possessory interest here."

"I beg your pardon." Yeshua's speech was calmer now, although he was still breathing heavily. "You're wrong to say she isn't betrothed. She and I are betrothed."

Darab defended himself. "It isn't so. I never knew this. You lie."

The Paragon

"I didn't know of this myself," Hadi said, "and I know everything about my caravan. Can anyone say he knew of this?" He alone was judge and jury now.

"I can, sir," Ptolemy affirmed. "It's true. Yeshua told me before Susia."

Hadi Ba'riel clenched his lips and exhaled hard through his nose. He had one hand wrapped around the other on the on the sword handle. He brought his clenched hands to his lips and held them there tightly as he bowed his head in contemplation. He rolled his eyes upward to gaze on his guard crouched in the corner.

Yeshua didn't speak.

"It's settled, then." Hadi turned to Yeshua. "Since you're betrothed, one of the two must die."

Yeshua still didn't speak. He felt begging for his wife's life would seem like expressing doubt in her fidelity.

"Sir, I beg you. I didn't know. She was willing," Darab sniveled.

"You're the liar. I heard her scream," Hadi said, and without hesitation struck a blow that half-severed Darab's head.

In his heart of hearts, Hadi couldn't say for certain whether or not the woman had been willing, or how he should truly view the private betrothal, but he couldn't tolerate any bad business like this on his caravan.

As he left the tent, someone in the crowd outside shouted, "Sir, what happened?"

"Justice," he replied.

"Take his body far from camp," Hadi ordered, "and let the vultures see to him." Hadi returned to his tent annoyed but at peace with what he'd done.

Yeshua was appalled. "What have I done? The most important thing I teach is not to kill, and I tried to kill him and then allowed him to be killed."

"What are you talking about?" Meryam raged. "He raped me. You did what any man must do."

"What I must do is stop him," Yeshua responded. "Yes, even if I have to kill him. But once I stopped him, I tried to kill him out of anger and vengeance, not out of necessity. I could have covered you with my body."

"I don't understand." Meryam was crying hysterically. "Am I not worth your anger?"

"Come to me, Wife." He held her tightly and cried with her.

Yeshua stayed with her through the night. They slept in exhaustion, and when they awoke, he spoke to her. "Meryam, I love you as my wife and friend. I find no shame on your part for what happened. I believe and I feel that Darab imposed himself on you against your will. I don't doubt you, but I have to do penance for my anger. Justice could have been served by banishment, and I could have asked for that."

"Justice was served," she shot back. "The justice is what satisfies me, not you." Her eyes flared like he hadn't seen since she told him about her father's brutality.

"I understand," Yeshua said, realizing the gross insensitivity of his words. "But since you're safe now," he counseled, "I hope at

The Paragon

some time you can find forgiveness for Darab, as you've sought it yourself. It might be difficult now, but don't let hatred fester. You know where that leads. Forgiveness is for your own peace.

"Now I need to seek my forgiveness by doing penance," he continued. "You won't see me for several days. Yonnah and Ptolemy will look after you. I've agonized that this penance may be a selfish thing, but I need to tame the beast. I love you and I'll miss you."

He went to Ptolemy and told him of his plan. "You can't do this. You'll die," Ptolemy argued.

"If I die, it's God's will. Look after Meryam while I'm gone," Yeshua said.

"And if you die, what do I say to her?" Ptolemy chided. "That he completed his penance?"

"I pray I don't die, but I have to do this," Yeshua said.

He went to Yonnah. "Yeshua," his cousin said, with the news of the secret betrothal eating at him, "there are things I need to say to you, but now isn't the time. I understand your need to do this."

"Yes," Yeshua explained. "You'll all leave me here, and I will walk to Merv. I believe it will take several days. I'll take no food, nor water, even if offered. I'll contemplate my need to tame my anger."

"I think you overrate your anger in this case," Yonnah countered, "but only you and God can judge you. I understand as a teacher you need to provide an example, but I pray you don't die. I won't come for you out of respect for your penance." Yonnah then left him to his atonement.

The caravan went on to Merv. It took them almost three days. Everyone was concerned for Yeshua. Some wanted to go back for him, but Yonnah spoke as a powerful preacher, in a way none of them had heard before, and he forbade it.

"This is the will of the Lord!" he thundered. "All of us need to repent from wickedness and do penance, more so he who would speak in God's name. Yeshua must purify himself, and let no one put himself before God and interfere." No one, not even Hadi Ba'riel dared defy him.

Hadi kept a slow pace, hoping that Yeshua would be only a few hours after them, but that didn't happen. They took turns watching from the high city wall on the next day, but he still didn't come.

In the desert Yeshua waited and meditated until the caravan had long been out of sight. It was past midday when he began his walk to Merv. In his solitude the desert had never seemed so vast, so empty, so bleak, his boundless griddle of purification by fire. In the beginning his pace was steady and deliberate. Although the sun was sinking, the heat soon began to take a toll.

His steps became a shuffle, the soles of his sandals scraping the dirt. His throat felt constricted and as parched as the ground he trod. He saw a small oasis ahead. He walked past it. It was a temptation, a seeming Eden of shade and water, but he wouldn't stop. He walked as far as he could until it was too dark to continue and then moved off the road and slept in the sand.

He awoke the next day before the sun. He was weak from hunger and dehydration, but it was time to move before the heat set in. He happened on a well, a hole in the desert floor without the stream or pool or shade trees of a true oasis. Nomads were gathered there to drink and water their animals.

"Sir, why are you roaming this wasteland alone?" one of the nomads asked.

"I'm walking to Merv as penance for a grave sin," he replied.

"Sir, you look terrible, and you have far to go. Is this sin worth your life?" the nomad inquired. "Isn't there anyone who'd be devastated if you die, as you surely will?"

He didn't speak for a second. "Yes, there are people . . . but I owe this to God before I can be what I need to be for them. If I don't do this, everything I've ever said or been will have no meaning." In the silence that followed, Yeshua peered expressionless into the void. I have a duty, he thought, to God, to the people, to my ministry, to myself. But don't I now also have a duty to my wife?

The nomad's voice broke his trance. "Please," he begged, "take a drink before you go on. Do your penance, but give yourself a chance to survive it. The desert is cruel."

Gathering himself, Yeshua answered in a rasp. "Thank you, friend, and God bless you, but no. I have to do as I vowed." He left the oasis as the nomads, faces grim, watched him fade away into the inhospitable landscape.

By now the barren crust under foot was like an anvil to the sun's hammer. The heat began to penetrate the soles of his sandals. Each step felt like he carried a hundred pounds of millet on his shoulders.

He rested again at midday, but when he continued, he noticed the sky to the south looked strange. There was an orange tint to it. The vague color seemed to coalesce. It became a churning cloud racing along the ground right at him, like a charging herd of wild beasts.

The wind began to pick up. The grains of sand began to feel like needles on his face. He wrapped up as best he could and pressed on. The wind intensified to a roar. He knew what was coming.

Soon, the sandstorm bore down on him with full force. He struggled to put one foot in front of the other and maintain his direction of movement. Soon it became too much, and he could no longer see anything in front of him. When it became unbearable, he screamed. "What am I doing? What am I doing?" His scream seemed but a whisper in the roaring wind.

He found a rock and crouched behind it to let the storm blow itself out, while he prayed for deliverance and forgiveness. By then night was descending. He slept, shivering in the desert chill, until sometime after midnight, when the moon rose brightly enough to light his way. He trekked on. This would be the only way he could make it: sleep by day, wait for the moon to rise, and then move from that time until mid-morning.

At Merv

On the third day after they'd arrived, Ptolemy spied a lone figure in the distance. The human form moved slowly, and Ptolemy was sure it was Yeshua.

"Look, Yonnah. I think it's him," Ptolemy shouted.

"Yes, I think you're right," Yonnah said.

The Paragon

Ptolemy ran for Meryam, who joined the other two. "Yonnah," Ptolemy said, "I'm going to get him. He's done enough penance. I don't want him to die a mile from the gate."

"No, don't do it," Yonnah admonished. "He won't accept your help. He's set his punishment, and he'll complete it. I'd say he'd be angry with you, but since his penance was to tame his anger, then his ordeal would have been for naught. Let him come."

Ptolemy refused to listen. He grabbed a horse and galloped toward the pitiful figure. "Yeshua," he urged, "you've done it. Come on. I'll put you on the horse and you can ride into the city with your head held high. Here, drink this."

Yeshua could scarcely part his lips enough to utter one syllable. "Go."

Ptolemy was both filled with admiration and frustrated by Yeshua's stubbornness. At the same time, another thought roiled his mind and knotted his stomach; why did he even care about this man who murdered his mother and whom he was sworn to kill? What was wrong with him that he could allow his heart to grow soft, to weaken his resolve?

He turned his horse around and spat in the dirt as if to expel a bitter herb, to expel the disgust he felt with himself and to rid himself of the dilemma that vexed him like a demon. But his dilemma was double. He would have to do his duty soon enough, and if he could not bring himself to kill Yeshua, honor would demand he take his own life. He kicked the horse as if it was himself and galloped back to the city to wait with the others.

The last steps were agony. Yeshua could no longer lift his feet. He was unsteady, and every fiber of his body was desiccated. He was covered head to toe with the dirt of the road and the storm. Putting one foot in front of the other, he entered the gate and collapsed. His friends were waiting for him and ministered to him. They gave him water and bathed him.

As he lie there, he looked up at his wife and mouthed the words, "Forgive me."

Of the three, only Meryam understood the words or their significance. He ate something and slept. He never spoke of the ordeal, nor did anyone ask him about it.

Seven

The fabulous city of Merv rivaled Maracanda as the largest on The Great Road. Yeshua knew from Hadi and others that the followers of the Buddha had established a large presence here, and they were more than willing to discuss and explain Buddhism to the transients who inquired.

Hadi didn't subscribe to any one religion. He was Zoroastrian in name, but the Buddhists intrigued him. He also had contact with Jews, including Yeshua, but found Judaism to be clannish and unwelcoming to outsiders, whom they called Gentiles.

The gods did as they pleased, as far as he was concerned, and his lot was to try as best he could not to anger them. Trying to influence them through prayer or sacrifice--that was a vain task, but he had an abiding interest in the opinions of his diverse trading partners.

The caravan would be here for a while, resting, trading, and enjoying the city life. As Yeshua regained his strength and vitality, he told Hadi he'd like to find a Buddhist temple. Hadi suggested one, associated with a small monastery, whose lama enjoyed a great reputation for both holiness and scholarship. Yeshua found it on the city's edge.

"Come in. Come in," Mandeep, the lama, greeted him. "I'm pleased to meet you, Yeshua," he said. "Your reputation precedes you."

Yeshua had no idea how this was so, or that he even had a reputation, but he expressed pleasure for the meeting as well. "I've come here to learn more about the teachings of the Buddha, and I hoped you could enlighten me."

"An interesting choice of words, I'd say," Mandeep responded. "No one can enlighten another. You find *enlightenment* yourself, but maybe I can educate you about our teachings and show you a small step on your way to that enlightenment. The Buddha's way is only one way to get there, but that's between you and me. Too many religions say they're the *only* way."

Yeshua was amused by their wordplay and accompanied the teacher to his room behind the main temple. It was neat but simple. There was a bed, a table, two chairs, and a small shrine on a ledge of one wall opposite a window that allowed the sun to directly illuminate it.

The shrine was a bronze statue of the Buddha, cross-legged, eyes closed, with all the edges rounded smooth, evoking peace. There was a fresh blossom floating in a dish of water in front of him, as if the Buddha were contemplating it. Yeshua had never seen an image of the Buddha before, and he examined it intently.

There was a second image of the Buddha in the room, a painting on papyrus. It was remarkable to Yeshua for something else he'd never seen. "Why is there a white circle around the Buddha's head?"

"That represents his aura," Mandeep explained. "Only a few people can see auras, but the white color represents pure spirit. Yeshua, why are you really here? Are you merely curious?"

"I come from the tradition of Judaism. Even within that religion, there are factions who believe differently from each other. I'm not satisfied with certain aspects of that tradition, so I seek a larger truth."

"Oh, it's the truth you seek?" the lama said with a smile. "I'm not sure you'll find that here. What do you mean by the truth?"

Yeshua shifted in his chair. He knew he was about to be challenged. This was something he enjoyed, even craved. "I suppose it's that which is fundamental and unchangeable for all time and in all places."

"Well, you're a smart man," Mandeep said. "Let me ask you this. Is it the truth you have free will?"

"Yes," said Yeshua carefully, not wanting to trap himself in a game of words. "I believe that's the truth. I'm free to make choices and suffer their consequences."

"Do you believe, in your tradition, that God knows everything, past, present, and future?" Mandeep questioned further.

"Yes. That's true," Yeshua affirmed.

The lama rose and walked over to a bucket. The puddle around it suggested a small leak. He filled two glasses with water as he spoke. "Then, if He knows it, isn't it preordained from all time, for all time?

How can this be?" Mandeep challenged. "How can free will be true and God's knowledge also be true? The ideas contradict one another."

"I struggle with this," Yeshua admitted. "I can say God allows me to choose, but He knows what the choice will be; but that doesn't satisfy me. Do you think one or the other is not true?"

"No, I think they are *both* true," the lama proposed.

Yeshua sat silently, mulling the lama's proposition. How could *this* be? He felt a warm breeze waft through the window and watched as it stirred the flower in the shrine's water bowl. The bronze Buddha seemed to be almost smiling at him.

"What does it mean to say, 'I have free will'?" Mandeep continued, beginning his thesis with a question.

"It means I'm able to make a choice to deal with a situation that confronts me, whether or not God approves of my choice." Yeshua felt as if he were back in class with the rabbis.

"And what do you think is the most important word in what you just said?" Mandeep riddled.

"'Choice,' maybe? Maybe 'God'?" Yeshua answered, following the path of the questions with great curiosity.

The lama smiled and took a sip of water, then he put his glass down while he looked Yeshua right in the eyes. "How about 'I'?" the lama suggested.

Yeshua thought for a minute. Mandeep continued, "When you say 'I this' or 'I that,' you've chosen a *perspective*, a way of looking at things. You've chosen the perspective of self, or 'I', or *ego*, if I can adopt the Roman's word. It's the perspective we choose most often. It springs from the operation of our senses and is most concerned with our individual survival.

The Paragon

"Our baser emotions spring from ego--greed, anger, jealousy--and even some of our more altruistic ones, which at their core sustain our self-image, our ego," Mandeep concluded. "Ego isn't our real self, but our view of our self."

Yeshua now paused for a drink, allowing a few seconds to formulate a responsive question. "What other perspective is there?" he quizzed the lama.

"Understand that I mean perspective to be something different from mere viewpoint. Two people arguing might both have the perspective of ego, but entirely different viewpoints, each focusing on himself. Perspective goes deeper. I think there's a gradation of perspective: ego, family, tribe, kingdom, or even caravan, for example."

Mandeep let Yeshua absorb the idea. Each man was apparently listening carefully to the other, not thinking what to say next while the other was still talking. "Or if you think in terms of time, there's second, minute, day, season, lifetime, and eternity. There's the perspective of planet. You do know we're on a planet that goes around the sun, don't you?" Mandeep suggested.

"Yes. I've learned this," Yeshua acknowledged, "but where I come from, I keep it to myself."

"And there's the perspective of the cosmos," Mandeep added, having saved his most emphatic pronouncement for the end of the proposition. "It's possible to take that perspective by using your imagination and stepping back to view the universe as if you encompass it and are observing it unfold. From that perspective, all that's ever happened or may ever happen exists forever, and all we do in our puny existence is vanity.

"Look at it this way," he continued. "To a five-year-old child, ten years is an eternity, but to an old man, ten years seems the blink of an eye. To the cosmos, it's nothing.

"Or consider a man climbing a mountain," Mandeep concluded. "The higher he climbs, the farther he can see. Eventually, his village is a patch of irregularity in the view of the valley below. His house, a speck of imagination. But his vista is limitless, to the ends of the earth, perhaps."

The flower began spinning in the bowl. Yeshua sat mesmerized for some seconds as his mind processed this new concept. He reasoned as he spoke. "So, both perspectives are real and true at the same time, and thus free will is both true and not true at the same time. The first is true, because my individualized self exists within the reality of my body, and from that perspective I truly have free will. The other is true because the cosmic reality, which I can know through imagination, exists forever, past, present and future, and from that perspective everything is truly predetermined."

Mandeep rose again and walked to the window and removed a large gray cat from the sill. Stroking it, he returned to the table. "This is Ishtar, goddess of our household. You'll notice we have very few lizards or mice.

"In any situation, Yeshua, the perspective you view an event from is a choice you make," the lama explained, finishing Yeshua's thought. "For example, when confronted by the death of a loved one, do you choose the perspective of ego and feel sorry for yourself; or do you choose the cosmic perspective and see the event as part of the flow of nature?

"I think we've talked enough for today," Mandeep concluded. "Will you return tomorrow?"

"Oh yes, if my mind cools by then." Yeshua's mind was spinning like the flower beneath the Buddha.

"One other thing, Yeshua, about choosing a perspective," Mandeep counseled. "In almost any argument where one says, 'This is true,' and the other says, 'No, that is true,' remember: both may be true. Each person may have chosen a different *perspective*.

"If you keep that in mind, you understand the other opinion more and argue less, or at least get to the root of the difference instead of talking past each other. The real issue becomes what in our individual experience leads us to choose our particular perspective over another."

Yeshua had spent his time in Merv resting after his ordeal in the desert. The physician who attended him said he'd been close to death. Since he was well enough to visit the temple of another pagan religion, Yonnah thought, he was well enough to talk about what had bothered him for two weeks.

He found Yeshua at the caravanserai and spent little time with pleasantries. "I see you're doing much better. What's the meaning of this supposed betrothal?" he demanded. "Is it something you made up to spare Meryam?"

"No, Cousin, it's the truth."

"Why didn't you mention it to me?" Yonnah asked, as the lines in his face tightened.

"I was going to tell you in due time," Yeshua responded, "but the events in the desert intervened before I had the opportunity. I hesitated because I felt you'd be angry over it, although I knew a day would come when I had to face your anger."

"And yet," Yonnah said, "you could tell this new 'friend' you found in a ditch, but not your own family? That disturbs me as much as the idiocy of the betrothal."

"Cousin, it's done and she's my wife. Since she has no father or family of any kind who's ever cared for her, we made a contract between us. I'll honor that contract and someday take her to my parents."

"Raging about this would be useless," Yonnah acknowledged.

"So, you're learning," Yeshua responded.

"Don't poke me when I'm about to concede an argument," Yonnah said. "This doesn't please me, but now that you've done it, I hope you don't regret it. This woman will be more difficult than you appreciate right now."

Yeshua would have said, "You know nothing of women," although neither did he in this intimate way. It would be a learning experience. Besides, Yonnah was correct. It wasn't the time to prolong the argument.

Instead he said, "I understand your misgivings, Cousin, and I'm sorry I didn't tell you sooner, but I hope, as family, you'll support my decision."

The Paragon

Yeshua returned to see Mandeep the next day. "Yeshua, let's walk today," the lama suggested. "Have you ever done any angling?"

"Oh, yes," he recalled. "My friends at home are fishermen, with nets, of course, but sometimes when I'd visit, we'd sit by the sea and throw in a line. I was never very successful, except one time . . ."

"Careful, my friend. No tall tales," Mandeep joked, and they walked out of town to the river that came from the distant mountains to feed the oasis. As they sat on the bank, Mandeep resumed their conversation.

"First, let me explain some things to you. We're not an organized religion. We're not organized under one orthodox doctrine, nor do we worship a god. Buddhism is rather a way of looking at things. We share that characteristic with our Chinese Taoist friends."

"And apparently, the Hindus," Yeshua added, casting his line into the river.

"True enough," Mandeep said. "We talked of perspective yesterday. That's my personal way of understanding the Buddha's teaching. For many Buddhists, the only real perspective is the cosmic. Ego doesn't exist. It's an illusion. For them there's only one essence, soul, or consciousness, but because of our bodies, we have an individualized experience of it. To them this individualized experience is illusion. The great oneness is the only true reality.

"However, I think there are two ways of looking at ego," Mandeep continued, dropping his own line in. "One is the self that operates in the physical world pursuant to the senses that lets us understand that world. Personally, I'm unable to deny the reality of that.

"The other," Mandeep explained further, "is our image of our self. *That* ego is based on how we see ourselves and how we believe others see us. That's the ego that isn't real and doesn't really exist. For most people, however, it's their whole reality, and these are sad, tortured people."

Yeshua noticed the water rippling a bit offshore beyond their lines. At this point the river had a lazy flow. The rest of its surface was still. There was no breeze today. The sun was getting warmer as it approached midday. The men were under a palm that shaded them, but the time for successful fishing would soon pass. Maybe those ripples would move their way. Maybe they'd get lucky.

"Now," the lama began again, "what shall we discuss today?"

"Let's take a thread from yesterday," Yeshua suggested. "You said emotions like anger have their root in the perspective of ego, and I believe I understand this. I understand an event is neither 'good' nor 'bad' to the cosmos, but any emotional interpretation of it arises from the value my ego ascribes to it. I'm prone to outbursts of anger, yet I consider myself a spiritual person."

"Yes, but think about it," Mandeep offered. "What angers you--some event, perhaps? Maybe someone does something to your detriment. Maybe someone insults you."

"I think a verbal insult is easiest to deal with," Yeshua said. "I know what a person says to me, even if it's completely vile, doesn't diminish me. I'm the same person after the insult as before. If anyone's diminished, it's the person who delivered the insult. He reveals to all he's crude and ignorant. If he chooses to do that, it's nothing to me."

The Paragon

Yeshua heard the bleating of a goat behind him. Two children were shepherding a small herd to the river to drink. He made eye contact with the youngsters, who smiled and said hello and led the goats farther up the bank from the fishermen's spot.

"Exactly," Mandeep agreed, recovering the thread of the conversation, "but someone physically hurting you or a loved one seems different. It makes you want revenge, or at least to express your unhappiness with great vehemence, doesn't it? Why is that?"

"In a way, it's normal," Yeshua responded, "but sometimes it becomes explosive and leads a man, me, to hurt others. I believe this is wrong."

Yeshua felt a little tug on his line and then a series of them. He was about to try to set the hook when the activity stopped. The breeze began to pick up slightly, but it was a warm breeze. It would be a hot day.

"We humans engage in a lot of counterproductive activity," Mandeep went on. "Take worry, for example. If you think about it, there are only two kinds of problems in the world: the ones you can do something about and the ones you can't. If you can do something about your problem, do so. If you can't, go about your business or your sleep and don't worry. Worry is useless, except to stroke the ego, because if you can do nothing, what will come will come.

"Revenge is even more useless," the lama continued. "It doesn't solve your problem but makes another problem. Someone wants revenge in return. You may think you're bringing balance to the world, but you're merely compounding the negative. The universe will bring things to balance without your help, and if you've sought revenge, that balancing will weigh heaviest on *you*.

"In any case," Mandeep summarized, "if you have a cosmic perspective--or call it the expansive perspective--your problem, no matter how great or who caused it, is not a problem to the cosmos, only to an ego. Only a person who chooses to see his real self as an individual and nothing more will respond with explosive anger. Anger hurts your own body and soul. It's counterproductive."

Yeshua pulled his line out of the water. As he suspected, his bait had been taken. They had brought some grasshoppers for that purpose, so he hooked another one and recast his line.

"I can understand that idea intellectually," Yeshua agreed, "but how do I keep mindful of it, so when a situation arises, I choose the expansive perspective and not the perspective of ego that makes me lash out?"

"Spiritual exercise." Mandeep deftly jerked his line, and the water began to splash until they saw a silver tail flopping and eventually a full, scaly body. Mandeep brought the fish to shore, and the two men admired his catch. It was slightly bigger than Mandeep's hand. He carefully removed the hook and released it.

"Some Buddhists think this is wrong," Mandeep confessed. "They'd say I killed an insect by using it as bait. I don't know. Maybe I'm a bad Buddhist, but I don't think so. Sometimes, when they're bigger, I eat them. The fish, I mean."

"As do I. It's my cousin who's the bug eater." Yeshua laughed and returned to Mandeep's prior thought. "You tell me, 'spiritual exercise,' but I meditate daily. I pray. How much do I have to do?"

"As much as it takes," Mandeep said. "If you want to be perfect, you need to spend as much time as it takes to keep you mindful of the expansive perspective. If you meditate eight hours a day, but lose your temper in the tenth hour, then you need to meditate ten hours a day.

"If, however," Mandeep concluded, "you can tolerate your own imperfection, meditate as you will, try your best, but realize you may sometimes fall short of perfection. From there, seek to amend."

"A man who meditates ten hours a day to achieve perfection cuts himself off from people, from love," Yeshua observed.

"Yes," Mandeep said, "and Lord Buddha came to understand that, but meditation and prayer are not the only forms of spiritual practice."

"What else, then?" Yeshua wondered aloud. He felt a nibble on his line. Patience, he thought. At last something struck, and he tugged to set the hook, but it got away, having taken his bait again.

"A monster, no doubt," Mandeep teased. "Yeshua, anything you do," he explained, "that you connect in your mind with the spiritual or expansive perspective can be spiritual exercise. For example, an artist doing his art, a musician playing his instrument, a dancer, a farmer tending his crops, the very act of intimate love, can all be spiritual exercise. What makes them so is doing them with an attitude of mindfulness of the expansive perspective, devoid of the perspective of ego."

"I understand," Yeshua acknowledged. "Let me think on this."

"*Thinking* about these matters is overrated, but do what you must, my friend. I'll see you tomorrow."

Joseph Emmrich

The next day Yeshua returned to the monastery. He'd spent any time he'd been alone mulling the ideas of perspective and spiritual exercise. These led him to questions of salvation and the afterlife. Once he and the lama greeted each other, Yeshua turned the discussion to what was most on his mind.

"Do you believe in resurrection of the dead or reincarnation like the Hindus," Yeshua asked Mandeep, "or that there's nothing beyond death, no heaven, no hell?" He mused that in Galilee and Judea, he was the one who was supposed to have the answers, but as the traveler, he was quite satisfied to be the one asking.

"So many questions that lead to more questions," Mandeep answered. "How many years do you have here? So, what do you believe about that?" Mandeep turned the tables.

"I believe with the Essenes," Yeshua answered, "or for that matter the Pharisees, that there will be a great judgment and the dead shall be raised. I believe we each have a soul, and the souls of the righteous will exist in a life of everlasting bliss."

"Let's go to the market," Mandeep suggested. "I have some things I need to buy."

"Excellent idea," Yeshua agreed. "I have some coins Hadi asked me to take to a merchant at Central Market, and there are one or two things I want to purchase myself."

The two men headed through the narrow streets toward the city center, occasionally ducking the putrid refuse being tossed out of windows, wincing at the demanding screams of hungry infants within, all the while continuing their conversation.

The Paragon

"As I was about to say," Yeshua continued, "there are other sects in Judaism, like the Sadducees, who don't believe in life after death. Still others believe the righteous will be reborn into a new and better life on this earth. All of us say we base our belief on the word of God and argue over it like Roman lawyers. So many intelligent men sincerely hold such different ideas it makes me doubt my own certainty."

"Even in Buddhism there are differing viewpoints about it," Mandeep responded. "I myself might say this talk of resurrection or rebirth refers metaphorically to the death of ego and rebirth into a new life in the Divine Spirit, albeit in this physical plane.

"Most Buddhists say," Mandeep continued, "as we discussed yesterday, there's no individual soul independent of the universe. They believe when a body dies, the permanence that remains is *karma* from the past life, which regenerates a new life form, like the flame of one candle lighting another. This continues until it achieves nirvana or unity with the One, and individuality ceases."

The men turned onto a larger street that would lead them to the market. It was a busy day. Pedestrians and ox-carts made their way along the thoroughfare. Yeshua and Mandeep had to avoid the traffic as well as avoiding the perils of waste, animal and human, underfoot. The acrid odor produced by rotting garbage was something the urbanites probably took for granted, but having come from the pristine desert, Yeshua found it unpleasant. He silently hoped he wasn't becoming the curmudgeon his cousin was.

"That sounds like the Hindus," said Yeshua, responding to Mandeep's last observation. "And what exactly do *you* mean by *karma*?"

"*Karma* is simply the law of cause and effect," explained Mandeep. "It's the immutable law of the universe. The difference with Hinduism is that most Hindus believe in an individual soul, more like your tradition. After death, the soul continues as an individual and comes to inhabit anther life form. I just want to be clear. I don't speak for all Buddhists."

"Nor I for all Jews. In fact, as I told a Hindu friend, we have a strain of thought in Judaism, written in the Sefer Yetzirah, that says a man has free will and nature rewards or punishes the choices he makes."

"That's approximately it," Mandeep concurred. "You know, Yeshua, we talk about things like the nature of the Divine Spirit or God if you will, but we're trying to explain in words something beyond words. When most people say, I believe in God, or I don't believe, they're talking about a Creator or Supreme Being. As you're beginning to see, there is a way of understanding the Divine Spirit that has nothing to do with a being. But this Awesome Mystery can't be defined in words. It can only be described by metaphor."

"How do *you* describe it, Mandeep?"

"Ooh . . . the unity of all things, perhaps; maybe the unfolding of the universe. You'll come to understand it in your own way, my friend," Mandeep offered.

Yeshua and Mandeep approached Central Market. It was jammed with city folk, people from nearby towns, and nomads, all come to trade. The first stalls they encountered were those of the farmers, who had brought the produce they grew on their oasis farms and had arranged the fruits and vegetables in colorful geometric displays. There were pyramids of bright yellow apricots, flats of orange carrots, and piles of purple eggplant. Circular bowls displayed onions, white, gold, and red. Amphorae overflowed with barley and olives. Garlic and dates hung from the cross-branches supporting the coverings that shaded the businesses.

Despite the engrossing distractions, Yeshua brought himself back to the topic at hand. "But, Mandeep, isn't it important to find words for the Divine Spirit?" he challenged. "The people aren't philosophers. They crave certainty in their lives and need to know what to believe. Most people follow a path of righteous behavior because they believe they'll be rewarded when they die. They'll be reunited with their loved ones in everlasting perfect bliss. If they're evil, on the other hand, they'll get eternal punishment. Why else to be good?"

"People do want words and certainty. That's a purpose of religion," Mandeep agreed. "Give them rubric and ritual, reward if they follow it, punishment if they don't. Personally, I followed the ethics of Buddha because it made life on this physical plane more pleasant for me and for those around me. By doing this, I was certain that whatever came after death, even if it was nothing, wouldn't involve eternal punishment for me, no matter what I've believed.

"I think like this," Mandeep continued in summary. "When I die, what will I see without eyes? What will I hear without ears? What will I think without a mind? When all those things turn to dust, how can there even be an 'I?' Some say the real 'I' is the individual soul. But apart from the body, how can it have any awareness? How can it sense anything?"

"I noticed you used the past tense when you spoke of following the ethics of the Buddha," Yeshua observed.

"I see you're paying attention," the lama said. "We can talk about that later."

They bumped and jostled their way through the crush of humanity that had developed in one of the main intersections. They'd come to the spice market, which was Mandeep's destination. The smells of the city had changed now, to the pleasant, pungent aromas of the seeds, powders, herbs, leaves, and barks that had been brought there from the far reaches of the Royal Road and its extensions into places only imagined.

Yeshua was familiar with some of these from his homeland and had learned more of them as he traveled. Some of the caravaneers dealt in them. He noticed things like cinnamon and cloves seemed cheaper here than in the west. Price differences like this determined how and where a caravaneer traded certain items. The better a trader understood his markets, the more money he made.

As Mandeep continued shopping, Yeshua noticed an old woman, wrinkled and decrepit, clothes tattered, and barefoot, sitting by the road. She was leaning against one of the buildings, begging for alms. "Baksheesh," she cried out, voice cracking, holding her cupped hands out in a hope, that as Yeshua looked on, went unrealized.

Yeshua went to her and crouched beside her. He gave her some dates he'd purchased. By now, he spoke a few words of the Parthian language. "What's your name, Sister?" he asked.

"Shirina," she replied, coughing from the depths of her lungs.

He smiled at her, and she relaxed and smiled back. "That doesn't sound good, Shirina. Are you feeling ill?" he asked.

"I've felt better," she admitted.

Yeshua looked around. Mandeep was still at the spice trader's stall. He noticed a sign that identified a physician's residence. "Sister, let me help you up. We'll walk over to the physician."

As she struggled to her feet, she protested, "Sir, I have no money."

"Yes, you do," he assured her.

He helped her across the street to the physician and gave him the rest of his own money. "Sir, please care for her the best you can, and make sure she has food. I trust these coins will be sufficient."

"Yes, thank you," the physician said. "You're very generous." Yeshua wasn't sure if his coins were enough, but the physician seemed moved, and Yeshua trusted him to do as he promised.

"Shirina, I need to go," he said to the old woman. "The physician will take care of you."

"A thousand thanks to you," she said, embracing him. "May Ahura Mazda bless you."

Before he left, he laid his hands on her. She immediately relaxed, and he added his own healing power to whatever the physician could provide. Then he plunged back into the crowd.

He couldn't spot Mandeep anywhere, saffron robe notwithstanding. He decided to go forward in the general direction they'd been walking. As the crowd thinned a bit, he noticed other beggars. There seemed to be a concentration of them in the area, but he had no more money except Hadi's.

He saw men with missing limbs and women with pocked faces, contorted in tearful misery, all but demanding money from him. A man with a bulbous growth on the side of his face blocked his path. He dared not stop. There were too many of them. A woman carrying a child--maybe two years old, who had no hands, only stumps--grabbed his cloak with her free hand. The brood of small children behind her grabbed him as well.

The rest began to mob him. He was afraid for his safety and felt them ripping at his bag containing the coin purse of Hadi's debt. They forced him down a narrow alley and took him down. They began to kick him and beat him with their fists. As he tried to cover his head, they snatched the bag.

Even then, the mob didn't relent until he heard a voice scream, "Leave him alone, you animals."

Yeshua didn't recognize the voice, but the man barged into the mob wielding a stick, continuing to bellow threats. He beat them indiscriminately, until there was enough space to lift Yeshua up. His screams were fierce and apparently frightened the mob. They ran away, throwing Yeshua's bag on the ground as they left.

He went to retrieve it. It was empty.

"Is this what you're looking for?" said his benefactor, holding up the coin purse.

"Yes, it is. How did you recover it?" Yeshua asked.

"It's all there," he assured, as Yeshua looked inside. "The truth is, I stole it from you before you helped the old woman," the thief explained. "I saw what you did for her, and it moved me to repentance. When you left the physician's, I tried to catch up to you to return it, but the mob of beggars and robbers intervened.

The Paragon

Physical robbery isn't my style. I'm a pickpocket. My name is Pakur."

"Thank you, Pakur. I'm Yeshua."

"Yeshua, you're a mess. Come with me. There's a fountain around the corner. We can wash the blood off your face. You know, you're not the first one that's happened to. They operate as a gang. Mostly, they just beg. The child with no hands--purposeful mutilation to appear more pathetic."

"I suspected that," Yeshua said. "Ouch!" Pakur wiped the blood from his facial wounds. "I've seen it before on the road."

As they talked, Mandeep came running toward them. "Yeshua, I lost you. Are you all right?"

Yeshua explained what happened to his friend and introduced him to his rescuer.

"A monk, then," Pakur observed. "Yeshua, are you a monk too?"

"I was for a time. Now I'm traveling with a caravan," Yeshua answered.

"Maybe I'll be blessed for my good deed," Pakur said.

"No doubt," Yeshua responded, "but it has nothing to do with our station in life. You risked your life for another. I'm not sure why you've chosen the profession you have, but you seem a better person than that. I can't ask anything else of you, but I'd hope you amend your life. There's peace of mind and happiness in serving others. Don't you feel good right now?"

"I do," the thief replied. "Poorer, I'd say," he continued with a grin, "but you inspired me in a way I've never experienced, and you tempt me to think of myself as a good person, which I have never been."

Now Yeshua grinned.

Mandeep spoke. "A friend of my friend is my friend, Pakur. I suspect, if he's up to it, Yeshua needs to finish his errand and return to the caravan and rest. Why don't you come with me to the monastery? I'll feed you. I've seen you before in the market. Maybe I can find an alternative to your present lifestyle."

"I'm feeling better," Yeshua assured them, "a little sore, but I'll be fine. Mandeep, I want to rest tomorrow, but I'll stop by the next day so we can finish our conversation."

"Very good, my friend," Mandeep said. "I'll see you then."

Two days later, Yeshua returned to the monastery. As he entered the walls, he saw Pakur working in the garden. "Hello, my friend." Yeshua greeted him.

"Greetings, Yeshua," Pakur shouted. "Apparently, I have a job."

Mandeep came out to greet him. "Hello again. As you see, we have a new helper. Mostly, the monks take care of the chores, but under the circumstances I thought we could use another hand. It's a nice day. Let's sit out here in the garden."

"So, my friend," Yeshua said, "I think this may be our last opportunity to talk. In two days we head for the Oxos and on to Maracanda, and I'll be busy with preparations tomorrow. We've been here so long it's like starting over."

"When you get to Maracanda . . ." Mandeep began.

"The Paragon?" Yeshua interrupted. "I know of it by now. I think it's the most famous landmark on the Great Road."

"On the contrary," Mandeep countered, "few know about it."

Yeshua let his fascination with the mystery pass in favor of what had been on his mind. "We were going to talk about ethics today," Yeshua reminded. "From what I know of Buddhism, I think the way you treat each other is like my tradition."

"As it is with most other traditions," Mandeep agreed. "The *basis* for behaving a certain way may be different in each tradition, or points of emphasis may be different, but most arrive at the same rules or suggestions, except perhaps on how to deal with those who wrong you.

"These rules, I think, are necessary for almost everyone," the lama continued, "but I think when you attain Buddhahood, you go beyond the rules. They no longer apply to you because your deep understanding causes you to act righteously without considering what the rule is. You're beyond *karma*."

"That's why you used the past tense when you spoke of your adherence to rules. How does a person attain Buddhahood?" Yeshua quizzed.

"Well, there are many paths," the lama explained, slowing the pace of his speech to emphasize what he was about to say, "and they lead to an Experience. Call it mystical union with the Divine Spirit. Once you have that Experience, you cultivate mindfulness of it like the expansive perspective. Have you had this Experience?"

"I long for it," Yeshua admitted, "but I'm not sure what it is or that I'll know it if I have it."

"Don't pine for it," Mandeep admonished. "Wishing or trying won't make it happen. Follow your path. Be open to it. It will come, and you'll understand it when it does."

The air was sweet in the garden, belying the city on their doorstep. It was simpler than the terraced marvels of Babylon and western Parthia but full of the color that attracted benign insects and chirping birds.

Although they hadn't asked, Pakur brought them tea. "Thought you might enjoy this. I made it with mint. I had no idea such a peaceful place existed in this city. I could get used to it. I still have work to do, so I'll leave you to your discussion."

"Thanks, Pakur," Yeshua said. "I'll find you to say goodbye before I leave." He was amazed at the apparent transformation of the man and humbled by his agency in the conversion, although he knew Mandeep had also played a part.

Yeshua's thoughts quickly returned to the Experience of mystical union. "So, you've had this Experience?" Yeshua asked.

"Understand, Yeshua, that it's different for everyone to whom it comes, but yes, I've been blessed," Mandeep admitted.

"Now, not everyone wants to or can become a Buddha," the lama quickly continued. "For them there are rules or guidelines, religion if you will. We have eight precepts that define a righteous path. If I were to simplify them, it would be thus: first, speak truthfully and in a non-hurtful way."

"Yes, I have a cousin who's great at the former, but horrible at the latter. I pray for his 'perfection.' 'Thou shalt not bear false witness' is our equivalent."

"Then, of course," Mandeep followed, "*act* in a non-harmful way."

"That's the gist of several of our commandments," Yeshua offered, "but in the Torah we've made good behavior so complex that I've been thinking we need to simplify our Law. I'd summarize it by saying, 'Love God and love your neighbor as yourself.'"

"Excellent. Simple," Mandeep responded. "I like that very much. I don't worship a deity, but I completely understand the concept."

The Paragon

"I have one more question of you." Yeshua was about to address one of his main difficulties with Buddhism. "Doesn't the Buddha say the essence of earthly life is suffering?"

"Some might use the word *anxiety*--one or the other," Mandeep suggested.

"And that suffering arises from desire, and the only way to free yourself from desire is by following a path of spiritual exercise," Yeshua continued, "until you attain Buddhahood and dissolve back into the universal soul?"

"More or less," the lama concurred.

"Then it seems the only purpose of Buddhism is to protect your ego from the pain of living and provide a hope of conquering death," Yeshua said, although he couldn't bring himself to accept that life was *only* pain.

"Isn't that the purpose of all religion, Yeshua?" Mandeep challenged, "That is, until you become a Buddha. I mean, the other reason that people need religion, besides a reason to be good, or to foster a sense of community, is to inure them against the fear of death. Contemplation of the cessation of your existence is almost beyond imagination and is certainly terrifying."

"I see that clearly." Yeshua paused and then added, "We use the word *salvation*--from death and the punishment that follows death, which we deserve for our sins.

"Some of these Buddhist ideas are like my own tradition," Yeshua continued. "Some appeal to me, and some trouble me. I hope to understand those better, but I've got to go now, Mandeep. I've enjoyed our conversations more than I can express."

"As have I." Mandeep embraced him heartily. "Yeshua, your present path, the path of ideas, is a difficult one. I think it's a lonely path. Few others walk it. It may lead you to Buddhahood, just as religion can, but Buddhahood is beyond any idea."

"I'm coming to realize this," Yeshua acknowledged. "My intellectual path springs from predisposition and upbringing. As I travel, the people close to me become more important. I'll be nothing and I'll bridge no divides unless I'm of the people and unless I'm close with the people who are dearest to me. Thank you, Rabbi."

Mandeep's smile seemed to express satisfaction and humility at Yeshua's honorific. "Something is dawning on you," Mandeep said. "When it comes in its glory, you'll know it. Go safely then."

Yeshua found and embraced Pakur. "You're on a good path, Pakur. Walk it for the long journey, and thank you again for saving me."

"It's I who thank you for saving *me*," Pakur rejoined. "Travel safely."

Yeshua left the monastery ecstatic over his experience in Merv. Not only had he witnessed a man turn his life to good, but he'd met a man who was more a teacher to him than all the monks or rabbis he'd known in Galilee and Judea.

The Paragon

Yeshua spent the next day preparing the caravan for its desert crossing, to the town of Amul on the Oxos River. On the following morning, when they were about to leave, he saw a figure wearing a saffron robe running toward the caravan. It was Pakur.

Yeshua was stunned. "Good morning, friend. Are you in disguise?"

"No, Yeshua. I've decided to join the monastery. I'm happy for you to know because it's you who set me in the right direction, but that's not why I'm here." The smile on his face faded and his tone became serious. "I have to talk to the caravan master right away."

Yeshua didn't even ask why but brought him directly to Hadi. "Hadi Ba'riel," Pakur began, "I've kept company with bad people. They live in the city and observe the coming and going of caravans. They sell their information to armed bands of robbers who maraud between here and the Oxos. They've had their eye on your caravan, and I believe you can expect trouble."

Hadi bit his lip. "Thank you, friend. How many are there?"

"As many as a hundred," Pakur replied.

"Very well, then; let's go. We'll be ready." Hadi looked anxious, but he knew they couldn't stay in Merv forever. He had to move. The caravan headed for the Oxos.

Eight

It would be several days to Amul and the crossing of the Oxos. They would leave the relative peace and stability of Parthia for a land contested by smaller competing empires. Currently, peace also reigned in these lands, as far as Hadi knew. The Parthians only wanted the roads open, in and out of their empire, and all their neighbors to the east, no matter how they felt about each other, wanted peace with the larger hegemon.

As far as being a threat beyond its own borders, however, Parthia was a paper tiger. It had neither the army nor the unified political will to project power. Although Parthia was in a period of relative peace with Rome, its army and treasure had been depleted by conflict on that western frontier, but the eastern satraps didn't realize that.

The caravan was headed for the land of the Sogdians, and they, particularly at Maracanda, had a tolerance for ideas. They were Zoroastrian mostly, with an increasing Buddhist influence. Hadi had a second home there.

The Paragon

Ptolemy was doing remarkably well. It seemed no infection had set in, but he was still dutifully using his crutch. He carped about the device, and Yeshua had to continually urge patience, hoping he wouldn't carelessly abort the healing process. Yeshua and Ptolemy spent considerable time in conversation, and Yeshua felt their friendship was deepening. Lately, however, Ptolemy seemed quieter, even anxious. Yeshua suspected the source of it and knew if it didn't pass, he would need to talk to Ptolemy about it soon, very soon.

Yonnah, Yeshua knew, still didn't completely trust either of his new companions, because of his nature and because of a sense of duty to be protective. He'd softened somewhat toward Meryam, especially since the incident with the camel, but he remained guarded, if no longer hostile.

Yeshua went out walking with Yonnah in the desert a little way from the caravan. "You grow lazy," Yonnah chastised. "You spend more time with your new friends than in God's work. You neglect your prayer and meditation."

"You exaggerate," Yeshua responded. "I pray and meditate daily, and I'm learning from these travels. I've come to understand that this time with these friends is more precious than all the teachings of the sages. You can learn all there is to know, but it counts for nothing if you can't care for people. I'd rather bring my love to one person than my knowledge to all mankind."

Upwind from the animals, the first breeze of the morning touched Yeshua's face like a wave of Seresian silk. He noticed his cousin's face, weathered by the road, and mused that his must be the same. He hoped it was a sign of wisdom gained rather than a passing into decrepitude.

"Your words chasten me," Yonnah said, "but I suppose my focus is more on the love of God."

"I understand," Yeshua explained, "but I sense God in my love for them, and for you, Cousin."

"Although I preach to the people," Yonnah said, "and pray they amend their lives and find God, I'm not drawn to their company as you are. I'll keep trying to understand what you're doing."

It was morning. Yeshua had already meditated and seen to his first chores. The heat of the day hadn't set in yet. The two men sat on the ground and leaned on a large stone, the remnant of some unknown ancient structure left, if not by the Greeks, then by their historical predecessors, or theirs, or theirs.

"Sometimes I find it difficult to understand how an ascetic can be so political," Yeshua challenged.

"It depends on what you mean by 'political,'" Yonnah replied. "I have no interest in the feuding among factions, only in the larger question of the freedom of our people from tyranny. However, I choose to speak about it from the wilderness. Being involved in government doesn't appeal to me.

"By the way," Yonnah continued, "some of the people you meet and listen to with such intensity, I don't understand. The Hindu man in Hecatompylos, twisting his body and laughing; wasn't he just a fool?"

"Not easy to say," Yeshua replied. "He's an ascetic, like you, but with a better sense of humor. He may act the fool, like a street minstrel, but I sense it's a type of affectation. There's something that motivates his behavior I don't yet understand."

"You say that as if you expect to," his cousin said.

"Sometime, I think I might," Yeshua mused. "The Hindus' belief in a god with three different aspects, Brahma, Vishnu, and Shiva--Creator, Preserver, and Destroyer--each so strong and distinct it becomes personified, regarded as a being. This interests me."

Yeshua now heard the animals stirring, the clanking of pots, and unintelligible conversation. It would soon be time to move on. Both men stood but continued their conversation.

"One God is enough for me," Yonnah averred, "and our people have a covenant with Him."

"'Our people.' Do you think Yahweh rules over the Parthians and the Hindus?" Yeshua questioned. "Or are their gods different? If they're different, why is Yahweh greater than Shiva or Ahura Mazda?"

"You'd walk the edge of blasphemy?" Yonnah both questioned and admonished.

"Blasphemy?" Yeshua responded. "Haven't you ever had doubts about your beliefs? I find that hard to believe. I tell you I grow ever more uneasy with a vengeful deity, and I begin to think all these gods are not only equal, but are the same God, called by different names."

The breeze was picking up, enough to begin blowing the finer particles of dust in their faces as they walked. The day's first flies began their ritual annoyance.

"How can you say Ahura Mazda is the same as Yahweh?" Yonnah argued, waving his hand across his face to shoo the insects. "They're nothing alike."

"Each is a way to understand the Divine Spirit," Yeshua answered. "Each takes the attributes the local people impart to him . . . or her."

"I haven't heard you talk like this before," Yonnah responded, "and it troubles me."

"Don't be troubled," Yeshua reassured him. "What about your own doubts? Never?"

Yonnah hesitated, not wanting to blaspheme. He pulled the end of his scarf across his face, apparently to get relief from the flies and dust, but it also gave him a second to formulate a seemingly difficult response. "I, like you," he stammered, "am troubled by the horrors Yahweh has allowed to be unleashed on us; the Babylonians, the Romans. There are many good people among us . . ." His voice trailed away, then snapped back to a speedy staccato certainty, like a man pulling himself from a path he knew he could not follow. "But if Yahweh deems we deserve His punishment," he concluded, "so be it. It's for us to repent."

Now, Yeshua heard a distinct voice out of the stirrings in the background. It was Hadi calling for him. It was time to end the conversation and get to work again.

"Of course, each of us needs to repent, but I'm not so sure about Divine collective punishment," he said to Yonnah as they walked. "I'm struggling with a new way of understanding the nature of God and then finding a way to explain it to our people. I pray it will come to me.

"In the ancient Hindu writings," Yeshua concluded, "the Rig Veda, which is four thousand years old, before Brahma, Shiva, and Vishnu, even before Yahweh, they addressed a supreme God. They prayed, 'Agni, you are Our Providence, Our Father; we are your brethren, and you are our spring of life.' The people prayed to him for their deliverance and daily sustenance. It's pure to pray to God in such a way."

The caravan picked up stakes for its last leg of travel across the desert. The Oxos River would be the next major landmark, and they were only a day or two from it. Ptolemy was curious when Hadi called everyone together. It was early in the afternoon.

"Friends in Merv," he began with a serious tone, "have warned me nomadic robbers are afoot in this part of the desert, and the government hasn't managed to stop them. As we've moved, I've sent men ahead to see if we're in danger. Our scouting party just returned and informed me a band of robbers is gathered at a well about five miles from here. We can expect an attack, and we can expect it tonight."

"How many of them are there?" someone shouted from the crowd.

"There are nearly a hundred," Hadi said, "but if they had the element of surprise, it would be like an army. We have only seventeen trained fighters, but if we have the element of surprise, we'll be like two hundred."

Ptolemy spoke up. Although he didn't want to give up his cover as a merchant, he offered to help fight in defense of the caravan. Hadi rejected his offer. "No, friend, I appreciate your desire to help, but a man on a crutch would only make a problem for my plan."

"What's your plan?" Ptolemy asked. His military training made him curious and potentially critical.

"The robbers will sneak up on us in the dark," Hadi began, "so it must be tonight, because once we reach Amul and the Oxos, they'll have lost their chance. Rather than continue to the next oasis, we'll camp tonight on ground favorable to us. The men have found a *wadi* a little farther on that parallels the road. The other side of the road has some high ground adjacent to it that also parallels the road, making a narrow corridor.

"Most of you will be on this high ground or safely behind it," Hadi continued. "We'll set up a false camp on the road before the narrows: a few tents, a few animals, and a fire. We'll wrap boulders in cloth soaked in oil and place them at the top of the high ground. When the robbers enter the narrows, we'll block their exits, set the boulders on fire, and push them down into the stalled column.

"We'll attack them with archers," Hadi went on, his voice becoming more intense, "kill as many as we can on the road, and push the rest into the *wadi*. Once they've fallen into the ravine, they'll be disoriented and probably injured. When they do, the rest of the guard will wipe them out."

Ptolemy was impressed. "Where did a merchant learn such sophisticated tactics?" he asked.

"I've read the accounts of Hannibal and Alexander," Hadi said, flashing excitement. "Surprise and favorable ground; conquer empires. We'll make these bastards sorry they took us on."

"Let's move," Ba'riel concluded, now transformed into a general. "We have a mile to go and then only a few hours to prepare."

The Paragon

As the meeting scattered, Ba'riel took Yeshua aside. "Yeshua, I have a role in this plan for you, if you accept it. I know your attitude about killing, and there will be killing. To my thinking, if *we* don't do the killing, we will all be killed. No one need die by your hand, but I'd like your help in what amounts to a war others are waging against us."

Yeshua considered what his friend was asking. "The way you've explained this, it seems we have no other choice. There seems to be no other way to avoid a fight, nowhere to hide, and no possibility of outrunning them."

"I assure you I've considered every option," Hadi said. "I don't crave bloodshed."

"Then I trust your evaluation," Yeshua said, "and I'll help, although I won't take a life. If self-defense makes killing necessary, although I don't like it, I accept it."

He wondered if the Buddha would fight rather than accept death. Maybe if it were only himself who would die, his answer would be different, but with the lives of his wife and friends in the balance, he would do what had to be done.

When Yeshua apprised Meryam of the situation and the plan, her eyes went once again to that place he saw the morning after the rape. He was taken aback by her look and now was somewhat concerned by it, although he didn't let his own expression betray that concern.

"I'll take up arms with the men to defend us," she volunteered. "You know I can fight as well as they can."

"Yes, Wife, I'm sure you can," he replied. "But I don't want you to do it". He felt he was walking a fine line. Although he was within his rights as a husband to order her, he knew that ordering would make more trouble than it was worth. At the same time, he realized that throwing herself into a bloody fray would be the worst thing possible for her.

"Meryam," he continued, "the last time you were in battle in Nehardea, although your body was cut and bruised, your spirit was wounded almost fatally. I ask you to remember that and satisfy yourself with staying with the other women, keeping them calm, and defending them with arms only as a last resort."

There were several more women in the caravan now. They had become wives to a few of the men during the journey. Hadi didn't allow prostitutes to accompany them, nor did he allow slavery. He had told Yeshua how, as a young man, he came to understand the cruelty of it, and vowed to forsake any opportunity for profit that the slave trade might offer him.

While sometimes the line between wife and slave was blurred, the mere formality of the relationship was an important distinction in the caravan.

"I understand what you're saying and asking of me," Meryam said, softening her tone and countenance. "I'll do as you ask."

The caravan put the plan into effect with military precision. By now Hadi Ba'riel had molded everyone, guards and merchants alike, into a cohesive group. Yeshua and a few others would tend the campfire and watch the animals that would be around it.

The Paragon

In addition to the boulders, the men gathered balls of dried brush to set aflame. Some would be rained down from the high ground. Some would be in piles, bound by and attached to ropes that, once ignited, could be dragged across the road by men in the *wadi* to block the brigands' path.

Everything was in place before dark. Hadi was pleased with himself and the people of the caravan. Now they waited. It was a moonless night, which would let the robbers think they had an advantage. This was their territory, of which they knew every inch, and they apparently had no qualms about moving in the darkness. The attack came in the middle of third watch.

Yeshua was in one of the tents of the false camp, having just stoked the fire. Ptolemy was in the tent with him; Hadi had allowed *this* at least. The thieves approached by stealth. When their whole column had gotten into the trap, Hadi sprung it. The men on the high ground sparked the fires that ignited the stones. The robbers looked up at the lights. In seconds their curiosity turned to dread as the lights came blazing down upon them.

The brigands fell into a general panic. Many became engulfed in flames and screamed in agonizing death throes. Others fell into the ravine as planned and began a desperate hand-to-hand combat with the caravan guards.

Others of the guard pulled the flaming bushes across the road to block the robbers' escape, but one of them broke through at the front and leapt the burning bush with his horse. Seeing no one, and not being able to return to help his friends, he dismounted and, brandishing his sword, stormed screaming into Yeshua's tent.

He raised his weapon over Yeshua and was about to do him in. Ptolemy was lying on the ground when the man entered. He saw what was happening, and it crossed his mind in an instant that the intruder could absolve him of all inner conflict. All he needed to do was nothing, and the robber would accomplish Ptolemy's ordered duty and settle the score for his family. He could defend himself well enough.

That, however, would have been the most extreme form of moral cowardice, and it left his mind the same instant it entered. Ptolemy grabbed his crutch and hurled it like a spear at the intruder. He threw it with great force and accuracy, striking the man in the side of his head, knocking him to the ground and leaving him stunned. Ptolemy leapt to his feet and in two painful steps set upon the invader, pounding him with blows like hammers and then snapping his neck in swift finality.

Yeshua was stunned. "You have skills."

"A lucky throw, my friend--lucky for you."

Yeshua began to consider if it was lucky for him or not. This may have changed some things. "How's your leg?" he asked Ptolemy.

"It hurts, but I'm fairly sure I haven't reinjured it." Ptolemy winced. "Quickly, let's see how the rest of the battle goes." They left the tent, but the battle was over. There were a few men groaning, on the road and in the *wadi*. There was blood and the charred bodies of men and animals. The smell of death hung heavy in the air. The burning objects still glowed, but now they were but luminaries to the grisly scene.

The Paragon

They found Hadi. "I trust you're all right," he said. "I understand that was a close one for you. We lost no one. There are a few injuries from hand-to-hand combat in the *wadi*. The robbers are all dead. You'll have a few more horses to take care of."

The next day the caravan approached the river Oxos at the crossing town of Amul. This was an important milestone for them. After the crossing, all that was left was to follow the tributary Polytimetus River to Bukhara and then finally to Maracanda. It should be less than one month to their destination.

Yeshua and Ptolemy walked together on the bank of the river. Ptolemy had given up his crutch, but long walks weren't yet comfortable for him, so they took a break.

As they sat together in the evening stillness, watching the great Oxos roll past, Ptolemy mused, "Since my father died, it's been my plan to go to Maracanda, but from there I haven't decided what to do."

Yeshua looked down at the dirt between his feet and scratched the ground with a stick. A fly, which he didn't bother to brush away, lit on his cheek and explored his face. Without looking up, he said, "Will you kill me there, or will you do it on the road before we get there?"

Yeshua knew it was time to broach the subject and clear the air. "Although I never felt you owed me anything," he continued, "I wondered now, since you saved my life, if you might view the ledger as even, and it might be time to do your duty."

Ptolemy looked shocked and troubled. He tensed for a moment but said nothing. The soft splashes of the river filled the silence. At last he spoke. "By now I know you well enough that I can't deny I'm charged to kill you. You must know I'm a soldier and have always done my duty, but you've never seemed like someone who was a Zealot."

"A Zealot? Who told you I was a Zealot?" Yeshua asked, taken aback.

"Antipas himself," Ptolemy said. "He told us a Zealot leader he tortured, said you and Yonnah were the men who murdered my mother."

"I've never been a Zealot. I condemn them, and I've never murdered anyone." Yeshua began to make some connections. "When and where was your mother killed?"

"In the market in Sepphoris some years ago," Ptolemy recalled. "I stood there and watched it."

"And a man came and pulled you to safety until soldiers came and took you away," Yeshua interrupted.

"How would you know this unless you were there?" Ptolemy asked.

"I *was* there," Yeshua affirmed. "The man who pulled you to safety was my father. We were working on the amphitheater. I saw it all. I cried for you and vowed I'd always oppose the Zealots. I've always thought there was something familiar about you."

Ptolemy turned to Yeshua, grabbed him by his tunic, and looked straight into his eyes. "This news lifts a heavy burden from my shoulders. I tell you this truly: in all my life I've never had a friend such as you, and I will not kill you. I would die for you. But now I have no need to reconcile friendship with a mother's curse."

The Paragon

Yeshua knew he spoke from the heart and embraced him, for neither had he ever had a friend like Ptolemy. "And what of Yonnah?" Yeshua asked. "You're not close to him. Would you kill him?"

"You needn't even ask," Ptolemy said with an earnest smile. "He's your family, and as I look on you as a brother, Yonnah is likewise cousin to me. He's the surly cousin, but cousin nonetheless. So, tell me, please, how did you know these things: my identity, my mission?"

The insect chorus was full-throated by now. The evening on the river bank was like a performance of the king's musicians. Yeshua laughed and intoned, "*Because I am all-seeing.*"

"Between you and me," he continued, "it's a matter of good observation and deductions. When you told me you were a merchant, I knew that wasn't true. Merchants are fat; you're athletic. You have scars on various parts of your body. Merchants buy their way out of scrapes. You have the cocky attitude of a soldier, and that was even before your display in the tent the other night. Your accent is like mine, so I assumed you're from where I am.

"Now what would a soldier," Yeshua wondered aloud, "basically a spy, be doing out here? If it was to spy on the king, he would be in Ctesiphon, where the king lives. When I first said my name, however, you swallowed hard. You might not have even realized it, but it wasn't lost on me. Why would a soldier in the service of the king, Antipas I assumed, react to my name without saying anything?

"I'd heard Yonnah and I were in disfavor because of our, or rather Yonnah's, preaching and promotion of me," Yeshua concluded. "It dawned on me that Antipas would have us killed, and you were here to do it, but I had no idea you were here for revenge."

A crescent moon now smiled on the two. Upstream, by the town, fires dotted each side of the bank. The smell of the smoke, wafted in the direction of the travelers. Since it included the burning of the day's trash, it wasn't completely pleasant.

"I stand amazed, and I beg your forgiveness," Ptolemy responded. "I said nothing, because as I grew to know you, I wanted to forget I was ever given or accepted so evil an order, and I couldn't comprehend how you'd ever been a murderer."

"I forgive your silence," Yeshua said. "I'd have done the same thing if I thought I was undiscovered."

"But what about you?" Ptolemy questioned. "You must have known soon enough I wouldn't kill you."

"Well, I was fairly sure you wouldn't," Yeshua replied. "Let's call this a small tease."

"Small tease?" Ptolemy blurted. "It ripped my heart."

"Better your heart than your soul."

"Bastard!"

"Brother," Yeshua answered. They both laughed in relief and release.

"There will never be a ledger between us," Ptolemy said.

"Ptolemy." Yeshua paused. "We joke, but I believe there was something more weighing on you, and that maybe you wanted to spare me from. The other reason I spoke up now is that I know you to be a man of honor, and if you couldn't do your duty, you might choose to kill yourself. I hope you've put that idea to rest."

The Paragon

"Yes, my friend," Ptolemy said. "You know me well. Don't be concerned. Our talk has satisfied my sense of honor, and my life as a soldier of Antipas is finished. Let's walk back to town. I hope Yonnah is feasting, because these bugs are feasting on me."

Yeshua never spoke about this conversation to Yonnah nor Meryam.

Nine

The bridge was under repair and impassable. This news frustrated everyone. The caravan was closing in on the goal of Maracanda. Crossing the Oxos was a milestone everyone had been looking forward to. While fording the river without benefit of the bridge this time of year was at least thinkable, it was still a tricky proposition, complicated by the presence of crocodiles. Although there were ways to distract the reptiles, Hadi took the decision to wait the few days until the repair would be complete.

When he heard the news, Yeshua went for a solitary walk around town to explore what would be 'home' for a while. The streets and alleys were dust, the buildings whitewashed to reflect the oppressive sun, and everyone was moving slowly to remain as cool as possible. There was a fish market on the north end of town that he wanted to visit, and his sense of smell told him it was just ahead. He would have gone on to explore it, but a heavenly vision distracted him.

The Paragon

She was the most beautiful woman he'd ever seen. Dressed in flowing white silk, she was tall and slender like the statue of a pagan goddess, yet her eyes made her accessible and alluring, perfection made flesh to him. He felt her kindness and spirituality. What could such a woman be doing here in the dirt streets of Amul? She should be in a palace or a temple.

Although they were a hundred feet apart and the street was full of other people, she looked up as if startled and stared directly at Yeshua. After so many months on the road and now in a relationship with Meryam, he was no longer shy about approaching women, but it was unusual for him to do what he did. He locked into her gaze and walked directly toward her.

She stood motionless, the hot breeze fluttering her dress, waiting for him to approach. "I'm Yeshua," he said, "and I feel drawn to you in a way I believe you understand."

"I'm Roxanna. I do understand. I've seen your aura. It emanates a powerful spirituality and purity of heart like I've never seen."

"I've heard about auras," Yeshua said. "I can't read them, but I seem to have growing empathic abilities, and I feel the same coming from you. Your beauty captivates me as well, so you might see another color flashing in my aura." He smiled, and she blushed, for apparently, she had.

"I'm a healer," she told him. "I've been wandering the Great Road like an itinerant monk, and from time to time I change location. I've been here at Amul for almost three years. This crossing point of the Oxos gives me a chance to meet people from many places. I know it isn't the most glamorous stop on the Road, but

I've found this mixing bowl of Parthians, Sogdians, Tocharians, and who knows who else to be full of interesting people and hospitable hosts. So, I stay for a while."

"I'm doing likewise," Yeshua said. "I'm traveling with my wife, cousin, and friend in a caravan bound for Maracanda. The bridge repair has delayed us. We'll be here a few days. I'm also a healer, and I'd be interested to learn about auras. I understand knowledge of them might be useful to me."

"It certainly would," Roxanna responded. "You've said you can't read them. I think you might learn in time, but even if you never develop that ability, your empathy will stand you in good stead.

"You can still use the knowledge of auras to promote better healing," she continued. "I'm not empathic the way you are, but I believe our two talents are closely related.

"I have a house where I also see people who want my services," she suggested. "I have time tomorrow if you'd like to come, and I can teach you some things about auras."

"I'd be delighted," Yeshua agreed.

"I'll see you tomorrow, then," she said. "It's just down this street."

That was interesting, thought Yeshua in an internal understatement. He began to wonder about many things. He was a married man, after all, but he couldn't deny both the physical and the spiritual attraction he felt toward Roxanna. He'd never met anyone with whom he was so attuned on such a deep level.

To make things more complicated, or perhaps more simple, each knew what the other was feeling at any given moment. He wondered if it would be wise to pursue this friendship and these lessons about auras.

When he returned to the caravanserai and found Meryam, he told her of the day's encounter. "This woman is spiritually powerful," he told her. "She can make me a better healer."

Meryam feigned lack of interest, but jealousy was in her nature. Most of the time there was no good reason for it. Changing her tune, she said, "I don't meet many interesting women on this journey. I'd like to go with you to meet Roxanna."

Yeshua knew this request came from her jealous heart but felt it wasn't the time to confront her about it. Her request, he thought, might be the best way for him to handle what could possibly turn into a dilemma of the worst kind. "Of course," he said. "We'll go tomorrow around noon."

Yeshua didn't tell her that her jealousy would be apparent to Roxanna. He just hoped all would go well. He hoped his wife's presence would temper his own desires and keep him mindful of his promises, and Meryam would leave the encounter trusting him.

Roxanna greeted them at her door. Although she was surprised to meet Meryam, she was completely gracious and friendly. They sat and had tea while she began to talk about auras, directing her explanation to Meryam. "The aura in simplest term is an emanation of energy that surrounds every living thing and is visible to a few as a glow of color."

"What color is it?" Meryam asked.

"It depends first on a person's underlying personality," Roxanna explained, "and it changes because of the emotions we're experiencing at any given moment."

"But I don't see auras," Meryam protested.

"Not many people do," Roxanna said. "It's a gift."

"So, you see these auras? Do you see ours as we sit here?" Meryam questioned.

"Yes, I do," the healer replied.

"Oh, my goodness." Meryam became embarrassed. She knew what was in her heart and was not comfortable with this woman knowing it, perhaps more accurately than she understood it herself.

"Meryam, I know you have jealousy," Roxanna counseled, "but that's a normal first feeling in a situation like this. Don't let your heart be troubled. I see your husband's aura as well, and I see a man who'll be steadfast in the promises he's made, particularly those he's made to you. Have confidence in that for now and for the rest of your life. Jealousy can only bring you pain. I hope you can overcome it."

"You speak to me as my husband would," Meryam replied. "I can't read your aura, nor am I empathic like him. Maybe all I have is the intuition that every woman seems to have, but I trust him, and I appreciate your words."

Meryam said these words to help her make a graceful exit. Her discomfort at her naked soul exposed to a stranger exceeded her curiosity about the art of it. She sincerely thanked Roxanna for her hospitality and returned to the caravanserai.

When she'd gone, Roxanna said, "Although her aura is far less agitated than when she arrived, her words and smile mask what still lingers in her heart. She's an interesting woman. I wish there was time to become her friend. If she grew to trust me, there'd be no jealousy."

"What do you see that tells you all this?" Yeshua asked. "I want to understand it and learn it if I can."

"You may or may not acquire the gift of seeing auras," she told him. "You have the sensitivity and a habit of meditation. Some people gain the ability by practicing over time and sharpening their visualization of solid colors in their meditations, but don't be seduced by the potential power of it. Seeing auras is not spirituality. It can be spiritual, if the effort required to achieve it doesn't cut you off from people."

Outside the door a donkey brayed, followed by an equally grating human voice. If it was meant to be singing, it was an epic failure, but as a ploy to attract customers, the cry of the produce man left no doubt as to who was in the neighborhood. He barked a short list of his fare, grown on his own plot, rousting the local women from their household chores to shop at his mobile market.

Roxanna excused herself to buy an eggplant. Yeshua joined her and bought some apricots for them to enjoy while they talked. "He's very reliable," Roxanna said. "He passes through every other day around this time, so I don't have to walk all the way to the market."

"As I was saying," she continued, "if you go to a cave and meditate all your waking hours, to acquire all these gifts of the hidden arts, what have you accomplished? If you can read auras, heal by laying on hands, foretell the future, move objects without touching them, of what value are these things spiritually to you or anyone else?

"No one should confuse these powers with spirituality," she warned. "Accept the gift if it comes to you, but don't crave it or devote your life to its acquisition. That's the same as all other desire. It's the root of suffering and anxiety."

Yeshua understood this. It was pure Buddhism, but these powers were so seductive he also understood there was no harm in being reminded of it. "You sound like my Buddhist friends. Are you from that tradition?" he asked.

"I am Buddhist," she pronounced. "I am Hindu. I am Zoroastrian and Taoist, Confucian and even Jew. I am all these. The gift of the Great Road is that on its path I can be all of them and not have to answer to anyone for it."

"Exactly," Yeshua said with enthusiasm. "This journey has given me such freedom to think. It's, as you say, a gift in itself; but tell me, what colors did you see in my wife's aura to see into her heart so accurately?"

"I saw the dominant colors," Roxanna began, "to be interacting shades of blue and green. This indicates, if not true spirituality, then a spiritual sensibility that places confidence in a teacher. It manifests as a life of doing good works to be true to the teacher's advice.

"I also saw an element of seeking to connect with the Divine Spirit, separate from the teacher," she continued, "and I saw flashes of that muddy green that indicates jealousy. It didn't appear to be a constant color. It only flashed from time to time, along with a swirling gray. The gray was mostly obscured by the pleasant blues and greens, but it shows a hidden predisposition to fear and depression."

"Your observation is astonishing," Yeshua said. "I thought the fear and depression were banished."

"No, not completely," Roxanna warned. "They lurk beneath the surface. As her husband, you should be mindful they exist and do what you can to make certain they're kept at bay."

"Yes, yes." There was a sigh in Yeshua's voice as it trailed into silence; then, snapping back to reality, he said, "I don't want to linger too long today."

"I understand," Roxanna responded. "Come back tomorrow, and in the meantime, I'll construct a color wheel for you. It will make it easy to see what emotions are related to what colors and how to understand the combinations. The shape of the aura is also significant and we can talk about that too. I'll see you tomorrow at the same time."

When Yeshua left, he realized they hadn't even discussed their relationship, but it was something the two of them had to address. He was powerfully attracted to her, but he'd made promises to his wife. He would continue to pray about it.

The next morning, as Yeshua was tending the animals, Ptolemy came limping up to him. "Yeshua, a while ago, as I was walking down by the market, I saw the most beautiful woman I've ever seen."

As he was about to babble on about her, Yeshua interrupted. "Would you like to meet her?"

"Are you joking?" The very idea that Yeshua, man of the spirit, backward with women, could introduce him, one who could have any woman he wanted, to this vision of radiance, confounded him.

"Of course," Ptolemy continued. "I'm not so forward these days, hobbling around like a cripple. At another time I'd have introduced myself, but I feel less virile in my present state. How do you even know her?"

"I myself was struck by her beauty and her spirituality," Yeshua answered. "Smitten, I might say. She's a healer like me, and there are some things she might teach me."

"And there are some things I'd like to teach *her*," blurted Ptolemy. "Oh, sorry. You talk about her with great respect, even love. I wouldn't interfere with any relationship you might pursue with her. If she shares your outlook and attracts you with her beauty, why don't you take her as a second wife or have some temporary tryst?"

"I don't pursue women like a hunter does prey," Yeshua responded, "but I must admit, the idea you suggest has crossed my mind--not adultery, but a second wife. I've made a promise to my wife, however, that I won't take another, even though it's permitted."

"But couldn't you persuade Meryam to excuse your promise by explaining to her how happy this would make you?" Ptolemy tempted.

The Paragon

Yeshua laughed. "Sometimes I wonder how much you actually do know about women, especially the one I'm with. No, my friend, I wouldn't do it. If a man can't keep a promise to his mate, what good is his word to anyone? His promise becomes empty words to be kept or not at his whim. Who can trust such a man? If he has a conscience, how can he tolerate himself?"

By now, Ptolemy could see Yeshua was sweating like an overworked mule. He was hauling cumbersome bundles of straw to the stalls, and the unremitting heat left him spent, even at an early hour. Yeshua soaked a cloth in the drinking trough and slung it around his face and head, reveling in the relief. He peeled it away and let it drape around his shoulders. Ptolemy began to pick up one of the bundles, but Yeshua stopped him.

"Roxanna can read a person's heart by seeing his aura," he continued, "so it would be pointless to try to conceal any feelings I have for her, but she wouldn't tempt me to adultery. She'd respect my relationship with Meryam, and I must respect it as well. I've prayed about this, and while acknowledging the attraction, I won't act on it. She and I share a bond and will be great friends, but we won't lie together."

"My friend," Ptolemy said, "you've tamed your penis in a way I can't comprehend. No one will ever question your steadfastness or loyalty. Maybe someday I'll have your wisdom and fortitude, but for now I'm like a bad dog. When can we see her?"

"I'm going around noon," Yeshua said. "Wear your infirmity like a war wound and be your cocky self. Her house is on the last street before the fish market, fourth on the right. Give me one hour for my lesson and to let her know I've invited someone else. I'm sure it'll be fine."

Joseph Emmrich

Yeshua went to Roxanna's a little earlier than planned. Above all, he wanted to clear the air. Even though they both knew generally what the other was feeling, words were necessary to make everything crystal clear.

She was wearing white again. "I almost always wear white," Roxanna explained, "especially if I'm seeing someone to heal. No one I've ever helped could read auras, but white, as an aural color, demonstrates pure spirit.

"The sight of these colors," she continued, "even to one who cannot see an aura, tends to evoke the corresponding mental state in the one who views them. So, a person who comes to me and sees this beautiful pure-white gown begins to feel, at least subtly, the presence of the Divine Spirit."

Yeshua could see how this would be so. Even this room of her house where she greeted people had a relaxing air about it. The walls were draped in silk the color of the daytime sky, coming to a point on the ceiling like the interior of a tent, yet evoking a limitless openness.

A milk-white, plush woven carpet caressed Yeshua's feet as he walked across the floor. They reclined on lounges arrayed with comfortable pillows. He felt as if he were floating among the clouds.

"This room itself," Yeshua said, searching for a word, "is ethereal."

"In my healing," she explained, "I use my appearance, my setting, and my soothing tone to relax a supplicant and give him confidence in me. If someone believes in me and believes I can heal him, then my chances at success are multiplied. You can't save someone unless he has reason to believe in you."

Yeshua found this idea to be profound, and as he looked back on his experiences caring for the sick, he saw how it must be true. She could teach him everything she knew about colors, but this lesson would resonate with him forever. He knew, of course, he would inspire people's confidence in his own way, but understood how it must be fundamental to his ministry.

She gave him a color wheel, explaining the spirituality of blue, the vitality of red, the intellectuality of yellow, and all the variations of shading and blending. She explained how the glow of one or two main colors revealed the basic personality and how the swirls and flares of other colors completed the picture. All of this information distracted Yeshua from what he wanted to say most, but eventually he focused on it.

"Roxanna, there are no secrets between us," he began. "Even if we wanted to have them, our gifts are such that it isn't possible. I feel your attraction to me, and you see mine for you. You also understand I love my wife. This is difficult to say, but I've made promises to her that I'll keep. This means I have to love you as a dearest sister. There can't be anything more than that."

"Yeshua," she responded, "you're a dear man. Your aura glows nearly pure white. I also see the bright yellow of intellect, the beautiful blue tint of morality, and the red of loyalty.

"I've known since yesterday," she continued, "this would be the path our encounter would take. I accept it must be so. I rejoice in our friendship. I consider it extreme good fortune the universe has allowed our souls to cross paths, and the energy of our love exists forever, irrespective of physical consumption."

"Indeed it will," Yeshua responded with a smile, "but before I go, I have a friend I'd love you to meet."

As if on cue, Ptolemy appeared at the door. Yeshua had mentioned Roxanna could read auras. He was certain Ptolemy didn't know what that meant, but as their conversation had taken another turn, Ptolemy hadn't asked any more about it.

This might be a fun surprise, Yeshua thought. "Roxanna," he said, "my dear friend, Ptolemy."

"My pleasure," she said. "Please sit down."

"The pleasure is mine, I assure you," Ptolemy responded, like a gentleman soldier. "I saw you as I walked along the river this morning. Now I'm blessed by the chance to meet you."

There *was* a surprise. Yeshua looked at her as she looked at Ptolemy, and he noticed her momentarily transfixed. "Do you remember I told you Roxanna could read auras?" he asked.

"Yes," Ptolemy said, "and I intended to ask what that meant."

"It means everyone gives off a glow of colors that indicates your mental state and feelings," Yeshua explained. "She can see your innermost thoughts."

"Is that so?" Ptolemy's tone reflected a complete lack of embarrassment over what he was feeling toward her, and although he couldn't read auras, he could see something in her eyes that seemed to welcome whatever colors he was emanating.

"You have a brilliant aura," she said. "It's as pure a red as I've ever seen. It proclaims vitality, virility, and loyalty, even though you appear to be recovering from some of injury. Inside, however, are swirls of a pure blue with flashes of white that indicate a nascent spirituality. There are flares of subtle shades within the red. Some of those show lust and some are the rose color of selfless love."

Ptolemy spoke in amazement. "The two of you know me better than I know myself. You put my lust in its place by exposing it, although you understand I'm still attracted to you, as I know my good friend is. Even without having your gifts, however, I'll presume to say I believe you're attracted to me as well as him."

"I wouldn't have thought I'd be so obvious to the untrained eye," Roxanna responded, "but you're correct. I'm blessed by this visit from two wonderful men, one who is promised to another, and one who is not ready to promise. I'm not pursuing a husband, but the only way I'll share myself physically is within the bonds of promises."

"I promise," Ptolemy said, laughing.

They all laughed because they all understood each other. Each one's separate friendship seemed to enhance their collective relationship, a bond that had instantly formed because everyone's feelings were completely exposed. They all felt they'd made something eternal no matter where they each went in life.

That evening Yonnah came in from the desert to see what was planned for the caravan. Yeshua told him about Roxanna. He reacted as Yeshua would expect. "So now you have another pagan friend."

"Yonnah, we're in pagan lands, and I like to make friends. Whom else would I choose? You have only one friend, and you verbally abuse him at every opportunity." Yeshua's tone was light. By now he could accept his cousin's rancor without reciprocating. He might respond with sarcastic humor, but there was no anger to it.

"I've come to understand you better as we've traveled," Yeshua continued. "You can preach to people, demand their repentance, even associate with them in a civil way. You choose not to, however, because you have difficulty forming intimate bonds with anyone, and you don't do well in crowded or enclosed places. I'd have thought this experience on the road might change you in that respect, but it doesn't seem to have done so, at least not yet."

"What you say is true," Yonnah responded, "but I think solitary asceticism is best for my soul. I couldn't withstand the temptations life would offer me if I became a man of the world. By now I'm used to this way of life. I embrace it, and I have no wish to change it. The best I can do is soften my preacher's persona when circumstances require me to be sociable. That much I'm learning."

"Your separation from people is no sin," Yeshua observed, "and in many ways protects you from sorrow. When sorrow occurs, however, as it inevitably will, it leaves you without anyone to share the burden and make it easier to bear. I pray you have peace in your life, Cousin. Oh, by the way, would you like your aura read?"

"Whatever that is," Yonnah groused, "I'm sure it's the last thing I'd like."

The Paragon

After some days the bridge was repaired. Caravans began lining up to make the crossing. Surprisingly, there was little argument over who would go next. During their last days in Amul, the friendship among Roxanna, Yeshua, and Ptolemy deepened. They visited with each other separately and together.

Roxanna taught Yeshua that even if he couldn't read auras, he could, in a meditative state or in directing the meditation of another, use imagination and visualization. "Yeshua," she explained, "you can have the other visualize the color of a desired mental or emotional state. For example, in healing a wound, you can use the color red.

"If you ever learn to read auras," she continued, "you'll see that certain colors indicate certain unhealthy conditions in the body. You'll learn with further study what colors to have the sick person visualize to counteract the unhealthy color and, therefore, the unhealthy condition. Maybe we'll meet again someday, and I can teach you myself."

"This is consistent with what the physician Varaza taught me in Ecbtana," Yeshua said. "Can you advance me in the laying on of hands?" he asked.

"Yes," she replied. "I know of Varaza, and I'd be honored to continue his mentorship."

"Have you met him?" Yeshua asked.

"No," she replied, "but I know his reputation. He's revered among some of us who wander the Royal Road, including you, apparently."

"Oh, yes," Yeshua agreed.

She observed his technique and evaluated his habits of practice. With Yeshua in the meditative state, she laid her hands on him as Varaza did, and gave Yeshua the new power to project healing energy remotely in space and time. "There is no past, no present, and no future," she softly intoned.

Her words and the sound of her voice took Yeshua more deeply into his trance. He felt as if he was nowhere and everywhere. "Simply visualize whom you want to help with the intention of sending them healing power," she explained.

Yeshua accepted his new ability with gratitude and humility as Varaza and now Roxanna reminded him.

Concerning their friendship, Yeshua tried to include his wife in the group. She seemed to appreciate his effort but never acted completely comfortable with Roxanna, nor with Ptolemy for that matter. Despite pursuing this new relationship, Yeshua remained a concerned and loving husband to her. He always viewed that as his first responsibility.

When they at last crossed the Oxos and looked back to Amul, the lady in white stood on the riverbank, waving adieu to them. Yeshua waved back, sad at separation but rejoicing in the glow of new friendship.

Ptolemy waved, feeling those same emotions, but also shaking his head as he marveled he could be in a town so long without getting a whore.

Meryam waved, because she thought it would please her husband, and she didn't want to appear jealous.

Yonnah never looked back.

At the end of the caravan, however, one more waved: Hadi Ba'riel.

At Bukhara

"Truth is One. Sages call it by different names."

Yeshua read the Greek inscription on the door lintel. It stood out among the shops on the narrow twisted streets. He recognized it from the Rig Veda of the Hindus. The caravan had arrived at Bukhara, the last city before the Polytimetus River turned southeast and set them straight for Maracanda, now less than two weeks away.

Yeshua thought he'd interrupt his errand for Hadi to see if there was anything of interest to him inside. When he entered, he saw a middle-aged man seated at a table surrounded by an array of codices and scrolls. He had a Mediterranean look about him and was not quite tall enough for his feet to reach the floor. Although there was a slightly musty smell to the place, everything else about the room was orderly.

Every item on the shelves that occupied all four walls seemed to be neatly in its appointed place. The room was otherwise devoid of decoration except for a small shelf at each window that contained a jar of flowers. In fact, the whole large room looked like a library.

The man was passing a piece of glass over the scroll he had unrolled. He seemed to be peering at the writing through the glass. Eventually, he set it down, leaned back in his chair, and stretched out his arms to yawn. As he turned his head to the side, he saw Yeshua and quickly gathered himself.

"Good afternoon, Friend," Yeshua said. "Whom do I have the pleasure of addressing?"

"I'm Arostos. I didn't hear you come in. I was engrossed in my reading. Welcome to my domain."

"Domain? I'd thought it might be some kind of temple," Yeshua said. "Maybe Hindu, because of the inscription on your doorway."

"No," Arostos replied, "this is no temple, and I'm no priest. You might say I'm a scientist of sorts or a theorist."

"A scientist of writings?" Yeshua asked.

"In a sense," Arostos answered. "I'm Greek, and I've lived here in Bukhara for many years. I came because it's a crossroads of religious thinking, closer to Seres and the Hindus than my homeland. I've always had an interest in comparing the religions and philosophies from civilizations different from mine."

"I'm Yeshua and come from Galilee. I have a similar interest, although I'm a teacher and intend to take home what I learn to renew the spirituality of my people."

"Oh, that's a far more ambitious task than mine," the librarian responded. "I'd always understood our Greek mythology in a metaphorical way, as do many Greeks, but I felt at some level others may have the same fundamental understandings as I do. When I found it was so, I inscribed the quotation from the Rig Veda as a kind of personal motto."

The Paragon

"I've had this same intuition," Yeshua said, "and the more I learn about how people are thinking, the more I become convinced of it. Have you distilled any fundamental principles from your studies?"

"I take it you're familiar with many of the writings," Arostos said, "so I leave it to you to discover what similarities you will, but I've observed some overarching notions.

"I think, first," he continued, "the understanding of the nature of the Divine Spirit is similar, although not identical, in the river valleys: the Nile, Euphrates, Indus, and Yellow, where men first farmed and came together to build cities. In the mountains and the desert, however, there's a different understanding."

"Yes," Yeshua agreed, "it seems that God in the fertile valleys is primarily a provider."

"Exactly," Arostos said. "And in the harsher climates, He or She is more wrathful. Those expressions of God reflect a way of life strong in hospitality but also strong in retribution.

"The movement of populations breeds the interaction of these ideas," Arostos averred, "and they change each other. People intermingle and intermarry. Those who want to maintain purity of thought battle against the tide. Where do your people come from?"

"Father Abraham was a man of the desert," Yeshua said, "but lately we've turned to cultivation and commerce, so this makes sense to me. Do you see other outcomes to this process?"

By now, both men were exchanging their viewpoints quickly and intensely. Yeshua was relishing the conversation. Arostos retrieved a pitcher and glasses and poured water for them to quench their parched throats.

"What's that piece of glass I saw you fiddling with when I came in?" Yeshua asked.

Arostos retrieved it and handed it Yeshua. "Come over here, and I'll show you what it does. This scroll has abysmally small writing that I can't possible read because of my eyes, but look."

As Yeshua stood over the scroll, Arostos passed the glass over the writing, and to Yeshua's amazement, it appeared larger. "It's a magnifier!" Yeshua said. "I've heard of these, but this is the first one I've seen. Where did it come from? How does it work?"

"I got it from a Roman trader," Arostos explained. "The Parthians don't officially let Romans cross their empire, but this one fellow slipped by, heard me complaining when he was in here looking around, and sold it to me. I don't exactly understand the science, but it pertains to the shape of the glass. It's been a godsend. What's more, with a little patience I can start a fire with it."

"I didn't mean to distract you from your thought," Yeshua said. "I was asking you about other conclusions from your studies."

"Oh, yes. I think people conclude," Arostos opined, "especially in lands of many cultures or where people have more education, their gods are myths or metaphors. They use a god to explain what's beyond words or to explain the operation of nature."

"Yes," Yeshua agreed in part, "but many still take their scriptures literally."

"Yes, maybe more in the west where we come from," Arostos said. "In the west, especially in your tradition, the Divine Spirit is typically a *being*, outside the universe, whose existence can neither be proved nor disproved. Although I would say if you accept the premises of Aristotle and view the world as he does, you can use rules of logic to prove the existence of a Supreme Being. That leaves the rest of us, who don't necessarily see the world that way, out in the cold.

"In the east, however," the librarian continued, "the Divine Spirit isn't a being but an all-pervading force within the universe. In some variations it's a nothingness from which the physical universe springs, is the universe itself, or is its oneness or process of unfolding. From it, divinities may arise who represent the forces of nature. You understand I'm generalizing here. There are no words to define this ultimate thing, only metaphors for what it does."

"You talk like my friend in Merv," Yeshua said.

"Lama Mandeep, I presume," Arostos replied, leaving Yeshua stunned.

"I understand," Yeshua said, putting aside his surprise that Arostos knew Mandeep, "but what you're saying about the way different cultures view the Divine Spirit corresponds to what I've seen on my journey."

"We Greeks do have Parmenides, who believed everything is one," Arostos added, "but we could talk about him all day. I leave him for you to explore at your leisure."

"We Jews have the Ayn-Sof, but few know the concept or embrace it," Yeshua said.

"I make one other observation," Arostos concluded. "It's this: the priestly class almost always degenerates from spirituality into formalism. It does so to make an alliance with the state to foster order and obedience among the people."

"You've described my home exactly," Yeshua sighed. "My friend, I wish I could stay longer and continue our discussion, but I have an urgent errand I need to do for my caravan master."

"Yes, of course, go," Arostos said. His expression drooped a little. "I don't often run across people I can talk to like this. It makes my day. It's been my pleasure, and give my best to Hadi Ba'riel."

Yeshua had ceased to be amazed by now. He didn't even ask.

"I see your surprise," the man of books noted. "Ba'riel is a friend and patron. I'm sure he helps more than me. He keeps his generosity to himself. He probably sent you on an errand that passed by my door. Don't tell him I gave away his secret. And Mandeep; we all know Mandeep."

Yeshua went out the door shaking his head. This last bit of information clarified some mysterious coincidences, and the discussion had helped him organize his thinking. He also thought about Arostos's apparent loneliness and Mandeep's observation about the path of ideas, a difficult path indeed.

The caravan made its way up the Polytimetus Valley. When they rounded a bend and first caught sight of the massive tan walls of Maracanda, everyone became excited. A cheer went up from the first to spy it, and the rest joined in, merely on the promise of seeing it soon.

Some of the men began to sing. "Sing to the glory of the Great Road, and praise whatever God delivered you safely."

The Paragon

It was a call and response. "Oy ya ya ya oy ya yea," everyone answered as one. It had no literal meaning but was merely an expression of approval. Anyone could take a turn.

"Praise to Hadi Ba'riel."

"Praise to Maracanda."

They praised the cities they'd visited. They praised the deserts, the mountains, and the rivers. They praised Ahura Mazda, Shiva, and the Buddha, and Yeshua even added Yahweh. The singing continued until they arrived at a caravanserai, a little down valley from the Alexander Gate, named for the founder of the magnificent walled city.

They entered the great hall, and everyone sat down for bread and wine. There would be a feast tomorrow after all were rested, but for now, they basked in their accomplishment and good fortune.

Yeshua and his companions stayed the night in the caravanserai. The next morning, on a recommendation from Markos, the owner, they found a place back down the valley in a neighborhood of people of mixed cultures. It was close enough to the caravanserai and about a forty-five-minute walk to the walled city further up the valley.

They rented a house from a Hindu woman named Amala, a midwife whose husband had just left with a caravan going east to Seres. She and her daughter would move in with her sister and rent the slightly larger dwelling to Yeshua. It had a large room with a hearth suitable for him and Meryam and a smaller room for Ptolemy.

Once Yeshua had settled in, his mind turned to the Paragon. It had become the object of his quest. He was excited to deliver the codex. He burned with anticipation at meeting all the sages who lived there, discussing great ideas with them and learning how to be a better teacher.

He knew from Markos, who not only owned the caravanserai but was also the owner and patron of the Paragon, that he could find it a little farther down the valley. Near a small bridge, he'd follow a path along a creek and then along another stream still smaller to its head.

The next morning, Yeshua followed the directions and saw the Paragon perched on a hill. It was the only structure he'd seen since leaving the farmhouses in the greater valley. The morning light made it glow through the wisps of fog that wafted around it.

It was smaller than Qumran, a compound built of brick, made up of one large building surrounded by several smaller ones, including a barn and a coop. It was walled to a height of ten feet with an open gate, and within the walls, besides the buildings, were gardens: some for food, some for flowers, and some for grapes. Yeshua walked quickly and broke into a run when he saw the gate.

He pounded on the door of the large building, grinning broadly in anticipation of whom he might meet. The door opened slowly. An elderly Seresman appeared. He spoke Greek. "Who knocks on our door, and what's your business?"

"I'm Yeshua of Galilee. I've made a long journey to better understand the ideas of great thinkers. Several teachers I've met on my travels directed me here."

"Galilee? What's that?" responded the man with a hint of annoyance.

"It's a small land near the Great Sea, called Mediterranean by the Romans," Yeshua said. "Maybe you know of Judea better?"

"No. Is it anywhere near Qumran?" the old man asked.

"Yes, it is." Yeshua said, his hopes now rising. "I've lived at Qumran."

"You have, then?" the man groused. "Why do you come here?"

"First, to deliver this codex of the Tao Te Ching in the Greek language from Ling Zhi of Susia." Yeshua unwrapped the codex and showed it proudly to the man at the door, who took it. "Thank you," the old man said and began to close the door.

"Wait, sir," Yeshua pleaded. "I beg to enter and talk with the sages."

"No room," the Seresman replied.

"But, my friend, I've spent months and come thousands of miles." Yeshua was crestfallen. He tried to peek past the man to get a small glimpse of the interior, to see what it looked like or if anyone was inside. He'd seen tools lying around the grounds and was sure the man wasn't alone. It was too dark, however, and the gap too small.

"I hope you have other things to do," the man at the door said. "There's no room for you now. Come back some other time. There may be room for you some months from now." Then he abruptly closed the door.

Yeshua was devastated. How could this be? How could everyone tell him to come to this place only to be rejected at the door? It made no sense. Was this some joke of God, or the cosmos, or karma? He was completely confused. He went back down along the last creek in the crease between the hills and found a flat spot under a tree. He relaxed, meditated, prayed for understanding, and composed his attitude before heading back to town.

He told Meryam and Ptolemy what had happened, and both expressed disappointment for him. "What'll you do now?" his wife asked.

"I'll plan to make some kind of life for us here for some months," Yeshua said. "I feel if I'm patient, I'll be allowed to enter. I'm not sure if they truly have no room, or if it's only no room for me, but the people I've met told me about this place for a reason. I won't give up on it now."

Yeshua wanted to tell Yonnah about the events at the Paragon, so he trudged up to his new cave, taking some bread Meryam had made. He found him in meditation and waited until he was ready to stop and converse. They knew not to interrupt each other when one was in this mental state. Yonnah's eyes were closed, so he may or may not have known Yeshua was there. In due course, however, he opened them, breathed, and exhaled deeply several times. Then he smiled as if ready to talk.

"Yonnah, I've come from the Paragon where I was denied entry."

Yonnah couldn't be his blunt self at a time like this. He knew how much this contact with the Paragon meant to Yeshua. From early on, it had become the goal of his journey, and he felt bad that after so many months and miles, it had come to this.

In his heart Yonnah felt the journey had been an indulgence and waste of time, but now was not the time to compound disappointment with scorn. Yeshua would surely understand how he felt without his having to say it.

He was unusually compassionate when he said, "I sense the depth of your disappointment and suggest maybe now is the time to return to Galilee and begin your ministry. Isn't this rejection a sign for you to abandon this pursuit? Haven't you learned all the knowledge that can be wrested from the sages of the Great Road? Do you really think there's more for you to discover so far from home?"

Yeshua paused, clearly thinking about his cousin's words. "No, I know there's something more. I intend to try again to enter the Paragon. I'll know when to do that, but the time is not imminent."

This disappointed Yonnah, who showed it in his face but said nothing. A breeze fired the embers of the small fire at the mouth of the cave. The fresh sticks he'd laid on them burst into a flame. Yonnah stood over it to warm his hands.

Yeshua could see his cousin's dejection. "I promise you I'll return to Galilee, and I look forward to the day we both preach to our people."

"Sometimes," Yonnah replied, "I feel the ideas filling your head from this journey will take your eyes off the plight of our people. I'm afraid these ideas will set you and me in different directions."

"I know, Cousin," Yeshua rejoined, "you're more political than I. If you want to preach with me when we return, you'd have to accept that. I can tell you, however, I'll be taking a new message to the people. I intend to propose a new covenant and a new way of understanding Yahweh."

"And I thought I was the radical," responded a surprised Yonnah. "Yeshua, I have to preach what I feel in my heart, as do you. When I return, I'll establish a ministry in Perea. It would please me to live by the river there, unless Antipas has built another Sepphoris on its banks.

"But you're proposing a *spiritual* revolution," he continued. "At last I'm beginning to understand where you're headed with your message. Our voices may not be as much contradictory as they are complementary. You're a wise and spiritual man . . . most of the time. I believe God will guide you as you hone your message, and knowing you as I do, I'd trust your ideas and urge my people to listen to you. This is the most confidently I've ever heard you speak, and it encourages me--the attitude if not all the conclusions. This journey apparently agrees with you, but I wish you'd end it."

"Not just yet, Yonnah," Yeshua replied. "Not just yet."

"Look at you," Yonnah observed. "Your hair grows thin and your face rough. Your beard has a hint of hoar. This is God's way of telling you it's time to return to Galilee."

"Not just yet."

Ten

The four itinerants settled in as if they were making a life in Maracanda. They needed to find some gainful occupations to support themselves for an indeterminate time. Yeshua had no idea how long he would need or want to remain here. His wife was content to be at his side. She had no other plan for herself. Ptolemy was content to remain in one place for a while to see what life had to offer. Yonnah, as was his custom, lived in his mountain cave, removed from people, although he came to town almost every morning to beg for alms and to visit with Yeshua.

Yeshua made business as a carpenter and practitioner of building trades as his father did. Ptolemy, ostensibly a merchant to all who knew him from the caravan, became an apprentice to Yeshua. They lived in a neighborhood that, besides being ethnically mixed, was composed of tradesmen, middle-class merchants, and farmers.

They had yard enough for a small garden, which Meryam tended, and she also learned weaving from Amala and other local women. She had no regrets about forsaking her former profession and still hoped to fulfill her life's desire. If she couldn't bear children, perhaps she could take in an orphan and be a mother to her.

As time went by, her husband became known as a healer. People called on him for the simpler things a physician could do. Often he referred them to Nagira, the lady on the hill, one of her friends, who specialized in herbal medicine.

He also applied the techniques he'd learned on his journey. She thought he ought to set up an official practice and be paid. He didn't do this for money, however, but those he helped always repaid him with food they grew or services they performed. The last man he helped with chronic pain repaired the wheel of the cart Yeshua used to transport building materials. That would do, she supposed.

She settled in to a life of habits, a welcome respite from the long months of arduous travel. The novelty of her new home eased the withdrawal of the constant stimulation of the journey.

Hadi had warned her and the others about the possibility of homesickness for the road. "You may be surprised to find," he told them, "the period after the journey can be as difficult for your spirit as the journey itself. The sudden change in one's way of life isn't easy on a person."

They heeded his admonition and found little difficulty in adjusting to their new life, except for Yonnah, who was beginning to long for Galilee. Although he'd urged Yeshua to end his journey, Yonnah still felt a sense of duty to him and for the task of seeing him safely home. How long he would continue to feel this way, he could not say.

The Paragon

One day as Yeshua and Ptolemy were finishing a small job for one of the families of their neighborhood, Ptolemy made a suggestion. "Yeshua, we have no job scheduled right now. Have you ever been hunting?"

"Hunting?" Yeshua replied, "For wild animals? No, never. It's not something my father did, or for that matter anyone in Nazareth. I don't know the first thing about it. I'm not sure it's something I'd enjoy. Killing for sport doesn't interest me very much."

"No, not for sport," Ptolemy responded. "For food. We could take two mules, some salt, and minimal supplies and trek up into the mountains."

"The salt is to preserve the meat?" Yeshua asked.

"Yes," Ptolemy answered. "We'd be gone maybe a couple of weeks. We could eat some of the meat ourselves, share some with the neighbors, and if we're lucky, sell or trade some in the market.

"I have the skills," Ptolemy continued. "I'm sure I can make spears and bows. I can even make traps. I'm intent on doing it, but I'd enjoy your company. Even if we catch nothing, it would be fun to explore. Tell me you'll do it."

"I'm a married man, Ptolemy," Yeshua said.

"But the man is master," Yeshua's friend cajoled.

"Technically, yes," Yeshua countered, "but this woman comes from different circumstances than most, as you well know, and I've explained our contract to you. It's not as if I have to ask her permission to do this, but I owe her a discussion. If I want to do it, I think she'll be agreeable."

"What do you mean, 'if'?" Ptolemy said, "Say yes, and I'll begin preparations. We can leave in two days."

Yeshua hesitated, but the adventure of it intrigued him, and maybe he'd get an opportunity to see how the people of the mountains practiced religion. He'd heard they were Buddhists but of an unusual sect that worshipped their ancestors and ancient wrathful deities.

"All right, then," he agreed. "Let's do it. Just don't act as if you're already prepared to leave before I talk to Meryam, and I hope you notice that the 'man as master' idea isn't part of the local culture. You might keep that in mind in the event some woman finds you 'interesting.' I mean in the event you ever get over your whoremongering."

"We'll see what Maracanda brings," Ptolemy mused.

Although they'd been joking, Ptolemy had been having thoughts about settling down with one woman. This time he'd spent with Yeshua had caused him to begin to think outside himself. He enjoyed helping Meryam and Yeshua take care of neighbors in sickness or in need. It made him think of having a family of his own.

Ptolemy was disappointed that Meryam remained a little cool--not disagreeable, just distant--considering the tribulations they'd all shared. He still believed she'd eventually warm to him.

Yonnah was Yonnah. He *was* disagreeable, even to Yeshua much of the time. Ptolemy accepted Yonnah for what he was. Such was his family, but in his heart, he began to consider the possibility of a wife and children. These thoughts were so new he hadn't even told Yeshua about them.

For his part, Yeshua had also been thinking about this. He had a wife who couldn't bear children, but in his heart he didn't accept the finality of what she'd told him. So it had become his daily practice, as a part of his meditation, to direct some of that meditation to images of family life.

He visualized Meryam as pregnant. He visualized a son playing with him around the house and splashing in the river. He saw them gathered around the table for the evening meal, desiring with all his heart that this should come to pass. He prayed for it.

Yeshua told Meryam about the hunting trip, and she was agreeable. "Maybe you can bring back a goat or an antelope. It's been a while since we've eaten any meat," she said.

The two men sought out Markos before they left. He offered some suggestions. "The animals are still in the higher elevations until the weather turns," he advised. "Each valley is controlled by its own tribe or clan. You need to get permission from the chief even to pass through, let alone hunt, but it is possible. The farther you go, however, the less civilized the population. Just be careful."

The two men set off on their trek. They rode up the valley until it became narrower and steeper and then set off along one of the tributaries of the Polytimetus into the heart of the mountains.

They soon came to a small village where they sought out the chief. He was an elderly man, robust for his age. He stood tall and straight and walked with a staff that wasn't necessary for support.

"We're hunters," Ptolemy explained in a combination of local and sign language. He seemed to have a facility for new languages. Perhaps that came from his mother. He'd always been the first on the caravan to learn a few helpful phrases wherever they went. Consequently, he took the initiative. He gave the chief a woven blanket as a token and asked permission to pass and hunt.

"You may pass," the chief communicated, "but there are too few animals this time of year to allow you to hunt. You must go to a higher valley and ask permission there, but be careful. Some are not so friendly."

The two hunters thanked the chief and moved on. They eventually left the valley and climbed to a ridgetop to reconnoiter. They saw an area Ptolemy said looked appealing. It was a couple of ridges away. They descended back into another streambed and camped for the night.

There were no villages along the route they'd chosen and no sign of people. Without anyone to request permission from, they continued their hike until they were well into the mountains. They were following game trails, although they hadn't seen any animals. Soon, however, they rounded a bend near a ridgetop and saw a small village in the valley below. They had climbed to an elevation where most of the trees and vegetation had given way to barren, rocky mountain walls and scattered angular boulders that had broken off and tumbled from above. They paused to catch their breath and to savor the crisp air and bright sun.

The Paragon

"Let's go meet the people and get permission to hunt," Yeshua said. "Besides, I'd like to try to learn about their beliefs."

"I'm not so sure," Ptolemy responded. "There were game trails all over the last valley and no humans to spook the animals. It might be better to go back. I can set traps. Wait, Yeshua; look across the valley." Ptolemy pointed out a herd of goats in the distance. They were frolicking and fornicating on some rocky outcrops, looking for all the world like dinner. "Let's go meet the people," he agreed.

As they made their way down the trail, which was now a broader path for humans and domestic animals, they got close enough to see activity in the village. Yeshua stopped. "Ptolemy, let's watch from a distance before we approach. I'm not sure it's a good idea to go there."

Ptolemy looked a little puzzled, and although he was the experienced one in this realm, he acquiesced to Yeshua's suspicions. They found a side trail that went back up the mountain at a place where a large boulder could hide them from view. They watched in rapt silence.

The village sat on the hillside up from the valley floor. The mix of stone buildings and more rudimentary shacks clung to a terrace along the path and to a second terrace several feet below the first. In the middle of the second terrace was an open public space, where everyone was gathered. The villagers were colorfully dressed and standing around a table in the center of the open space. Adjacent to the table was a fire, burning down to a mound of hot coals topped with an iron grate. There seemed to be many more people than the number of dwellings would suggest.

One of the men, who stood apart from the crowd and near the table, appeared to be wearing ceremonial robes and a headdress. He was reciting some prayer or incantation. It wasn't in a language they understood. An acolyte stood next to him holding a wooden staff topped with a carving that was diamond-shaped and contained a circle within a circle, like some kind of eye.

"When I first saw the village," Yeshua said, "there was a blur of color around the people. I thought there was some problem with my eyes, but then I thought it might be an aura, emitted by the group, and now I'm sure that's what it is."

"What does it look like?" Ptolemy asked.

"It's horrible," Yeshua replied. "It's a tempest of grayish blues and dark blues that are almost black."

"What does that mean?" Ptolemy asked, his voice now echoing the concern his friend expressed.

"It's a kind of religious feeling but dominated by superstition and fear," Yeshua explained. "It's something we want no part of."

When the one in robes finished chanting, a man and a woman stepped out of the crowd. They were each holding a hand of a small boy. Yeshua guessed him to be six or seven years old. They took him to the man in the center and laid him on the table. The child had been docile to that point, but when they bound his hands and feet, he screamed and writhed in a futile effort to free himself. The woman who had led him up to the table began to weep inconsolably. The man bowed to the man in robes and led the woman back into the crowd, at one point nearly dragging her. The other women surrounded and comforted her.

The Paragon

The man in robes took a dagger from his waistband and raised it to the heavens with both hands.

"Oh, dear God," Yeshua exclaimed in an agonized whisper.

The man in robes, a priest no doubt, began to chant again, and turning his demonic gaze on the squirming child, plunged the dagger into the boy's heart. He then began some call and response prayer with the crowd. Yes, you could call it a prayer now, because this was a human sacrifice to the god they worshipped.

Yeshua and Ptolemy slouched back against the rock and cried. Finally, Ptolemy said, "We need to get out of here. I have an idea we won't be welcome today, and we don't want to see what happens next."

Yeshua agreed, and they started back the way they came. One of the mules brayed, and apparently, some of the villagers heard it. Yeshua and Ptolemy heard someone yell something at them. They turned to look back and saw that some of the men were coming after them. They mounted the mules and headed back over the top of the ridge and down the other side.

They looked back and saw the villagers were still pursuing them. They rounded a bend in the trail and saw a shepherd with his flock coming down an animal path. They watched him pick up a lamb that appeared to have wandered dangerously off the trail. He hoisted it around his shoulders

They begged for his help, and he seemed to understand their plea. He motioned them to go down the trail. After they passed, he brought his flock down onto the trail behind them. This effectively blocked their pursuers.

Yeshua and Ptolemy didn't stop moving until they reached a vantage point where they could look back across the valley. They saw the men were no longer giving chase but were arguing with the shepherd. They weren't putting their hands on him or harming the sheep, but they couldn't get around the flock. The mountain wall on one side of the trail, the precipitous drop-off on the other, and the feigned impotence of the shepherd to make a path for them thwarted their pursuit.

The villagers shifted their frustration with the shepherd back to anger at the hunters. The stymied men screamed at them across the valley. Yeshua didn't understand the words, but they seemed to him a bitter curse. It chilled him to the core.

Ptolemy and Yeshua continued to move, crossing another stream and finding a cave just as darkness was falling. They settled into it for the night but built no fire. The next day they made their way home.

"I'll have to tell my wife what happened," Yeshua finally said, "but I won't tell her the victim was a child. Even if I have to lie, I'll never tell her that. I thought those people were Buddhists. Buddhists don't do that. That was pagan savagery."

"Yeshua, I was as horrified as you," Ptolemy said, "but don't you know there are many places where people offer human sacrifice?"

"Yes, I know it," Yeshua answered, "but to see it done and not be able to stop it, and to see it done to a child. This makes me sick."

"Let's stop in the caravanserai and have a jar and some food before we go to the house," Ptolemy suggested.

The Paragon

"I agree," Yeshua said. "I want to talk to someone about this, and I think Markos is the man who can best help me understand it."

When they got to the caravanserai, Markos was in the dining hall. He could see the men were dirty and shaken to their bones. "Yeshua? Ptolemy?" he asked with a tone of concern. "What brings you here and in this condition? You look as if you've seen a vision of hell."

"That's exactly what we saw," Yeshua said. He told Markos about their experience. "Aren't these people Buddhists?" he asked Markos.

"Yes, they are--in name," Markos answered, "but their mountain religion existed long before Buddhism came here. Their gods require a human sacrifice of someone's first-born son, one for every valley, once a year, for thanksgiving and prosperity, and as you may have surmised, consumption of that sacrifice. If you came to them as a lost stranger, they'd welcome and take care of you. If you walk unannounced into a sacrifice like this, however, you're a demon to them."

"How can they possibly call themselves any kind of Buddhist?" Yeshua questioned again. While he had, indeed, guessed the purpose of the fire and the grate, the recollection of it nauseated him.

"Well," Markos replied, "it's easier for people to change some of their beliefs than it is to change all of their habits."

These words scared Yeshua as much as what he'd seen. "I'm beginning to understand what I want to teach people, but what will become of those teachings when I leave a place or when I leave this Earth? Is that what becomes of peaceful teaching?"

"If you have a good message," Markos counseled, "you can't be afraid to teach it. Keep it simple. Do your best."

"I'm coming to understand that," Yeshua acknowledged.

"But for your information," Markos warned, "if you happen down the wrong street in the walled city, you may find a temple where the same thing goes on. I suggest you don't wander into anyone's ceremonies out of curiosity, unless you're invited or unless you know exactly what to expect. They believe anyone not of their faith who witnesses their ultimate sacrifice has committed a grave sin, and they will make you pay.

"One more thing," he continued. "These people don't come to the city except once or twice a year during the great holidays. If they do come, they won't forget you, and they'll look for you, so you should beware during those times."

Yeshua took the warning to heart and went home to tell Meryam what happened. As he finished telling it, he said, "I don't want to talk about this anymore." She respected his wish, and he never had to reveal the full horror of it.

A week had passed since Yeshua returned from the hunt. He and Meryam were alone at the house. Meryam was uncomfortable as she awoke.

"I didn't sleep so well last night. I don't feel well at all," she complained.

"I can make you a weak tea," her husband offered, "and I'll go see Nagira to get some herbs and broth for you. Rest now. Be as comfortable as you can. Nagira has an herb for every situation."

The Paragon

While he was gone, Meryam dragged herself out of bed and out the door and vomited. Amala saw her and attended to her until Yeshua returned. He thanked her, and she left with a smile.

"Here, try a little of this broth, and when you finish, I'll lay my hands on you to help you feel better." He had her lie flat. He spoke the words to calm and relax her. He put his palms on her head and eventually her abdomen.

"Yeshua."

"Shhh. Relax," he said.

"Does it make a difference in what you're doing," Meryam asked coyly, "to know that you're doing it for two?"

"What do you mean?" Yeshua said, obtuse to the hint.

She looked down and put her own hands on her belly. Yeshua's eyes grew large. "Yes, Yeshua," she said, "I'm with child. I thought it might be so, but I was afraid you might not want this baby. If you don't, I know what to do."

"Oh, no, Meryam." He hugged her fiercely and lay next to her in her bed. "I'm filled with joy, as I pray you are. This is a divine blessing. I'm so excited. What can I get you? What can I do?"

"Nothing, nothing for now," she replied. "I'm comfortable. The sickness will pass. This may change our plans, but since you're happy, that puts my mind at ease. I'll be fine. I'd like to rest now."

"I want to tell Ptolemy," Yeshua said.

She rolled her eyes. Always Ptolemy. "Yes, yes, go tell your friend; and good luck to you telling your cousin."

The smile momentarily left Yeshua's face. "Everything will work out," he said. "Everything will be fine.

When Yeshua went out the door, the first thing he did was yell thanks to God. He couldn't restrain his excitement. He had to find Ptolemy and tell him. He started down the hill toward where he thought he'd find him doing his fitness regimen and indeed saw his friend running in his direction.

"Ptolemy, come quickly!" he yelled.

"Why are you so excited?" Ptolemy asked.

"Meryam is with child," Yeshua answered.

"By Zeus, that's great news," Ptolemy said. "It's good we're at Maracanda, and not on the road, but it looks as if you'll stay here a while."

"Yes, yes," Yeshua replied, "at least long enough for the baby to be born and be old enough to travel, but right now I'm so excited I'm not thinking of anything else, except having a child full of joy and good health. I'll treat Meryam like a queen and try to keep her happy at all times."

"Yes," responded Ptolemy, drawing out the word as he formed a delicate response. "I know you have little experience in these matters. I don't have much myself, but you'd better understand she won't be happy all the time no matter what you do. A woman with child goes through changes that aren't understandable to a man. Revise your expectations and be sober about this. Jump around like a fool for a bit and enjoy this moment, but you, as well as she, have no easy task ahead."

"Right," Yeshua responded, filing the advice in the back of his brain. "Ptolemy, please do me the favor of not telling Yonnah until I do. He'll be furious with me. I can deal with him, and there'll be some moments of unpleasantness, but let me find the right time."

The Paragon

"By now that goes without saying," Ptolemy agreed.

"Right now I'm exploding with energy," Yeshua said. "Let's run to the river."

Yeshua took off. Ptolemy glanced to the heavens in amusement and followed. He quickly overtook his friend. He was fully recovered from his broken leg. Ptolemy arrived at the river first and ran into it but found himself in muck almost to his knees. Yeshua followed him until he was stuck, unable to move.

Both men were laughing uncontrollably. Ptolemy grabbed a handful of the slime and chucked it at Yeshua, making a direct hit on the middle of his chest. Yeshua returned fire, striking Ptolemy in the back of the head as he turned away. Children playing nearby ran over to watch and laugh at the men and soon joined in throwing mud at the two of them and at each other. It was a filthy, glorious melee.

Soon enough someone's mother came running over, and she was not amused. "Get out of there right now!" she screamed at her child. "All of you, out!" Adding, "You men should be ashamed of yourselves."

"We beg forgiveness." Ptolemy spoke up. "His wife is with child for the first time, and he rejoices."

She was unmoved. "I pity her. For then she'll have two to deal with." Yeshua cast his head down with a sheepish look. He didn't make eye contact with the woman for fear he would disrespect her by bursting into laughter.

When she left, Ptolemy played the wise one. "Come on. Let's clean ourselves in the river and go to the tavern for a small jar of wine while your wife rests. Then you can return to her and behave as a normal, concerned husband should."

As they left, one of the children came running back. "Misters, will you come back and play with us again?"

"Yes, we will," Yeshua answered, "but I think we need to make peace with your friend's mother first."

"That was *my* mother."

After a celebratory drink, Yeshua stopped back at the house. Meryam was comfortable, so he told her he wanted to find his cousin and tell him immediately. He knew from his experience of keeping the betrothal a secret that he ought not to make that mistake again. He realized he also held the secret of Ptolemy's true identity, but he felt he must remain silent about that.

He didn't have to trek up to the cave, but rather found Yonnah at the river, not far from the site of the day's earlier indiscretion. Fortunately, neither children nor parents were in the area. He would rather meet them again when he was prepared to make amends.

"Yonnah," Yeshua began, "although I fear your reaction, it would be useless to keep this information from you." He held his breath for a moment and then blurted out, "Meryam is with child."

"She is what?" Yonnah's head seemed to explode at the news. "My cousin, Messiah to his people, has impregnated a whore? The secret betrothal was bad enough. Whose is it, truly?"

Yeshua boiled and forgot his newly found tolerance of Yonnah's caustic tongue. "Damn you, Yonnah. Even you had gotten beyond that reference, and now you bring it back. You know what she means to me and that she's amending her past life."

The Paragon

"Think of your parents," Yonnah countered. "They decide whom you'll betroth. They'll find someone suitable if it's a wife you must have, some arrangement that will help the family. This will be the grandchild you'll give them, a bastard born out of wedlock?"

"You test my forbearance, Cousin," Yeshua said, fighting to restrain his temper. "How do you know we'll even get back to Nazareth alive?"

"Because you promised your parents," Yonnah seethed.

"So someday it will happen," Yeshua said, "but now we're here at the gates of Maracanda. Where's the rabbi who'll enforce the Law and the Prophets and tradition when life goes on around us here?"

"You are the rabbi," Yonnah argued. "You know the Law. You must keep it by your own discipline."

"My discipline is to love and responsibility," Yeshua responded. "We've been betrothed to each other since before Hecatompylos. My parents aren't here. You, then, are my family. You know I want this above all else. I call on you as my family to bless my marriage and my child in the name of Yahweh, because in your heart you know our union is pure; and I expect you to be happy for us."

Yonnah was stunned into silence by this demand. He would pray on it, and it was possible he couldn't refuse it.

"What of your ministry?" Yonnah said, turning back on his way up the hill. "Will you go to Galilee and preach to everyone to marry whom they wish?"

"I won't preach it, but I will not condemn it."

Joseph Emmrich

Yonnah was not a priest. He abhorred what the priestly class had become in Judea and Galilee. They kissed the feet of Antipas and the Romans. The authorities reciprocated, not only with forbearance, but with riches that the clergy flaunted while their people suffered. The people had no use for priests like this.

According to custom, there was no ceremony for a wedding, but Yeshua and Meryam wanted to proclaim their betrothal contract publicly and have the family, represented by Yonnah, approve their union. Yonnah gave this approval grudgingly, but he resolved to do it for his cousin and put his best face on it. Maybe not a happy face, but his best face.

Amala had lived in the neighborhood for about a year and, while friendly with everyone, told Yeshua she still felt like a bit of an outsider. It was natural, therefore, for her to befriend the newcomers. She offered to have a celebration at her house after the blessing, and Yeshua and Meryam accepted.

On the day of the ceremony, which he had to invent, Yonnah led the group down to the river: Yeshua and Meryam, Ptolemy and Amala, and Markos and Hadi Ba'riel and their wives. Yonnah began. "We come to the river, the water of life, where sins are washed away and new life begins. Let us all walk into the river."

They all followed into the flowing water, and Yonnah continued, "Yeshua and Meryam, you have made an agreement between you to betroth one another. Do you affirm that agreement before your family, your friends, and God?"

"Yes, we do," they responded together.

"Yeshua, as the representative of your family . . ." Yonnah said.

"And Meryam, as your chosen representative . . ." Amala added.

"We witness and bless your union," the two officiants said in unison.

"Now come to my house and we celebrate," Amala concluded.

Before they walked back up the hill, Yeshua took a moment to draw close to Yonnah. "Thank you, Cousin," he whispered. "I'm impressed by the beauty and simplicity of your ceremony and your willingness to include Amala."

"Was nothing," Yonnah huffed. "Believe me, I did it out of duty, not pleasure. I couldn't deny your request."

The hermit left the others to their celebration. He prayed he could find a way for his heart to embrace his words.

Ptolemy noticed Yeshua settling into his new reality. Everything had changed. A few days after the wedding, he and Yeshua were working on a job for the mother who had berated them at the river. They'd offered to help her with a door that needed repair, which they did for no charge. When they took a break, Ptolemy said what had been on his mind for some time.

"Yeshua, let's not leave this place." As Ptolemy sat with Yeshua on the riverbank, Ptolemy, too, realized things were changing more quickly than he'd ever expected. Now they'd be here for some months: at least, as Yeshua had said, until the child was born and became old enough to make the journey back to Galilee. Ptolemy hoped, however, he could persuade Yeshua to change his mind.

Ptolemy continued. "It's pleasant here, and we could start anew. I'll find a wife. We'll raise our families, be farmers, carpenters, or you a healer. You'll, hopefully, have the company of the Paragon. Galilee means oppression and the wrath of Antipas, who'll paint you as a Zealot.

"I'm not an ignorant man," Ptolemy went on, "although I'm not as enamored of ideas as you, but I see how you live and treat people, and it motivates me to do the same. Let's stay here. You know you won't be able to avoid politics at home, and I think you have little stomach for politics."

"My dear friend," Yeshua responded, "my cousin is correct. I've always planned to return to Galilee, but it's also my duty and destiny. I have something of value to give to my people."

"I understand duty, if not destiny," Ptolemy answered. "You seem to make your own destiny, and I believe you could be of value *here*, but I respect your devotion to your duty even as I've abandoned mine. Yeshua, if it's your choice to go to Galilee, I'll follow you there."

"Your devotion warms my heart," Yeshua said, "but make your life where you will. Our friendship has set you free. You've discovered your sense of duty and devotion were misplaced. You have greatness in you. Because you give love, people will love you and you'll prosper. You don't need to follow me to Galilee." Yeshua did not say, I fear Antipas will behead you, and I would be devastated.

"I know what the risks are," Ptolemy answered with finality, "but I will go with you."

The Paragon

The months of Meryam's pregnancy were long and difficult. Although the winter was mild, that did little to make her more comfortable. She frequently had morning sickness, and her energy was generally low.

Yeshua had no experience with a situation like this. Amala, as a midwife, was able to monitor Meryam's condition and keep her in good health but could do little to maintain her spirits. Yeshua, for his part, laid hands on her at the beginning, but soon Meryam became irritated at the practice and asked him in no uncertain terms to stop. He obliged and spent as much time as he could in or near the house, making himself available to see to her needs, but Amala became her primary attendant.

"Amala," Yeshua said to the midwife one day, "I'm frustrated that I can't help my wife feel better or at least make her smile."

"I understand," she counseled, "but there are changes going on inside her that make this a difficult time for the spirit as well as the body. You must be patient and resolute and keep up your own spirits. When the baby is born, this will pass." She said this out of hope rather than conviction, because she noticed Meryam's depression was deeper than most, and it concerned her as well.

"Your advice is like Ptolemy's," Yeshua replied. "I have no choice but to accept it."

Yeshua and Ptolemy continued to work on projects, but Ptolemy began to occupy his spare time with the study of Tao yin, which was like Seresian yoga, and martial arts. He was taking lessons from a Seresian man in the city. Ptolemy had read from the codex of the Tao Te Ching Yeshua had transported.

He talked to Yeshua about his new training. "My teacher," he said, "incorporates the lessons of the Tao Te Ching into our sessions. With this physical training, the words come alive. We move like graceful animals. I know it isn't our tradition, and I hope you aren't insulted by what I'm doing."

"Of course not, my friend," Yeshua responded. "I'm pleased you've found an interest you can be passionate about. I like the words of Lao Tzu myself. There's no difference between those words and my thoughts about how to treat others. His words don't contradict anything I believe."

"I'm happy you feel that way," Ptolemy said, "but to change the subject, I'm concerned for Meryam."

Since the pregnancy, Ptolemy had moved into another house in the neighborhood, but he had contact with both Yeshua and Meryam every day.

"Yes, my friend," Yeshua said, "so am I. Amala has urged I be patient, and it's been as you cautioned me from the beginning. Her time is near, and for now all I can do is pray every day for her health and welfare. God's will be done."

Meryam became progressively more depressed. Yeshua tried to keep her spirits up. "Why are you so worried?" he asked sweetly.

"I'm afraid," she said. "Afraid of being pregnant after being told it was impossible, afraid over what my past life might do to the child in my womb."

The Paragon

"I can't believe, after all you've been through, God would let anything bad happen now," he said. Of course, he knew God would do what He would do, but he never stopped trying to lift her spirits. Although Meryam continued to reject him, he never left her presence without telling her he loved her.

The days went by slowly, but eventually winter ran its course and the streams were again full. The first blossoms at last burst out of the mud, and the rains signaled the time of renewal. Everyone knew the wait would soon be over and the world would have a new face, born from the love of parents strong of will and warm of heart.

Amala was all smiles by now, for she had borne a heavy burden herself during these past months. Yeshua was beginning to experience a sense of relief. Meryam knew her time was at hand, but that knowledge was doing little to alleviate her physical or mental discomfort.

The day of the birth was a warm, bright day. Amala came over in the morning to check on Meryam, and she seemed to know right away the time had come. "Yeshua," she ordered, "wait outside until I tell you to come in."

Amala called for her daughter, Raika, to assist her. She responded with hot water and clean linens. Yeshua went out as he was told. He sat for a while until he could sit no more. He walked up and down the road. All his spiritual training did little to calm him, although he was sure things would have been much worse without it.

Occasionally, he would hear Meryam moan or cry out as if possessed, but it was maybe two hours later when he heard the first infant's cry. He heard the women talking excitedly, but then he heard concern in their voices, and then, no crying. He was afraid he knew what was happening but denied it in his heart.

He obeyed Amala's admonition not to enter until called, but she called him soon enough. He ran into the house to see Meryam writhing on the bed wailing. He saw Amala standing over the crib in the corner and ran to her first.

He looked down at his son, who wasn't breathing. Amala and Raika were both crying. He put his hands on the baby. He tried to revive him like the baby in the earthquake, but to no avail. He picked him up and held him close. There was no more to do.

As common as infant death was, no one ever expected it would be his child who didn't make it. Yeshua set the baby down and went to his wife. This was no time to lose his composure in the torrent of grief sweeping over him. He held his wife still and sought words of comfort. He couldn't bring himself to say everything would be all right. It wouldn't. He could only say, "I love you, and we'll get through this tragedy."

"Why has God done this to me?" she screamed.

Of Yeshua, she demanded, "Why couldn't you save him?"

He knew there was no good answer that could satisfy her. That would call for a wall of reasoning against a tide of emotion. Best to let the tide run its course. There would be time enough for talk later.

After she passed into sleep from exhaustion, he went outside and cried. Yonnah, Ptolemy, and Amala all came to comfort him. He appreciated that but needed to be alone, so he went by the river to try to let the sound of its spring flow mend his broken heart.

Yeshua knew in his mind all the reasons that his heart should be still. In his tradition, one would say, it's God's will, or God has a reason for everything. Who are we to question God? God never asks us to bear more than we can endure. He knew in the Eastern traditions that his earthly attachments, loved by his ego, accounted for nothing when reality was viewed from an expansive perspective.

All these thoughts from all these traditions, however, seemed hollow in this terrible moment. If he were a thousand miles away and heard of the death of a grown son, maybe he could shed a tear and then become dispassionate. Here and now, however, reflecting on the image of the dead child in his arms, he could scarcely bear it.

Yes, he knew the child was dead, and that it was himself he was feeling sorry for. He was crying for Meryam, though, even more than himself. He knew how great her devastation must be after having no hope, after enduring those long months of physical and mental pain; and he wept for his son, who had no chance at life. What would that child have done? What would he have become? There was no comfort to be taken, as one could in the death of an older person, in the celebration of a life well lived.

Meryam, once she awoke, was in a dark place. She looked over at the crib where the child lay wrapped in bloody linens. Her spirit roiled inside her. There would be retribution for this.

Her thinking made no sense. From whom would she exact that retribution, and why? Demons were controlling her thinking, but she concealed their presence behind a strange, soft smile that didn't match the anguish in her eyes.

The following day Yeshua took the body and went, along with Yonnah and Ptolemy, across the river and up the hillside to a remote grassy area. Meryam, of course, was not well enough to go with them, nor for emotional reasons did Yeshua believe she should. Amala said she was lucky to be alive.

"Yeshua, I think this is a good place," Yonnah said. "The earth near that boulder is soft for digging."

Yeshua said nothing, but lay the body down and picked up the shovel. Before the spade first pierced the earth, Ptolemy gently took it from him and dug the hole himself. Yeshua handed the boy's body, wrapped in fresh swaddling, to Ptolemy, who took it and placed it at the bottom of the hole.

The three men stood over the grave and Yonnah spoke to God, saying simply, "Receive the soul of this little one, O Lord, who had no time to know you, nor any time to offend you. Bless his parents in their time of grief and all of us who mourn with them, and grant us all eternal life together in your holy presence."

"Come with me, Yeshua," Yonnah concluded. He took his cousin by the arm, glancing at Ptolemy, who knew it was his duty to finish the somber task.

As the weeks passed, Meryam seldom left the house. Yeshua knew something was wrong, but Meryam was unreachable. "My wife," he'd say, "I share your grief, but I sense you're sinking deeper into yourself in an unhealthy way. Will you come with me to tend the garden or help Amala. She's been sick for a few days? Won't you at least talk to me?"

"I'm fine," she'd say, sometimes expressing ennui and sometimes disdain for her husband. "Can't you see I'm in mourning?"

All he could do was watch her carefully and reassure her of his love at every opportunity. This was not good. He kept looking for any chance to break through the barrier she'd constructed around herself but was finding none.

Eleven

As the days and weeks passed, Yeshua began to heal. The death of his son would be with him the rest of his life, but at least he'd become able to laugh again. Ptolemy and Hadi had helped him in that regard, although there were still times when he grew silent and could feel the weight of his own heart. Sometimes he'd go to the river and sit without meditating or praying.

Ptolemy loved his friends, including the two who were weak in reciprocation, and was in their company daily, but he liked having his own place. Though only a short distance from his adopted family, it allowed him time to think and focus on what he was learning in town. One day, after practicing his forms, he stopped to visit Yeshua and Meryam. Since Meryam was sleeping, he suggested, "Yeshua, come with me to the caravanserai and enjoy a jar of wine."

"Give me a moment to make sure Meryam is comfortable," Yeshua said, "and I'll walk with you. She tends the garden now and weaves, but there's no joy in her life like she once had, and

The Paragon

she's constantly tired. I keep trying to break through to her, but something inside is resisting."

"There's time enough for problems," Ptolemy said. "I drink less wine since practicing martial arts, but today I'd enjoy your company and a small libation."

"I've noticed a change in your attitude lately," Yeshua observed. "Many of your former habits seem, well, muted. There's an increasing calmness about you, and you express your self-confidence less brashly. Is this all due to your new training?"

"That surely has something to do with it," Ptolemy concurred, "but I hope I don't renew your pain when I say that observing what you've gone through has been very sobering for me. As your friend, I've felt your sorrow and your trial in my own bones. Life is short, and I want to be the best person I can become."

Yeshua and his friend walked to the tavern, joking along the way. They found a table in the great room that was crowded by the arrival of a new caravan from the south. The crowd was raucous, fueled by first libations after a long journey. Yeshua and Ptolemy had to raise their voices to be heard by each other above the din of the rest shouting orders to the staff.

There were many who had the look of Pahlavas from the mountains and Sakas from the land beyond the Indus, but a solitary man in the corner had a more familiar look.

"Look at that man dressed as a monk. He looks more like us, more like you, even," Yeshua joked. The man's head was down, focused on his food.

Ptolemy stared at the man and then turned white. "Yeshua, you must go this instant."

"What's wrong?" Yeshua asked.

"*That's my father!* He mustn't find you, but I fear he may. I want to greet him, but besides my joy, it's my problem, our problem, greater than words can express. I don't know what to do yet, but trust me for now and go."

Yeshua understood and wasted no time leaving. Ptolemy watched the man he was sure was his father to make certain he never looked up to notice his friend. When Yeshua was gone, Ptolemy walked to the corner table and stood by the man hunching over his plate. "Pardon, sir, do I see a ghost?" he asked, trembling.

The man looked up. "By Zeus and all that's holy. It's I who am haunted. Is it truly you, my son? I thought you lost or dead."

"As did I you, Father." The man jumped to his feet, and the two embraced.

In Nehardea
Many Months Before

Kefir struggled with all his might against the goons who'd invaded their room. They threw a hood over his head and began dragging him down the stairs. He screamed at them. "You bastards! I'll kill every one of you whoresons!"

As they stumbled down the stairs, one of the men kicked him between the legs, and another followed with a kick to the midsection that rendered him unable to speak or catch his breath.

The Paragon

He could feel himself thrown into some conveyance, now bound, hands and feet. He couldn't hear his son anymore.

They sped away from the tavern. "They've killed Ptolemy," at last he was able to moan. "Why have you killed my son?" he screamed. No one answered him. Kefir knew, of course, it was revenge for the fight, but that didn't stop him from a forlorn repetition. "Why did you kill my son?" he wailed.

Kefir had no idea how many of the thugs were still with him. Although he was parched by now, no one offered him anything to drink nor even spoke to him, but he didn't remain in the cart for long.

His captors delivered him to a dock on the river. They yanked him out of the cart, threw him onto a boat, and chained him to some part of it. The smell of the pitch that made the reed vessel river-worthy made him nauseous in his present condition. The odor was overpowering, new probably. When they finally removed his hood, Kefir could see the oarsmen had scarves tied around their noses and mouths.

He could also see he was the only human cargo, along with jars of wine and pistachios. Besides the two oarsmen, there was one other whose job seemed to be to watch him. Kefir lay crumpled on the floor, unable to see anything else but the first color of the morning sky. He could feel he was floating down the river. His captors finally gave him a little water but refused any communication.

At length, Kefir was allowed to sit on a small bench, still chained and still watched by his evil-eyed overseer. Although the guard was a squat man of middle age, his massive arms seemed capable of bending the bar to which Kefir was secured. Escape was on his mind, but it wouldn't be possible now.

He knew from hearing the men talk that they were headed to Apologos, the city at one of the mouths of the Euphrates where it poured into the Persian Gulf. The king of Parthia had never convinced the Greeks or Romans to call it *his* gulf. Apologos was a gateway to the Orient by sea and to Egypt as well.

When they arrived, Kefir almost forgot his situation as he laid eyes on a city as large as Caesarea Maritima, queen of the eastern Mediterranean ports, and the equal of it in commercial activity if not in aesthetics. He wouldn't have expected anyone to create a port as magnificent as Herod the Great's *magnum opus*, but this place was wretched.

The stifling smell of rotted fish and refuse forced the nostrils closed. There was no grandeur to the random and ramshackle structures of unfinished brick that lined the waterfront. No one had enforced any order to the architecture, and the process of commerce that arose from it was screaming chaos.

A quick transaction yanked Kefir back to reality. The round little man with the big arms led him away in the company of another whose clean tunic made him appear to be the businessman. The businessman had a lackey whose military bearing and fit physique marked him as security. They led Kefir to another part of the port where the larger ocean-going ships were docked. They boarded one of the vessels.

"Congratulations. You speak Greek, I take it," the businessman finally said to him. He spoke with a woman's voice. He was younger than Kefir, and his tone oozed sarcasm like the oil from his foppish curly hair. He certainly wasn't the captain of the vessel but from his pompous, condescending attitude seemed to be in charge of the commerce.

"Today's bad news, as you may have guessed," he continued as he leered at Kefir, "is that you're now a slave. My name is Dakkim. I own you for now. I'm taking you to Barbaricon, where you'll be resold for more money than I can believe. This journey will take many weeks.

"The good news is you'll be allowed to eat," he continued. "You'll eat well, I might add, if you choose to row. If you choose not to row, you'll be thrown into the hold, fed little and, much as it would hurt our profits, be lucky to make it alive."

"Bugger yourself, man-lover," Kefir spewed, and he spat at his unctuous antagonist.

The military-looking man, who was standing next to him, wheeled and in one motion snapped his elbow into the side of Kefir's head, knocking him to the ground, unconscious.

Kefir awoke in hell. That blow seemed personal, he thought in disgust. He had to be in the hold of the ship. He was still chained. He could feel the cold grip of the iron, but it was pitch-dark, and his prison stank with smells whose origin he didn't wish to imagine. He called out to see if there was anyone else with him in this nether world and heard one response. It came in a language he had never heard, and conversation ended before it began.

After uncountable hours had passed, the hold was opened. The bright light of day shined into his dungeon. "Do you wish to row?" peeped the voice of the man he'd insulted. Kefir refused to answer.

"Feed them," Dakkim ordered.

One of his minions threw down two scraps of bread and a small skin of water. His now-visible companion lunged to grab all the bread, while the two on the deck above began to laugh. Kefir could see he was physically superior to the bread hog. He could kill him but instead grabbed the skin of water and motioned that they ought to trade.

They did, and the door above slammed them back into invisibility. It was many hours before the door opened again. Kefir was hungry beyond pain. The other fellow apparently didn't speak any language Kefir knew even a few words of. His world, therefore, was bereft of sound as well as light, save for the gurgle of water on the hull and the occasional splash of a mis-stroked oar.

Kefir soon realized what the result of his intransigence would be. He would likely die, but at best he would be too weak to escape, so when the door opened again, he announced, "I will row."

"A wise choice," Dakkim said. "You're lucky I've forgiven your insult and lucky you were the first to cooperate. There's only one seat left for a rowing crewman. Your friend below will remain there unless someone else dies. Maybe we can give him double bread. Hopefully, he'll survive."

Kefir knew that wouldn't happen. He rowed as if it were a duty and got fed like a free man. Sometimes the sails allowed them rest. He prospered physically but seethed with hatred inside. He wanted to kill the smarmy trader, but if that proved impossible, he would kill someone else.

The Paragon

After some weeks, thankfully without serious storms, they landed at Barbaricon at the mouth of the Indus River. The other man in the hold had died, and his body had been cast into the sea. "Pity," Dakkim said as the deed was done. "He'd have been worth at least a little something."

Barbaricon was even worse than Apologos. This wasn't Parthia, whose cities, other than the Gulf port, tended to magnificence. Here the buildings were dilapidated, and beyond the crumbling structures of the harbor front, there was a sprawl of shanties like the most wretched parts of Damascus a hundred times over.

Kefir and the others were taken to a holding den for the slave market where other men and women from other ships had been brought. It was a horrible place: miserable human beings, chained and piled one stinking body on another, worse than the ship's hold.

After several days there was an auction. Kefir and the others, maybe a hundred and a half, were brought shackled, under guard, to an area outdoors. He saw a large elevated platform surrounded by a crowd of buyers and onlookers.

First, they brought the women out, one by one, naked, with men in the crowd hooting, touching, acting like pigs, as if it were some pagan festival. There was a time in his life, Kefir thought, when he could have been one of those screaming, filthy jackals. But this experience disabused him of any such thoughts forever, he vowed.

Most of the women--you couldn't even call them women; they were girls, young girls. Kefir could see their fear. Most of them were crying, and these men bid on them as if they were animals.

When the first auction was settled, the crowd cheered the winner as if he'd achieved some great success or won some fabulous prize. He ascended the platform like a potentate and dragged the girl away. Kefir could see the terror in her eyes. He didn't know if she was old enough to know what was about to happen to her. He couldn't watch after that.

Eventually, it was time to sell the men. They brought Kefir up. He was also naked. There was no hooting, but there were plenty of comments about his body. He had no idea what manner of life he was being sold into. Another wretch said someone would probably buy him as a kind of gladiator.

"Gladiators aren't used in great public spectacles here," the man said, "but in private battles. The owners place wagers on the outcomes, like dogs or cocks. If you fight well and survive for some years, you'll be treated well, maybe win your freedom."

"That will not happen," Kefir swore. "I'll escape before any bastard puts me in a contest, or die trying, and let me also swear this while I have someone to listen. As a soldier, I'll never have any part in taking slaves again. I'll kill a man before I allow him to be taken as a slave."

"Jew, tall for a Jew." He heard murmurs from the crowd.

"Looks like a soldier, quite fit."

"No, too old."

"No, experienced I'd say."

Finally, he heard a man say, "I offer five gold pieces," whatever that was in this place. That closed the auction. Kefir

The Paragon

learned this was the lackey of some satrap to the north, and he began a journey along the Indus River until it began to rise into the mountains.

He tried to keep his wits about him, and looked to escape at every opportunity, even though that escape would be into a strange land where he didn't speak the language. His new home was a grand fortified compound, on a bluff high above the river, protected from invaders by the surrounding hills.

The satrap, whose name was Balavan, had in fact bought Kefir to gamble in games of combat, but Balavan was ill-served by his palace guards. They were idiots and thought iron bars alone would do their job. They drank too much. Kefir knew the day would come when he could escape.

Conditions in his new cage were disgusting but seemed almost comfortable compared to what he'd experienced in transport and at the market. He broke his vow not to fight because he saw the opportunity to escape lay in present cooperation.

He was, of course, a great fighter and had skills enough to defeat even younger opponents. It grieved him to have to kill *them*. Balavan appreciated his efforts and the money Kefir won for him, and he showered him with extra rations and even a woman or two.

Kefir refused the master's offer of a separate and more comfortable confinement. "I want to remain with my cohorts," he protested, knowing that choice offered his best chance to get out. He never wavered in his focus to escape and to kill doing it.

Eventually, he saw his opportunity. He knew when the guards would be drunk. His fellow prisoners spoke little if any Greek, but the group drew pictures in the dirt and used sign language to organize their escape.

They staged a fight in their cell, and when the two interior guards came in to break it up, the fighters jumped them and killed them with the guards' own weapons. Kefir knew there were other guards outside but not exactly where.

He found two sleeping and dispatched them with great delight, with hacks across their throats and extra hacks for pleasure. He wanted to look for more to kill just for the sake of killing. He wanted to kill his enslavers even more than he wanted to take revenge on the Zealots, but he forsook the opportunity so as to make good his escape.

All the escapees went separate ways to increase their chances of success. Kefir made his way north, farther up the valley. When he reached a town, he saw a Buddhist temple. He thought it might be a place where the rabbi or priest, or whatever he called himself, might speak some Greek and might have the inclination to help him, and it was so.

The lama, Kimbu, not only fed him but also gave him monk's robes to wear. "I thank you," Kefir said, "and I know, because I'm an escaped slave, that helping me could be a problem for you. We're nearly a full day's ride from my prison, but I suspect my master will look for me at least this far."

"You're probably right," Kimbu said, "but you're safe here. Since you want to go to Maracanda, I suspect you know the way is over the mountains. It's too late in the year to attempt the crossing. The road is impassable now.

"You're welcome to stay here," he continued. "We live simply and quietly. I think the peace would be good for your spirit. I sense your agitation goes beyond the strain of escape and fear of recapture. Please stay."

"I accept your offer with gratitude beyond words," Kefir responded.

On one occasion, Balavan's men came to the monastery asking Kimbu if he'd seen any suspicious strangers. Kefir hid in a secret room in case the men decided to search, but the monk's denial and blessing satisfied them.

At the monastery's altitude there were snowfalls during the winter, but most of these came without the ferocity of those at higher elevations. Kefir had never seen such beautiful snow, draping the trees, softening the sounds of the earth.

The rippling of the cascading brook erased the banging of the ocean against the galley. The crisp purity of the air he breathed cancelled the memory of the stench of captivity. The white perfection of the snow itself smothered the memory of bloodshed.

The monks he lived with never proselytized. There were only a couple whom he could even share language with, but their way of life added to the cloak of tranquility that was swathing him. He was purged of his bloodlust, but his sense of duty remained--a duty that included dispatching two Zealots for his king, but now he could kill them with dispassion.

He left the monks, still disguised as one, when the first caravan of the season passed through. He embraced Kimbu. "I leave here a different man," Kefir said. "I thank you again."

"Go in peace, Kefir," Kimbu replied. "There is more change yet within you, but your new journey is well begun."

It would take some weeks to reach Maracanda, but he would find the Nazarenes if they were there and do his duty. If they weren't, he knew the way home. He was a free man now.

In the Tavern in Maracanda

"I thought you were gone forever from my life," Kefir said to his son, "dead or enslaved in some dark corner of the earth. I should have known you're as much a survivor as I am."

Kefir told his son the whole story except for the part about how his heart had changed. Ptolemy also told his father the story of his near-death and rescue by the caravan but didn't tell him who it was that had saved him.

"You've been here awhile." Kefir observed. "Have you found the Nazarenes?"

"No, I haven't." Ptolemy lied. "I'm sure they're not here, and I've been making a plan to return to Galilee. For now, I have to move from the house where I've been staying. Maybe you and I can find a place together for a short time until we can join a caravan to the west. Let's go home very soon."

"Yes, soon enough," Kefir seemed to agree, "but I want to look around and ask some questions to assure myself they're not here or to find where they may have gone. I trust your diligence, but I'm the one charged with the responsibility, and I'll need to report my personal efforts to Antipas, that those efforts and our tribulations may appease his wrath."

"Don't you think Antipas has forgotten about us and our mission?" Ptolemy asked.

The Paragon

"Perhaps for now," his father replied, "but our return will be reminder enough. C'mon. We'll find a place and begin one last search."

Markos overheard them talking and approached. "Ptolemy, you don't come so often or drink so much."

"I grow older, Markos," he joked.

"Maybe only wiser," the innkeeper responded.

"Wiser is my friend's job," Ptolemy said, afraid for a second he'd said too much.

"I hear you need a place to stay for a while," Markos said. "The caravanserai is full up, but feel free to sleep in the stable at no cost until you find something better for yourselves."

"Thank you, Markos," Ptolemy replied. "This is my father, who I thought was lost to me. Father, Markos."

"A pleasure, sir," Kefir said. "I thank you for your hospitality."

Ptolemy was relieved nothing in the conversation had given away anything he wanted kept secret.

Twelve

"Son, today let's go different ways and try to find the Nazarenes if they're here." Kefir suggested.

"Why can't we just leave and tell Antipas about our painstaking efforts to find them?" Ptolemy countered.

"Have you lost your sense of duty and honor because we're far from Galilee?" his father asked. "We've sworn an oath to Antipas. I intend to do it to the best of my ability, and I expect you to do the same."

"Very well, let's do it." Ptolemy acquiesced. "I'd suggest I start here and inquire farther down the valley. There are other caravanserais and inns up valley, along the road past the city gate. I haven't been to those since I got here."

"Good, then," his father said. "I'll make a fresh inquiry."

Ptolemy lingered until Kefir had gone out of sight and then ran to Yeshua and Meryam's house. No one was there. Amala thought perhaps Meryam had gone to the stream to launder clothes and Yeshua had gone to the Paragon.

At the Paragon

Yeshua knocked on the door as he had before. "Teacher, I've returned to beg entrance. I come only to learn from the sages. I've waited patiently, and as I've waited, I've endured an unspeakable sorrow. I'd like to learn how these men face tragedy. To say it's God's will or God's punishment has left me empty. I need their counsel."

Yeshua had a suspicion about the old man. He waved his hand in front of his eyes and, when he got no reaction, knew the man was blind. Yeshua said nothing.

"Sir, I regret there's still no room," the teacher said.

"But, teacher, your monastery is large and I need only a space on the floor, or maybe I could just visit briefly."

The man gave Yeshua a stern glance. "It does no good to question my integrity. When there's room you'll know it, and you'll come back. For now, there's no room for you.

"As to your sorrow," he continued, "ask yourself, when the codex of the universe is written from beginning to end, how large a page will your sorrow be granted? Will you even get a paragraph, perhaps a sentence, or even a single word? Your tears are a torrent because you look inward. You should understand this. When you view your tragedy as would the author of the codex of the universe, you'll heal completely. Go now."

Yeshua left the Paragon and walked to a grove of trees just off the path. He prayed and meditated, contemplating his own impatience, arrogance, and ego indulgence. He sat there for a long while. Although time and his own spirituality had put him on the path of healing, the teacher's words and his refusal to allow him entry were a slap in the face of his soul. It was a slap that brought him back to clarity.

The teacher had spoken to him as God had to Job: "Who is this that obscures divine plans with words of ignorance? . . . Where were you when I laid the foundation of the earth?" Both traditions came to the same place.

The words of sympathy others had expressed to him were comforting, but he'd wallowed in them. He'd never forget the brief life of his son and would perhaps muse wistfully of what might have been for him. But now, at last, he could forgive God, Meryam, and himself, deeply in his heart, for what had happened. A great load was lifted from his shoulders.

It was at this moment, when peace was at last softly enfolding him, that he saw Ptolemy running up the path. "Yeshua, my brother, I couldn't dissuade my father from looking for you. I tried to convince him we should leave, return to Galilee, and lie to Antipas about our great efforts to find you in Maracanda.

"I'd leave here and never see you again," he continued, "if it would save you. But he's convinced you murdered my mother, and his enslavement seems to have sharpened both his wrath and his sense of duty to Antipas. You have to leave here now because he'll find you. There's no stopping him."

Yeshua exhaled in resignation. "Ptolemy, I won't run. I can't leave. I came this far for a reason. It seems now I understand that reason more clearly, but there are matters I need to see to completion. I'm not sure what that completion will be, but I know I have to stay a while longer."

The Paragon

"Then I know what I must do," Ptolemy declared. "If he discovers you, I'll confess my lies to him and beg for your life in the name of your saving mine, but I fear he won't relent. I'll never take arms against my father, but he'll have to kill me to kill you. I pray we do not all die."

"I'll need to tell Meryam and Yonnah what I've concealed from them until now about your identity and about your father's intentions," Yeshua said. "I'll tell the neighbors to lose any memory of us, and we'll keep to the shadows until you and your father leave. It's possible I may not see you again. Know that you're my brother and I'll love you always." They embraced, restraining tears.

"Go now," Yeshua said. "I'll follow soon."

After Ptolemy ran back toward town, Yeshua started up the path but diverged to cross the valley to the spot he knew Yonnah frequented. Yonnah spent these days in meditation and solitude, frustrated by not being able to preach to anyone who would understand his tradition and anxious to return to Galilee to begin his ministry seriously.

Yeshua approached him and quietly interrupted his meditation. "Yonnah, I have urgent news. First, I must confess to you I've kept a secret since you rescued me in the desert. Ptolemy is a soldier, not a merchant. Antipas sent him and his father to kill us. He told them we were the Zealots who killed his mother in Sepphoris. Yes, Ptolemy was the boy in the market I told you about.

"He and his father," Yeshua continued, "were taken by slave traders and separated in Nehardea. The friendship between

Ptolemy and me is true. I knew from the beginning what his mission was, but he renounced it and loves us as family.

"His father, however, is alive, has escaped his captors, and has come to Maracanda to find and kill us. We believe he won't relent, even when Ptolemy tells him we saved his life. I want you to take Meryam and flee Maracanda. I'll face this problem, and if I survive, I'll find you in Galilee, if not on the Great Road. I cannot leave here now, and my remaining here will give time for you and Meryam to escape. I can at least avoid him long enough to buy you time."

Yonnah's head was spinning as he tried to process all this information. "You couldn't have told me the truth about Ptolemy before?"

"It would have served no purpose," Yeshua said. "I never lied to you or Meryam. He became a friend, and the past was the past--until something of that past inserted itself into the present."

Any anger Yonnah may have felt was subsumed by the need to respond with action. "I know you want to save us, but I will not go, and I'm fairly certain Meryam won't go either. I have no wish to die so far from my homeland, but I won't abandon you. We must have another plan. Maracanda is the greatest city on the Great Road. For now, we live on the outskirts, but we could plunge into the labyrinth of the center and become lost."

"Perhaps," Yeshua agreed. "Let's go to Meryam."

When they arrived at the house, Meryam seemed alarmed. Yeshua embraced her. "Meryam, I love you so much, but we have some difficulty facing us."

The Paragon

"Yeshua," she said, "one of the neighbors told me there's a stranger in town asking questions about two travelers from Galilee."

"We need to tell the neighbors to say nothing," Yeshua warned. "Ptolemy has just told me that the stranger is his father. They were sent by Antipas many months ago to find and kill us. When we rescued Ptolemy, and he and I became friends, his heart was changed, and now it's he who warns us against his father's obsession."

Meryam's expression grew dark. "Fool! I never trusted that man, and I don't trust him now. The friendship you gave him was misplaced. All those hours you spent with him, distracted by him from your family and your quest. Now we'll all die from your mistake and his treachery."

"Meryam," Yeshua said, "I have no time now to salve your jealousy, which I don't understand, or to convince you of Ptolemy's true friendship and remind you he's the one who warned us. We need to act now. I've asked Yonnah to leave and take you to safety, and he has refused to leave. I urge you to flee and save yourself, and we can find you if we survive."

"I won't flee without you," Meryam said. "What good will running do? Will I be safe in Bukhara or in Merv? Will I go into the desert with the serpents and insects and live like your cousin?"

"We've thought instead to go into the city," Yeshua said, "and lose ourselves among the unknown alleys and million faces. There's a good chance we wouldn't be found."

"If that's the best plan you can think of," she responded with disdain, "let it be so."

"It is," Yeshua said. "I think in a week or a month the danger will pass and Kefir will return to Galilee and Ptolemy with him. Tonight, Yonnah and I will go within the city walls to see if there's a friend to hide us. Darkness will fall before I can return, so I'll stay there until first light.

"You'll be safe, because Kefir doesn't know you or where you live," he continued, "nor that I'm your husband, but to be safe, I think you should spend the night with Amala. In the meantime, you can go to our neighbors and urge them to deny any knowledge of us. I'll come for you in the morning."

Yeshua and Yonnah left for the walled city. Meryam did as Yeshua asked and spoke to her neighbors. She returned to the house to gather a few necessities and was about to go to Amala's home when she heard a knock at the door.

"Who's there?" she called out.

"I'm a stranger to you," a man's voice answered, "but I mean no harm. I'm looking for some old friends from my homeland."

She opened the door and without introduction knew who stood before her. She saw the resemblance to her husband's friend in his face, and in his gait when she invited him in. "I've traveled by caravan from Galilee," he said, "and I've learned from my conversations at the caravanserai this may be the house of Yeshua. I've known him in Galilee, and I'd love to greet an old acquaintance so far from our homeland. I pray you allow me to remain and await his return."

Meryam's heart grew ugly, and she formulated a plan even as he spoke. "You have the right house. What's your name?" She smiled demurely.

"Kefir, please," he answered.

"Kefir," she acknowledged, "but Yeshua won't be back for two days. Tell me where you're staying, and I'll tell him you've called and send him to greet you. I'm sure he'd love to talk to you. He's gone into the city with his cousin Yonnah. Perhaps you know him as well."

"I've heard of him, but we've never met. I'd be delighted to make his acquaintance. I'm staying in the stable behind the caravanserai closest to here. I've only just arrived, and this is temporary quartering until I can find an available room."

"Very well, Kefir, I'll send Yeshua to you."

He took his leave. Stupid bitch, he thought. She's talked her way into widowhood.

Kefir went back to the caravanserai. He was pleased with himself and ordered a jar of wine.

Meanwhile, Meryam left her house, not for the home of Amala, but for Nagira's. Some of the herbs she grew were a nasty lot, and now they would be quite useful. She didn't have much time to effect her plan. She asked her friend what was possible.

"Right now, I have nothing that will kill in a small, tasteless dose," Nagira said, "but I have something that will bring a death-like sleep, especially if someone has had some wine to drink."

"I'll make that work for me," Meryam responded. "I thank you. Of course, we tell no one of this, not even my husband."

"Oh, it's not for your husband, then? It is for most who come to me." Although Nagira liked Yeshua well enough, she'd always side with the woman in domestic disputes.

"No, sister," explained Meryam, "it's to save my foolish husband and myself. Don't inquire further."

Meryam went back down the hill and sneaked in the darkness to the back of the caravanserai. She waited until the boy who worked there came out to dump a bucket of filth onto the pile behind the building. She spoke to him. "Zardon, come here. I want to have a word with you."

"Meryam," Zardon answered, "I have no time. I have to get back to work."

"Come, come," she insisted. "I have a job for you, for which I'll give you this gold coin. Here, take this powder and slip it into the drink of the one called Kefir and Ptolemy's as well. I want them to sleep soundly tonight."

"No, Meryam," Zardon protested, "I won't do it. You'd poison them?"

"No, Zardon," she explained. "It's only a sleeping potion. You'll cause them no harm. I promise."

"Sister," the boy repeated, "I cannot do it."

"Zardon," Meryam insisted, "take the gold coin, and consider that if you don't do it, Markos will know what you did with his daughter on the hillside last week. Would you like that?"

"No, sister," he lamented, "I would not. He'd kill me."

"So, do this for me," she said. "Don't tell anyone, and everyone will be happy."

Ptolemy had joined Kefir at the caravanserai. The two sat at a table drinking wine. Kefir's wide eyes crowned a broad smile.

The Paragon

"Son, I have good news. I've located the house of this Yeshua on the road down the valley. He'll return in two days and we'll finish him off. Then we can return to Galilee with the next caravan. The other one will be with him. They make it easy for us."

Ptolemy was completely dismayed. He was afraid of his father's reaction, but he had to tell him everything now. If there was any chance, this was it.

"Why do you look troubled, son?" Kefir asked.

Ptolemy exhaled. "Father, you cannot do this. I told you how I was rescued in the desert after I fell. It was Yeshua who saved me, and his cousin who returned to save us both. I owe him my life, and he's become my fast friend. I couldn't kill him then, and I will not now.

"I've told him I won't take up arms against you," he continued, "but I can't let you kill him. You'll also have to kill me to do this duty. I beg you to consider, if I mean anything to you, that you owe him my life. I know your heart has been hardened by your captivity, but think about this. Please don't kill them."

"Doesn't it mean anything to you anymore that these men murdered your mother in the streets?" Kefir countered.

"They weren't the ones," Ptolemy responded. "Neither Yeshua nor his cousin has ever been a Zealot. In fact, Yeshua was working with his father that day in Sepphoris, and it was his father who saved my life then."

"And you know this, how?" Kefir asked.

"Yeshua told me," Ptolemy said, "and he wouldn't lie to me."

"Son," Kefir replied, "I don't know what power this man has over you, that you'd believe a lying, murdering Zealot over

Antipas, the tetrarch of Galilee, who has blessed you and me and made us secure for the rest of our lives."

"Can't you see it?" Ptolemy pleaded. "It's Antipas who's the liar. Did you ever speak to that supposed informant yourself? Did you ever see him and know he really exists? Have you asked yourself why the other two murderers weren't revealed under torture? Why men who were once Zealots became Essenes? Antipas told us what we needed to hear to motivate us to go to the ends of the earth."

Kefir went silent, seeming to contemplate his son's words. In truth, revenge meant less to him now, although he hoped it still might motivate his son. Zardon, the young server, brought them another jar of wine. Kefir picked it up and poured some into his glass and some into his son's. As the ruby liquid splashed into the bottom of the goblet, he finally spoke. "You may owe this man your life, but I owe everything we have to the king who commanded me to do this.

"Our family would have nothing without the generosity of Antipas," he continued. "He's the one I owe. You need not have any part of this. I understand your loyalty, but I must do what I must do. If neither gratitude to Antipas nor the memory of your own mother no longer motivates you, then I fear I don't know you anymore."

"Father, what does my life mean to you?" Ptolemy asked. "I'd hope it means more than all the wealth of Antipas, including the pittance he's bestowed upon us; and I swear to you, these men did not kill my mother."

Kefir sat in silence, staring into his wine glass, twirling the liquid gently into a vortex. "Ptolemy, now that I know your heart, I must be completely honest with you as well. In the last months of winter that I spent with the Buddhists my heart was also changed. I've never been a religious man. I never raised you to be religious, and I didn't become a Buddhist.

"However, in my time with the monks," he continued, "a peace came to my heart that purged it of a desire for vengeance. What I have left from the past is a sense of duty that I count a good thing."

Kefir paused. His words became halting. "Our conversation is causing me confusion, and I grow strangely tired. I suggest we get some rest, and I'll reconsider all this in the morning."

"Father," Ptolemy responded, "I'm tired as well, and that's all I ask of you. I believe you'll understand, and I hope you relent." Ptolemy knew his father, and he believed there was now hope for this all to end happily.

The two of them staggered to the stable holding each other up, each laughing at the other's drunkenness for having drunk so little. Before long they were deep in dreamless sleep.

It was during the third watch when Meryam crept back to the caravanserai, with both purpose and rage in her eyes. She was like a she-wolf preparing to turn an intruder into a meal. Everyone had long been asleep. She sneaked into the stable and found the stall where the two men were sleeping. She carried a lamp in one hand and had the instrument of her plan tucked in her sash.

Meryam set down the lamp and went to each horse, calming it with a sweet treat. At the same time, she untied the ones who were lashed to the frame of the stall and unfastened the gate behind them. If all the horses were saved, no one would care about the foreigners.

She crept to the soldiers' stall and stood over Kefir, thinking how he probably had contempt for her and certainly had underestimated her. She carefully removed the dagger she'd sharpened from her sash, raised it high to give it sufficient momentum and then, with all her strength, slammed it into Kefir's heart.

She looked with disdain at Kefir's lifeless carcass, pleased with herself as she twisted the knife in the name of certainty. The flowing blood excited her, yet she would have more.

She ripped the crimson blade from Kefir's chest and turned to Ptolemy who, like his father, had been deprived of his soldier's instincts and alertness. She stood over Ptolemy, eager to kill. She again held the knife high as if to celebrate her triumph before the deed was done; then she stabbed him once.

His eyes opened suddenly, startling her, but that was all the response he could muster. He peered into the depths of her eyes with an expression of puzzlement and pain beyond the merely physical and slumped, finished. She stabbed him once more and again and again. How dare he look offended?

She left the dagger next to Ptolemy. If there were ever any question of how this happened, it could be said they killed each other in a fight. She kicked the lamp over.

The straw caught fire instantly. In her haste she lost the sash to her cloak at the door of the stable. She didn't give it a second thought but, as the stable became fully engulfed, disappeared into the night.

The Paragon

Early the next morning Yeshua passed the caravanserai on the way home. He'd found a place in Maracanda where they could hide. He saw the smoldering stable, now burned to the ground behind the tavern. He had a sick feeling in his heart. He knew his friend was staying there but hoped he wasn't caught in the flames.

He ran to the stable. Markos and his staff were shuffling around the ashes grim-faced and silent. Two men perished, they told him. They had dragged the bodies out, charred and hideous. He knew immediately who they were. He sank to his knees and wailed from the depth of his soul.

"How can you let this happen?" Yeshua screamed to heaven, and he wept inconsolably. His newfound peace was crushed.

At length, Yeshua stood and looked again at the bodies. He saw the knife. He noticed the stab wound in Kefir's chest. Some distance from the bodies, he saw a tasseled cloth sash he was quite familiar with, and he knew immediately what had happened.

"By God, this is enough!" Yeshua bellowed. His voice was lower, from some deeper part of his being, and he stalked deliberately down the road. Yonnah followed him, beseeching calm, but Yeshua could not be mollified. He threw the door to the house open and saw Meryam, sitting on the mat smiling, at least until he confronted her.

"Woman, what in God's name have you done?" he screamed.

"Do not rage at me," she replied coldly. "I've saved our lives."

"You've murdered the friend I loved!" Yeshua cried. "We could have been spared without any of this bloodshed!"

"It seems you loved him more than me," she shot back.

He raised his hand to her but didn't strike. "How dare you quantify my love in that way? I've loved you truly as my wife and have given you no cause to doubt it. I've also loved my friend. Don't you understand love is infinite and not something to be divided up--a portion for you, a portion for him, a portion for Yonnah? You've betrayed me and ripped out my heart. Get out. Leave my presence. Nay, I'll leave yours. I don't want to be in a place that reminds me of you. You're a vile creature, and I regret anything I've ever done for you."

Meryam was seized with an awareness of what she'd done, and his words struck her with the hammer of judgment and condemnation. They came from the one who meant the most to her, and she cried tears of anguish and desperation. With her face in her hands, she saw a vision of Ptolemy's final stare, like a ghost. "Forgive me!" she wailed. "Forgive me!"

Yeshua left before he did her harm and went down by the river to the place where he often sat in meditation. Yonnah followed him. They were both silent until Yonnah spoke. "I know you're experiencing unspeakable grief. I've grown to appreciate your friend and the way he amended his life to embrace doing good works for others--as you showed him by example.

"I've also accepted your wife," he continued, "because I know you love her and because she, too, is a changed person for knowing you. Now she's wronged you in a way more terrible than if she lay with another man, but you can't let your pain become paralysis. You have to decide what to do with her before she kills herself, because I see that's where her desperation now leads her. For her, the loss of you is the loss of all.

"You've always preached forgiveness," Yonnah went on, "but what will you do now? If you don't forgive, how will you be able to preach that message to our people or to anyone? Is ours destined to be a culture of revenge forever?"

"Do you forgive the Romans, then, and the Sadducees?" Yeshua whispered.

Yonnah was inwardly relieved that at least Yeshua was thinking again. "My quarrel with the Romans has nothing to do with forgiveness. Once they've left us alone, we can talk about forgiveness, but for now forgiveness is not my problem. It's yours.

"You need to decide if you'd abandon the very idea of it," Yonnah continued, "or if you'd forgive in word only, or if you'd really forgive in your heart. Once you've decided that, the next question is what you'll do with Meryam. If you forgive her, you'll take no revenge against her, but will you renounce her and leave her? Will you keep her but keep a cold distance from her in your heart; or will you embrace her again as your wife and lover? If you wait to answer these questions, the problem of what to do with her may be decided for you. But the question of what forgiveness you could have given will roil your heart until the day you die."

Yeshua sat staring into the depths of the river, torn between the experience of grief and the necessity of clear thinking. He vomited and then lay back on the slope, eyes closed, trying to breathe deeply and calm himself.

"Good day, sister." Yonnah greeted a solitary woman coming down the trail toward them.

It was Amala. "I come to offer comfort if I can. Yeshua, I am so sorry for the loss of your friend. I've left your wife with the other women, and I can tell you that she, too, is in great distress.

"You're a wise and learned man," she continued, "and I can't tell you what to do, but I also know this is the first woman you've been with, and there are some things I've seen in my life that might help you decide. I've seen many times after the birth of a child, even one who lives, a woman may go to a dark place in her soul. It can be as if a demon possesses her. All happiness goes from her life, she sleeps without end, and she's like a stranger to those whom she should love."

This description rang true to Yeshua's experience with Meryam in the weeks since their son died, but to murder over imagined things as if taking revenge on the husband who loves her?

"These demons can be powerful," Amala counseled. "Sometimes they're the same ones we spend our whole lives contending with and keep caged most of the time, but often some tragedy opens the gate and they emerge bold and hungry. With Meryam, we women can shower her with love as friends and even bring her some herbs that can help to salve her spirit. But if this demon is truly to be cast out, or at least put back into its cage, only you can do that, Yeshua. Without you she will not heal."

Yeshua heard her words. He also recalled the words of the teacher at the door of the Paragon. In the present moment it was difficult to look at these events as would the author of the codex of the universe or even to comfort himself with the belief he would meet Ptolemy again in the afterlife.

As she turned to leave, Amala said, "Yeshua, your friend had a great life, in a large measure because of you. Enjoy that thought. Would he want you to withdraw and grow dark?"

"Thank you, Amala," he said. "Yonnah, I appreciate your being here for me. I'll be well. I need a few moments alone, and I'll return home."

He lay there awhile in the shade of the tree, breathing deeply, considering the words of Yonnah and Amala. The soft breeze filled his nostrils with the smell of blossoms, and they fell on him from the tree like manna for the spirit. He opened his eyes to see soft clouds rolling and swirling gently above him. At last, he took a deep breath, forced himself to stand, and began to put one foot in front of the other up the hill to home.

"My wife, don't be afraid or desperate," he said when he entered. "My rage has passed. We need to talk about these things and arrive at an understanding. But before we do, I need to restore my body and spirit with sweet sleep. I'm exhausted." Then Yeshua fell into a sleep that lasted nearly two days.

Two Days Later with Yonnah

"Yeshua, I've grown sick of this journey. I've watched all the promise it held for you collapse into a rubble of tragedy. There's a caravan leaving in two days bound for Damascus. I intend to go with it. I beg you to come with me. Haven't you had enough hardship and pain? Aren't these deaths of your loved ones a sign from God for you to abandon this journey?"

"Yonnah," Yeshua said, "you speak of hardship. You invite hardship."

"Yes, Yeshua," Yonnah replied, "physical hardship is salvific for me, but the pain of separation from my roots and my land has become unbearable. I need to go lead if you won't. We hear news from other caravans that nothing has changed in Galilee. You've convinced me I don't need to watch over you, but I can't drag you back. Please reconsider."

"Yonnah," Yeshua responded, "my time on this journey isn't finished yet, but it will be soon. I feel this in my heart. There's still something for me here. I can't seek it, but when it comes, I'll know it. Then I'll return and make you proud. I understand our people are beaten down and need hope. You've been a faithful friend to me, and I shall see you soon."

"I trust you," Yonnah said, "and I'm pleased to hear you acknowledge the need to address the suffering of our people, but please don't linger. If Antipas remembers me, it will only put him on the lookout for you. We can only hope he's distracted by one of his grand projects."

Thirteen

After some weeks, after Yonnah had departed, and as his reconciliation with Meryam continued, Yeshua went walking on the great hill down valley from the city. The spring breeze swept through him, it seemed, cleansing him to the core. He removed his shirt to let his skin soak it up, filling him like water does a sponge. He inhaled it, as in a meditation, and then breathed it away. In its wake it left an internal calmness and an upwelling of physical vigor. Yeshua smiled at nothing in particular, maybe just at the feeling, and began to walk more briskly, even as he climbed higher.

He continued, stopping once in a while to drink from a stream or to pick some berries for nourishment, until he reached a vantage point that gave him a view of the city and valley below. He could see both channels of the Polytimetus that split near his neighborhood, forming a massive island, until they rejoined each other some miles downstream. He could see the valley opening onto the vast plain that would become the desert they'd crossed.

An impressive storm, anvil-shaped, rolled out of the mountains, about to drench the city. Yeshua would be spared its chilling rain, but this eye-level view, with bolts of lightning firing in its path, took his breath away. It was late afternoon, and the sun was low enough to paint a rainbow among the dark purple clouds.

Then Yeshua began to feel as he'd never felt before. It felt at first as if he were no longer viewing the scene, but *was* the scene. His awareness of the cosmic perspective leapt from the realm of imagination into physical reality and extinguished his ego. He no longer was aware of any sound. He had a strange perception of lines of energy flowing from his body to every point in his view and flowing back into him, as if he were creating the scene and it was creating him.

He rose to his feet and spread his arms. Every inch of his body tingled in response to this hidden force flowing between him and all that he saw. He soon felt no distinction between him and a nearby tree. The tree appeared as an infinity of points that circulated to him and then back. It was the same experience whether he focused on a rock, the shrubs, a small scurrying rodent, or the distant storm. And as he felt the unity of everything in space, he also understood that all time was one, that the time of ordinary experience was an illusion, that past, present and future existed as one forever.

Yeshua was overwhelmed with awe and ecstasy. Excitement and inexplicable peace filled his spirit all at the same time, for in that moment he began to understand that what he was experiencing was Mystical Union with the Divine Spirit.

He realized in an epiphany that came like a great sea wave that *he* was God, that he was one in the same substance with every single thing around him, and that he participated in the creation of all of it. What had once been merely an intellectual concept that he'd assented to in his mind, now became a powerful physical reality that made him shudder at the core of his being.

But this exhilaration soon gave birth to a profound sense of humility, both for the gift of the Experience, and for the realization that not only was *he* God, but so was every other person. He now understood viscerally what he'd come to believe. The greeting of the Buddhists, *Namaste*, "the Divine Spirit in me greets the Divine Spirit in you," was beyond words, beyond metaphor. *All men, all things,* were one entity in this Divine Spirit. This was why each person had to treat every other person like a brother.

He could no longer separate the feelings: joy, excitement, humility, peace. It overwhelmed him so that he sank to the ground and wept, laughing along with the tears. So this is it, he mused, and then a bright light that seemed to have no source flashed all around him. He stood, still crying and laughing. The lines of energy were no longer visible, but everything he did see was in sharper view, richer in color.

Now the sounds returned, each with greater clarity and more distinguishable from the others, but together seeming like music, filling him even more with the wonder of creation. His senses became one. He saw the music. He felt it. He smelled it.

When the Experience finally released him, Yeshua started running down the hill. He tripped and picked himself up, laughing all the more. A gentle rain from the edge of the storm soaked him. As night was falling, he ran all the way to his house, where he found Meryam. He began babbling to her about the Experience for which, ultimately, there were no words.

"It was Brahman, the Tao, Ayn-Sof--God in Essence!" he shouted.

"I have no idea what you're talking about," she said, "although I sense the passion you express it with. It makes me happy to see such enthusiasm in you, and there's a glow about your complexion I've never seen before."

Yeshua needed someone to understand. "Meryam, I'm going to sleep now, if I can, and tomorrow, as the sun rises, I'm going to the Paragon. I don't know when I'll return. Be patient with me. I have the feeling we'll be leaving Maracanda soon." He slept little and awakened with a snap as the first cock crowed.

Yeshua ran to the Paragon, hoping he would be allowed entry on this his third visit. "Do you have any room yet? I have just . . ."

The same old man grinned broadly. "Oh, yes, *now* we have room for you. I'm Yun Shen. For now, I'm the senior teacher here. Come in."

Yeshua instinctively took the blind man's arm as if to lead him, but it was Yun Shen who led. He took Yeshua through an inner door and into a hall with a grand wooden table, circular, low to the floor, and carved with symbols from the different religions and spiritual traditions he'd encountered on his journey and some he hadn't. There was an imposing but simple circular iron fixture suspended by chains over the table. It contained twenty-four cups on its perimeter, which could accommodate either oil or candles the monks made themselves. There were about ten people of various ethnicities seated around the table, including two women.

The Paragon

Yeshua looked twice because he recognized one of the women. It was Roxanna. He ran to embrace her. "What are you doing here?"

"I've visited from time to time," she said, "and I thought by now I might find you here. I also expected to see Ptolemy in town, but I know about his death, and I was devastated by the news. I trust you're doing well, and how's your wife?"

"We've both been healing," Yeshua said. "We're doing well now."

"Sit, sit. We were expecting you." A woman named Archisha, who appeared to be Hindu, motioned him to a large pillow at the table.

Yeshua was completely puzzled.

"Markos told us you had the Experience yesterday." They all began to laugh. "Now you know what you're talking about. I'm Azar. We've all had much the same Experience no matter what our belief system is. We know you're a thinker and a man of words, but your words and your thinking are only a path, one of many paths that offer a gate to this Experience for which there are no words. Personally, I'm in the Zoroastrian tradition."

"Yet you laugh about it," Yeshua said, "and I laugh with you."

"Yes, it makes you happy-happy, and so we laugh, not from disrespect, but from a sense of happiness, and from the irony that while it's so profound, it's at once so utterly simple." It was Jitendra, the yogi from Hecatompylos. How did he even get here? Yeshua wondered.

"And Yeshua," Jitendra added, "while I think of it, your friend and teacher, Mandeep, wishes he could be here, but sends his love."

Bo Jian, another man from Seres, introduced himself and said, "A man can find his path to the Experience by many ways: reading and thinking like you, being an ascetic like your cousin, or even immersing himself in rubric and ritual like a priest."

"Still other ways," Yun Shen chimed in, "are devoting one's life to good works or practicing an art with mindfulness of the Divine Spirit, perhaps a martial art. So many paths, so many different people, like all of us."

"My friend honors my path," Bo Jian, a martial artist, responded. "We haven't met before, but I was your friend's teacher. He was an exceptional person, full of energy and curiosity and with a good heart. I'm sure that isn't news to you."

Yeshua smiled, and emotions of pride, sorrow, and joy welled up in him. He sensed reciprocation from Bo Jian. "He grew so much in such a short time," Yeshua said. "I suspect someday he might have sat at this table. I thank you for all you did for him."

"Have some wine. We celebrate. And I just made some bread. Enjoy." The man who spoke, named Gyorgi, who appeared to be of local ethnicity, gave no outward sign in dress or mannerism of his spiritual tradition. Gyorgi spoke as he walked into the room, carrying a large tray of bread, filing the room with the scent of the baked grains and aromatic herbs he'd mixed into it. It made Yeshua's mind drift for an instant to his mother's hearth.

Gyorgi continued speaking. "Once you've had the Experience, you're beyond religion. It doesn't matter which tradition, if any, you choose to participate in after the Experience. I work in the fields locally, and I'm something of an outcast, because I don't affiliate with any religion."

The Paragon

"Religion has nothing to do with what you experienced on the mountain," Mukti, a Buddhist, offered.

"Well, except to say the practice of a religion can be a path to the Experience," Jitendra countered.

"If a man's prayer and ceremony are truly spiritual practices," Mukti answered. He continued, turning to Yeshua. "Even with that, religion is only a path, not the end in itself. Surely you read that in the codex you brought us."

"Here," Yun Shen, a Taoist scholar, said. "The first lines: 'Don't confuse your traditional path--*tao,* small *t*--with the Mystical Path of the Universe--*Tao,* big *T*. Small *t*, big *T*: Lao Tzu loved word-play and paradox."

Manisha, the man in the saffron robes, was clearly a Buddhist. "In other words," he said, "your way is only one way to the Way. I know you're destined to be a leader for your people. Now you have to find the metaphors to help them understand what is not understandable. Good luck with that. But enjoy yourself. It's not as if you have to die over this."

Yeshua raised his eyebrows, and his laugh went to a half smile. "In my culture that's exactly what I'll have to do."

Yeshua's thought was interrupted by squawking and wing flapping. Yun Shen had left the door open, and the rooster was chasing some hen's around the table. For good measure a goat had come to the party, and was begging for a treat. Yun Shen induced the menagerie to leave with a trail of goodies, while everyone watched the parade with rapt attention. He closed the door behind them and returned to the table taking a bow. "My fault," Yun Shen said, to general laughter. "Please continue, Bo Jian."

"Keep your stories simple, Yeshua," Bo Jian urged, echoing Markos. "You won't even recognize them once others retell them."

"Like all those primitives in the mountains, so-called Buddhists." Manisha, who spoke, and all the others were clearly informed about Yeshua's experiences in Maracanda.

"And wait until those Greeks get a hold of them, with all their logic and philosophy. I know. I *am* one, a Stoic, but we can talk about that some other time. I'm called Theophanes. It's a pleasure to meet you."

"The pleasure is mine," Yeshua said, "but Manisha enkindles an unpleasant memory. Roxanna, I believe I saw the aura of the group performing the human sacrifice."

"Sometimes," she acknowledged, "the strength of a collective aura makes it easier to see. Was it hideous?"

"It was," Yeshua replied; "a chaotic display of mostly blue-blacks and gray-blacks. I could scarcely imagine such a dirty blue."

"That's consistent with what was happening there," Roxanna said. "Have you seen other auras since?"

"No," he said, "that was the only time."

"A start at least," she replied.

Archisha and Gyorgi, who had left the room, re-entered with large trays of food. An aroma, pungent and pleasant, had filled the hall in advance of their presentation. There were large bowls of vegetables, grown at the compound under Gyorgi's supervision and cooked with the exotic spices of Archisha's homeland. The fare was simple and delicious, and even those among them who had an ascetic disposition enjoyed the banquet fully.

The Paragon

After they'd eaten, Yun Shen addressed the group. "We do have an item of business to take care of. As you all know, our new brother has brought us a precious gift. Our revered brother, Ling Zhi, poet and scholar, who, since the disaster in Susia, has undertaken a journey to Alexandria, has sent Yeshua to us with a codex of the Tao Te Ching in the Greek language. I suggest we all put our signatures to it and take it to our vault for safekeeping."

Yun Shen opened the codex again. Everyone had read it and universally praised the translation of the poetry and the beauty of the Greek calligraphy. There was nothing like it in the world: inscribed on paper in codex form, with the tai chi, symbol of the interaction of yin and yang, embossed on the leather cover. Now each in turn put his name at the bottom of the eighty-first verse under that of Ling Zhi. This last verse read in part:

One of whole virtue,
Is not occupied with amassing material goods.
Yet the more he lives for others, the richer his life becomes
The more he gives, the more his life abounds.

"Our Hindu brother and sister," Yun Shen said, "have special fondness for verse four, because in describing the Tao, it reminds them of the Rig Veda and Brahman."

It seems so obscure.
Yet it is the Ultimate Clarity.
Whose offspring it is can never be known.
It is that which existed before any divinity.

A warm breeze flickered the candles above them. Yeshua looked out and could see the distant hills from which it came. It caressed them all, and Yeshua marveled at the fellowship that these people from beyond those hills now shared like a family. The thought warmed his heart as the breeze warmed his body.

Manisha spoke up, breaking the spell. "All of us have our own scriptures, but the Book of Tao is so fundamental, it appeals to all of us in some way. As a Buddhist, whose tradition is concerned with suffering and anxiety, I'm drawn to verse thirteen."

People are beset with great trouble,
Because they define their lives so narrowly.
If they forsake their narrow sense of self and live wholly,
Then what can they call trouble?

"We all have our favorites," Manisha continued, "and we change from time to time. Would you care to share a favorite of yours with us, Yeshua, something that rings with familiarity to your own tradition perhaps?"

"These verses are dense with wisdom," Yeshua replied. "I've enjoyed becoming familiar with them.

"We have a prophet, named Coheleth," he continued, "who wrote a text that's like a poem, and when I read verse twenty nine, I thought of him."

The things of the world are constantly changing.
There is a time for things to move ahead, and a following time for things to retreat;

The Paragon

A time to withdraw internally, and a following time to expand externally;
A time to grow luxuriantly and a following time to decay;
A time to rise up, and a following time to sink low.

"These words," Yeshua said, "are almost the same as Coheleth. I wonder if he talked to Lao Tzu." They all laughed. But who knew? "And maybe I can add, 'a time to travel afar and a time to return home.'"

Yeshua continued, "I'd like to make a personal gift to the Paragon. I'll leave my scroll of the Torah, the Law of my tradition, with you, if you'd have it, along with some notes I made on my journey. The Torah is different from the Tao Te Ching in many ways, but it represents my spiritual roots, vengeful deity notwithstanding."

Everyone laughed again, approved enthusiastically, and followed Yun Shen into a room beyond the hearth room where they'd been conversing. The next room was full of scrolls and a few codices. Once a person had the Experience, there was little use in learning more about spiritual insight because the fundamental truth stood revealed. Such works, however, served the purpose of keeping the recipient of the great gift mindful of its meaning. So while some of these works were for continued edification, most were tomes the monks themselves were working on.

"We share a goal here," Theophanes explained. "We enjoy each other's company, but we don't just sit around laughing about the Experience. We all want to let the world know, each in his own culture, that there's a commonality to all spiritual insight and the Mystical Experience. Those of us so inclined like to write about it, not so much about the Experience itself--outside this room, most people would think we're crazy--but about what the experience represents."

They didn't stop at the library, however. Yun Shen led them into another room that had shrines along the walls to each tradition represented by the group and some representing the traditions of past residents. There was also a hearth in this room, but it appeared not to have been used for a while.

"Follow me," Yun Shen said. "Markos rigged this device when he built the monastery." Yun Shen went to the hearth. He took one of the fire irons, as if he could see, removed a stone from the floor, and inserted the tool into a hole where the stone had been. Having done that, he said, "A little help, please."

Gyorgi came to his aid and pushed at the hearth enough to reveal an opening that each one in turn squeezed through. A few had lamps to light the way. They descended a staircase to a depth Yeshua guessed to be about forty feet and found themselves in a tunnel. The bottom of a chain loop hung from some unseen connection above them and Manisha, the last one down, pulled it hand over hand as if weighing an anchor. It rolled back the hearth above them, re-concealing the entrance.

They went only a few yards until they came to a slight protrusion that no one would have guessed was another door. It operated the same way as the hearth upstairs. A simple key allowed the stone to be rolled away, giving them entrance into what could only be called a vault.

The Paragon

It was here they kept their treasures: some rare volumes in many languages, like a Seresian translation of the first part of the Rig Veda, as well as an ancient scroll of it in Sanskrit. Everything was wrapped tightly in cured skins, and each had its own wooden box lined with ceramic tile that fit snuggly into spaces hewn out of the stone walls.

"We wanted to show you this, Yeshua," Yun Shen said, "to let you know of its existence, and to let you know this is also an escape route should we ever be beset by robbery or war. This area is well above the water table, and if you follow the tunnel, you come out to a hidden place well on the other side of the hill.

"The tunnel is almost a mile long," he continued. "In an emergency, both the entrance and the exit can be sealed and made impenetrable. It's like the pharaohs' tombs, as legend has it. Anyway, it's simple. Each end has a big wooden lever. Pull it down and run."

They placed the Tao Te Ching in a case and secured it. Then they returned to the hearth room with the circular table for one more jar of wine.

Needless to say, Yeshua enjoyed his day at the Paragon. He was curious enough to ask, as he took his leave, how they all seemed to know so much about him. "We have our sources," Yun Shen said, laughing. "I'm sure a man of your insight can figure out who they are easily enough. One last thing. I'm sure I don't need to tell you, but keep up your spiritual exercise or you'll lose what you've gained. Having the Experience doesn't mean you can quit."

"I understand," Yeshua agreed. "When we talk about spiritual exercise, we might better say 'spiritual discipline': something to be done every day, above all other things."

"Perhaps you can be like Jitendra," Roxanna said. "He seems to live perpetually in the state of the mystical vision. He occasionally contributes a lucid sentence, but mostly his brain is in some other realm." She smiled and shook her head, as if in amazement at the yogi. "The rest of us need to keep up spiritual discipline to remain mindful of the true reality."

"Obviously, you can't live life in the physical world if you're constantly in the ecstatic state of the Mystical Union," Bo Jian added, "but it can always be in the background, informing all your daily actions."

"I understand, my friends," Yeshua said, "and thank you all so much."

"Oh, Yeshua." Yun Shen had one more thing to say. "I do apologize for teasing you on your first two visits." They both laughed.

It was time now, Yeshua thought as he made his way home: time to return to Galilee. Spending a long time at the Paragon would be a beautiful and rewarding experience, but he had a duty to fulfill and promises to keep.

At Yeshua and Meryam's Home

"Yeshua, how can you expect people to understand this Experience even I don't even understand and even you can't find the words for?" Meryam asked.

"I don't," he said. "Most people will never find it or even seek it. In fact, if you seek it, you won't find it. It comes when you're not seeking, and it will surely come for a few. Until it does, however, or for the others, they'll need something tangible they can hold on to. They'll want, even need, some certainty they're living correctly according to God and will be saved from sin.

"I can be their way and their truth," he continued. "I can take the place of that blinding light I experienced. For them it can be as simple as loving the Divine Spirit and putting your neighbor ahead of yourself out of love. Be patient with me if I tell you stories on the way home. I need to think of some."

"Won't God be angry with you for changing the covenant with the people?" she asked.

"No. No, He will not", Yeshua answered. "God-Manifest to me is like a loving father, and I see there's a Holy Spirit, which is the personification of the power of God-Manifest in the universe. I also understand that I and all of us are one with God--both God in Essence and God-Manifest--and complete His three-part nature. I pray everyone comes to understand all of us are one with God and in that unity are children of God and brothers to each other."

"So if God is the Divine Spirit or the Oneness of all things," said Meryam, having listened and thought intently, "how can God be said to be a man and not a woman as well? How can the God you talk about have a gender at all?"

"My wife becomes a theologian." Yeshua said with amusement. "I joke with you, but you've seen the truth. Everything I tell people will be in the form of parables, like the Buddha did, even about the nature of God.

"I won't be speaking to theologians or philosophers," he continued, "but to uneducated Jews who grew up in an intolerant tradition, and one in which God is a male. If I stray too far from their tradition, the very people I'm trying to reach won't hear me. Those who listen carefully will understand."

Yeshua went to the caravanserai. Hadi Ba'riel had remained in Maracanda for all this time. He kept a home here and it wasn't unusual for him to extend his stay. "So, my friend, you're leaving the city. This hasn't been an easy time for you, but you're in luck. I'm returning to Damascus. If you can give me about one month to organize a caravan, I'd be honored if you and Meryam would accompany us."

"What good news!" Yeshua exclaimed. "I'm sure Meryam will be as excited as I am."

"As long as she doesn't abuse any more camels," Hadi said in mock warning.

"You knew about that?" Yeshua said.

"Of course," Hadi replied. "I feigned ignorance to justify waiting for you in the middle of nowhere."

Yeshua went back to his home and told Meryam about their opportunity to return home with Hadi, and the prospect of it seemed to comfort her. They spent the next few weeks organizing their own departure. Yeshua took his Torah to the Paragon. He spent a lot of time there, visiting with Roxanna and the others. Some had other occupations or pastimes in the city and would often stop at Yeshua's house for tea on their way. Yeshua and Meryam gave away or sold what few possessions they'd accumulated and said goodbye to friends and neighbors.

The Paragon

When there were only a few days left until their departure, they sat with Amala outside her house, drinking tea. Her husband had yet to return from Seres, so they tried their best to reassure her he'd be home soon. "These journeys always take longer than expected," Meryam said.

"It's probably a sign of some business success," Yeshua added.

He said these words to comfort her but couldn't put strong conviction behind them. He well understood the dangers of the Great Road.

As they sat, Yeshua became aware of commotion in the streets. He saw young Zardon running down the hill and called out to him. "What's going on?"

"This is the time of the Sun Holiday," the boy said, breathing heavily, "and last night I served some rough-looking men who inquired about the Paragon. I thought nothing of it but mentioned it to Markos this morning. He believed they might have some evil purpose, so a few hours ago he went to check to make sure everyone and everything was safe. Now look yonder."

Yeshua looked out over the hillocks in the direction of the Paragon and saw smoke rising in the distance. "Let's go, then!" he shouted, and he began running with Zardon for the monastery.

Other men, friends of Markos, joined them. Someone had run to call the city garrison for help. As they neared the first turn-off, Yeshua saw a familiar form coming toward them. It was Bo Jian. His face was ashen and he winced with every labored step.

Fourteen

The Paragon
Three Hours Before

Bo Jian was in the dining hall, cleaning. The morning was peaceful. The windows were wide open. The new day's sun had banished the fog and pre-dawn chill. The fragrance of the garden filled the rooms. The others were out in front of the monastery. Some were meditating. Some were tending the vegetables or the animals.

Before Bo Jian heard anything, the hair on the back of his neck began to tingle and he felt a sudden icy chill through his spine. He couldn't imagine the reason for this, but as he wondered, he heard Yun Shen call out.

Yun Shen's voice was raised. It sounded stressed, strange for so calm a man. "Who visits us?" he called out to strangers Bo Jian did not yet see.

Bo Jian thought by the volume of Yun Shen's voice that he asked the question to alert *him* rather than to gain information. Bo Jian looked out to see men whose eyes were wild with anger. He didn't know who they were or why they'd come.

The Paragon

Yun Shen apparently knew they were trouble, terrible trouble. He shouted to Bo Jian in their Seresian language, "Bo Jian, bar the doors and windows NOW, and save what you can. Do not come out here." He didn't look toward the monastery as he spoke, giving the intruders no indication anyone was inside.

There were twenty men, all with weapons. Two or three were archers who were ready to fire. Bo Jian, a martial artist, thought about going out to fight them, but Yun Shen's command was so forceful he did as the old teacher ordered him.

He barred the door and windows on the ground floor. He ran up the stairs to bar the other windows but first looked out to see what was happening. All the monks except Yun Shen were lined up in a row. Half the men were guarding them, screaming at them. They came close to each one, breath to breath, as if they were trying to identify someone, while the others prowled the grounds to see if there were any more to be rounded up.

There were several of them around Yun Shen, a man of seventy-five years. They dragged him across the yard and hurled him at the door of the monastery, apparently demanding he open it. He stood and faced them, saying nothing. Then the one who seemed to be in charge kicked him hard between the legs.

He crumpled to the ground and doubled over. Then one of the others kicked him in the head. Yun Shen groaned and began to bleed; then another kicked him in the side. With that, they all joined in like jackals, kicking and stomping on him, screaming at him.

The other monks, having nothing to lose, began to run to his aid. The invaders cut them down, killed them all, and hacked them to death without mercy. Bo Jian had been in war, but he'd never seen such brutality, such bloodlust. He couldn't stand to watch anymore. Everyone was dead, and he knew he had a task.

He barred the remaining windows. The leader of the horde looked up, saw Bo Jian, and led a charge to the door. Bo Jian ran to the library and grabbed as many of the scrolls as he could carry. He knew he had a little time because the door was strong. He rolled back the hearth and threw the scrolls down the stairs.

He made his way below but fell five feet from the bottom and uttered an expletive of pain. He thought his ankle was probably broken. He pulled the chain to close the hearth behind him. He gathered the scrolls, hoping to take some of the priceless works with him. He realized, however, he had nothing to carry them in, and he still wasn't sure if he could escape the barbarians.

He did what he thought was best to save everything. He put the scrolls into the vault. By now he could hear men above in the passage room. He believed they wouldn't find the tunnel and vault, but he wasn't certain. He pulled the lever and limped down the tunnel as fast as he could.

Sand and stones came cascading down from the area of the stairs. No doubt the men above heard or even felt it. He hoped they thought it was an earthquake. In fact, it sounded as if the entire building was collapsing on top of him.

The rush of air from the descending fill extinguished his lamp. The dust it bellowed made it difficult to breathe. Bo Jian hobbled as fast as he could, feeling his way down the tunnel. He could hear the debris fall coming closer, and then it stopped. I must be past halfway, he thought.

The Paragon

He continued until his path was blocked. He felt around in the darkness until he found the key for the exit stone. He rolled it open and found it led into a cave. There was a little light coming in from the outside. It was enough to see the lever on the wall behind him.

He pulled the second lever and made his way quickly past the stone. He could hear the rumbling again, so he got out and rolled the stone back. Bo Jian made his way through the cave. When he got to the entrance, he had to push some stones away to make a hole large enough to wriggle out.

When he emerged, he sat a minute, trying to gather himself. He thought he knew where he was, but when he looked behind and saw dark smoke rising over the hill, he was fully oriented. He moved carefully, trying to keep concealed in case the horde was still in the area, and made his way to the road, where he found help, but too late.

Bo Jian saw Yeshua, Zardon, and the others coming. "They're all dead," he said, "all dead." One of the men stayed with Bo Jian. Yeshua and the others kept running to the Paragon.

Yeshua knew in his heart he didn't want to see what awaited him, and it was awful, the horror of it beyond his imagination. The Paragon had been laid to waste. All of it, inside and out, the stable and outbuildings, the trees and gardens--all were smoldering rubble. The main building itself was inexplicably crumbled. Six bodies in the yard were beheaded and burned. Yeshua could try to guess who they were, but he couldn't be sure, except for one. Who could do this to any of them? he agonized, but above all, who could do this to Roxanna?

A separate body near the door was not burned but was an even more ghastly sight than the others. It was Yun Shen; but there was still one more. On the other side of the yard with only a spear through his heart, spread in the dirt, was Markos, the benefactor who created this once-exquisite monument to love and peace.

Yeshua immediately noticed something else about the spear, and it struck him as if his own heart had been pierced. He knew he'd seen it before. "Oh, God," he uttered in a whisper that expelled all his breath and part of his soul. His stomach seemed to push his heart into his throat. He breathed quickly and heavily to keep composed. This was the standard of the priest in the mountains who'd sacrificed the child.

He staggered under the weight of the possibility that he was responsible for all of this, that it was meant as revenge against him for intruding on their brutal sacrifice, that he was an infidel or even a demon to them, and that all his brethren had to suffer punishment.

Zardon had run to Markos's body and was kneeling in the dirt, crying over it. Yeshua went to him and embraced him, but in truth he needed the embrace himself. He could now, after the Experience, see this from the cosmic perspective--less than a pinprick in the fabric of the universe. It softened the emotional blow. Disgust replaced anger. Dismay replaced hatred. Resignation replaced self-pity. But a human hug had imparted the strength to allow the metamorphoses.

There'd be a time he'd entertain the perspective of ego and shed tears, for as much as he loved his brothers and sisters for the

Experience they shared, he also loved their individual selves--their minds and their emotions that sprang from ego. He would allow his ego to react out of respect for theirs.

Yeshua and the others went back to town to get his cart for the bodies. He stopped where Bo Jian was still lying.

"Bo Jian," Yeshua said tearfully, "I recognized the standard of the priest who sacrificed the child in the mountains, plunged into the body of Markos. I'm responsible for this."

"Markos, too, is dead?" Bo Jian could see the distress on Yeshua's face. "No, my friend. Banish that thought immediately. If an earthquake had caused this destruction, wouldn't you say it was an act of nature that you had no control over? This was an act of nature. The act of a man is an act of nature. Man is a part of nature. You only have control over your own actions, and you did nothing wrong. Not one of those who perished, if they ever knew the reason for this atrocity, would count it against you; none of them. I know it."

"Thank you for those words," Yeshua said. "They offer me comfort."

Yeshua sat silently for a minute, contemplating the enormity of this crime, and then another concern crossed his mind. "Bo Jian, I must ask you, what of the scrolls and the codices?"

"They're buried forever," he said. "I don't see how any man will ever be able to find them or retrieve them. I had no idea what I unleashed when I pulled the levers. I'm sorry they're lost to mankind, but the ideas they contain will never be lost. They live on in other volumes. The ones we had were merely material objects.

"The Experience, which we've all shared," Bo Jian continued, "will live on as well. We aren't the only ones. I believe from our present group only you and I, Jitendra, and Mukti survive. The two of them went to the city, but there are others who've had the Experience. They live across the earth. Maybe someday all men will be privileged to have it."

Jitendra and Mukti came to Yeshua's house the next day. He told them the full story of what had happened. They knew he was returning to Galilee, but for now they didn't know if they'd stay in Maracanda or return to their homeland. They made heartfelt goodbyes and acknowledged their unbreakable bond.

Yeshua sought Hadi to express sympathy for the loss of his great friend. "Yeshua, it's a greater loss to the world than to me alone, but you should know that at least the inn will continue as a renowned institution. Markos's wife will keep the business going, and I believe Zardon will join the family and help manage it."

"Did you put an idea in anyone's head about that?" Yeshua asked.

"Me?" Hadi scoffed with a glint in his eye. "What makes you think I'd be involved in matters like that?" He laughed the laugh.

"*Because I am all-seeing*," Yeshua intoned, thinking of the way he answered Ptolemy at the Oxos. He laughed wistfully along with Ba'riel and then added, "My friend, as you know more of me than I would have imagined, I know how you've used your wealth. You're rich enough that you don't have to traipse across empires anymore, but you've used your fortune to help those spreading the ideal of brotherhood among men. I'm lucky to have you as my guide. You knew most of the people at the Paragon, didn't you, and supported it with Markos?"

"Yes, Yeshua, I did," Hadi said. "I knew those who came from the west at least--except for the yogi. I've met them and maintained friendship over the years. Along the way I visited when you weren't with them. I didn't want to interfere with any relationship you might form. You relate to them in a way I never will. You're one of them. I'm merely an admirer."

"You're much more than that, my friend," Yeshua said.

Yeshua sought Zardon. "Young man," he said, "I haven't spoken to you about this, although I should have. I know the full story of the death of Ptolemy, and I want to be sure you don't carry any guilt in your heart for what happened. I want you to know I forgive you, and I'm sure, as you pursue a life of good works, Ahura Mazda grants forgiveness as well. There's no way you could have known what was to happen. I thank you for your hospitality, and I wish you a happy life."

"Thank you, Yeshua," Zardon said. "I should have approached you to ask forgiveness. You've lifted a burden from me. Markos believed you would be a special person for the world. I have no doubt of it."

On the day of their departure, Yeshua walked Meryam to one of the horses and helped her up. "I love you, My Wife."

"And I thank God for it." She smiled as she said the words, as if she meant them in jest, but she was truly serious. "I love you, My Husband, more than you can ever know."

Meryam's words warmed Yeshua's heart, but he didn't respond at first. He mused how the things he'd desired most, including Meryam's love, had led to suffering, and yet he wouldn't have forsaken those desires. It was ironic, he thought, that his life had been enriched by them, that they had led him on a course with its triumphs and tragedies that he would not change, and that if some bad outcome were changed, a worse outcome might follow. He smiled as he wished he could discuss this with the Buddha.

Although there was still a place for humor in Yeshua's heart, deep down he realized what was in store. "Meryam, I hope you fully understand what coming home to Galilee will mean for you. I understand now my life is destined to be one of tragedy. Life will be difficult for anyone who follows me. They'll have to see me put to death, and when I'm gone, they'll probably be persecuted for associating with me."

He thought about the danger Meryam would be in. He even considered that it might be better for her to keep their marriage a secret in Galilee. He also knew this wasn't the time to broach that subject.

"I struggle with what I'm about to do," he continued, "not for myself. I know I can endure any suffering. This journey has tested and hardened me. At the same time, it's opened my eyes to the glorious truth, but I struggle over the idea of taking others down my path. I'll be leading them into hardship and tragedy."

The Paragon

"Yeshua," she said, "you are the truth, and the truth will set us free, and that's all that the people want. They want it more than comfort in life. You'll bring the gift of love, and no tyrant can take it away."

"Thank you, Wife," he said. "You give me courage."

This was the first time Meryam felt in her deep heart that Yeshua needed her. His words warmed the well of her soul, and it was in that moment that she truly began to heal.

"Let's go, my Magdalena, we're off to Galilee," Yeshua said, making the home she'd lied about a term of endearment.

She giggled about it, understanding it represented, not the old, but a new way of life for her. Even though she realized it could be brief, it brought her peace.

They made their way to the caravanserai, and Yeshua told Hadi they were ready to go. Ba'riel was finishing up last-minute preparations. "How's Meryam, Yeshua? Do the demons still haunt her?"

"My friend," Yeshua said, "she'll have to deal with her demons every day of her life, as we all do. Her demons brought her so low she was about to lose her soul. She realized that and has fought back courageously. I support her the best I can, and I believe she can succeed."

"You help her in ways you may not even appreciate," Hadi said, "but what of your own demons?"

"Every day, my friend," Yeshua answered, "*every day* as part of my meditation and prayer, I remind myself that, in understanding my true nature, anger makes no sense. What's the use of being angry at a universe I myself help create? That's my mantra, and I expect it will serve me well--most of the time."

He grinned and went on. "When I return home, I know there will be plenty to be angry about, but I'll have little time for anger. I expect a short ministry and a short life, although I think I can make a difference in the lives of the people in the time I have. Maybe even after I've gone."

"Yeshua," the master of the caravan said, "you're a young man--older than you once were, but you're only now leaving behind the attitudes of youth, where impatience and anger arise from a young man's nature. You're a spiritual man, and because of that, as an older man, your tempests will turn to rain showers. Keep your discipline, and fear not. Allow me to predict a heroic future for you and success for your teachings. A jar of wine, my friend. The road is long. Good travels to us all."

END

Map Keys

I've tried to use all the geographic names that were in use in the First Century CE. For those who want to follow on a current map, here's a guide:

Paneas has also been known as Caesarea Paneas or Caesarea Phillipi, but is in ruins today.

Nehardea no longer exists, nor does Ctesiphon (silent C), but they were both near present Baghdad, Iraq.

Ecbatana is Hamadan, Iran.

Rhages is Tehran, Iran.

Hecatompylos is near Dahmgan, Iran, and the ancient site is called Sahr-e Qumis.

Susia, also known as Tus, is near present Mashad, Iran.

Merv, also known as Alexandia, or Antiochia Margiana, is now also called Mary, Turkmenistan.

The Oxos River to the Greeks, was also known as Oxus, and today as the Amu Darya.

Amul is now Turkmenabat, Turkmenistan.

Bukhara is the same and is in Uzbekistan.

Maracanda is Samarkand, Uzbekistan.

The Polytimetus River is now the Zeravshan.

Seres and Sinae are ancient names for regions of China.

Author's Acknowledgement

The quoted verses of the Tao Te Ching are based on the translation by Ni, Hua-Ching.

Made in the USA
Monee, IL
27 December 2022